Facts On File Encyclopedia of

Black Women

IN AMERICA

Dance, Sports, and Visual Arts

Encyclopedia of
Black Women in America

Facts On File Encyclopedia of

Black Women

IN AMERICA

Dance, Sports, and Visual Arts

Darlene Clark Hine, Editor

Kathleen Thompson, Associate Editor

☑® Facts On File, Inc.

Facts On File Encyclopedia of Black Women in America: Dance, Sports, and Visual Arts

Facts On File, Inc.
11 Penn Plaza
New York NY 10011

Library of Congress Cataloging-in-Publication Data

Facts on File encyclopedia of Black women in America / Darlene Clark
Hine, editor ; Kathleen Thompson, associate editor.
p. cm.
Includes bibliographical references and index.
Contents: v. 1. The early years, 1619–1899 — v. 2. Literature —
v. 3. Dance, sports, and visual arts — v. 4. Business and professions —
v. 5. Music — v. 6. Education — v. 7. Religion and community —
v. 8. Law and government — v. 9. Theater art, and
entertainment — v. 10. Social activism — v. 11. Science, health, and
medicine.
ISBN 0-8160-3424-9 (set : alk. paper)
ISBN 0-8160-3644-6 (Dance, Sports, and Visual Arts)
1. Afro-American women—Biography—Encyclopedias. I. Hine,
Darlene Clark. II. Thompson, Kathleen.
E185.96.F2   1996
920.72′08996073—dc20   96-33268

Text design by Cathy Rincon
Cover design by Smart Graphics

Printed in the United States of America

RRD FOF 10 9 8 7 6 5 4 3 2 1

This book is printed on acid-free paper.

Contents

VISUAL ARTS

How to Use This Volume

SCOPE OF THE VOLUME

The *Dance, Sports, and Visual Arts* volume includes entries on individuals in the following subject areas:

1. *Dance* includes biographies of both dancers and choreographers. Some individuals who were considered to be primarily entertainers (Florence Mills, for example) are included in the *Theater Arts and Entertainment* volume of this encyclopedia, and some singers who are also dancers are profiled in the *Music* volume.

2. *Sports* includes both athletes and coaches.

3. *Visual Arts* includes those engaged in painting, sculpture, drawing, quilting, architecture, and related forms. Many creative individuals excel in a number of areas and you should check the general index at the back of this volume to see if the person in whom you are interested has a biography in another volume of this set.

HOW TO USE THIS VOLUME

This volume consists of three separate sections: *Dance, Sports,* and *Visual Arts.* An introduction begins each section, followed by biographies of individuals important in the field. At the conclusion of the biographical entries, a chronology lists important events in the history of black women related to the subject category.

If you are looking for an individual or organization that does not have an entry in this volume, please check the alphabetically arranged list of the entries for all eleven volumes of this encyclopedia that appears at the end of this book, in addition to the tables of contents of each of the other volumes in this series.

Names of individuals and organzations for which there are entries in this or other volumes of the encyclopedia are printed in **boldface**. Check the contents list at the back of this book to find the volume in which a particular entry is located.

This volume concludes with a bibliography that lists general reference books on black women in America. The bibliography also has separate sections on black women in *dance*, *sports* and *visual arts*, respectively.

DANCE

Introduction

The story of black women in dance is one of generations of dancers whose gestures, thoughts, and emotions have been handed down from one group of women to another, from one era to another. The generations overlap, of course, and the earliest traditions continue to have an effect on contemporary African-American culture.

In each generation, women dancers often performed without recognition and created without demanding attention. Despite their enforced powerlessness, they gave voice to dance and touching clarity to movement. The result of the process they began was a multitude of talented black performers who would change the American artistic landscape with the strength, beauty, and power of their art.

THE SILENT GENERATION

The first, silent generation of dancers laid the foundation for their heirs by maintaining a connection and intimacy with the earth, dancing under a full moon, remembering the power of ritual in their African birthplace, marking moments for remembrance. They danced in celebration of birth or marriage, and in commemoration of death. Even in the latter case, dance helped to affirm life and the possibility of a better life.

The first generation representing a myriad of African ethnic groups, was able to inject its varied heritage into the numerous religions of the New World. Because of these women, dance established a permanent home in the churches and temples of black people. Although it survived in a synthesized form that melded the traditions of several cultures, it became firmly rooted and nurtured.

THE ANONYMOUS GENERATION

The second, anonymous generation reveals itself in the literature of African Americans who through epic memory recall the pain of enslavement and the role of music and dance in the soothing of that pain. In his novel *Black Thunder* (1968), Arna Bontemps writes about Juba, a dancer who is beaten for her participation in a slave uprising: "A crowd of frightened Blacks materialized in the dusk. They followed at a safe distance, the whites of their eyes, the palms of their hands, their rounded white mouths, distinct in the shadows." Later the crowd sends up a soft, dove-like lamentation: "Pray Massa, Pray. Oh Pray, Massa Pray." With each lash of the whip as it goes into Juba's flesh, the crowd moans, "Pray massa pray" or "Lord a mercy." It has been suggested that African-American dance traditions grew out of the moans, groans, and movement of the enslaved Africans.

But dance did not express only the pain of the people. It could, and often did, come

1

out of the joy they felt in each other. At slave festivals such as "'Lection Day" or "Pinkster Day," women and men danced to the music of banjoes, fiddles, and fifes. Or they danced to the accompaniment of singing, drums, and "patting"—a method of producing music with foot-tapping, hand-clapping, and thigh-slapping. One way or another, they danced away sorrow and celebrated their families, friends, and loves.

Sometimes the festivals lasted for days, with almost nonstop dancing and singing. From contemporary reports, it seems that the music was almost entirely African. Hundreds of African Americans participated in the festivals in Albany and Manhattan. There were also many white spectators. Both men and women entered into the dancing, singing, and music-making wholeheartedly.

In New Orleans every Sunday and on church holy days, there was a similar kind of celebrating. Huge crowds of slaves gathered to sing and dance. Thousands of whites gathered to watch them. Historical reports say that the dancing began at three o'clock in the afternoon. Each ethnic group, or tribe, danced in a different part of the square and used its own orchestra of drums, banjoes, and rattles. The dancing would go on until nine o'clock and was so strenuous that dancers frequently had to be replaced as they fainted from exhaustion. The drumming and chanting that accompanied the dancing were performed by both men and women, as was the dancing itself.

These early forms of dancing often came directly out of the African cultures of the people. They were performed by and for African Americans. If white people chose to watch, they could. But the dancers were not entertaining them. They were wholly involved in their own pleasure and that of the people they lived with and loved.

THE MINSTREL GENERATION

The third, minstrel generation began to shape a more formal tradition in dance. The dancing and singing of black street performers in New Orleans inspired the most popular form of American entertainment in the latter two-thirds of the nineteenth century—the minstrel show. It appeared on the scene in the 1830s and remained the major entertainment form in show business for decades.

Black women did not participate in the early minstrel shows. Nor, for that matter, did black men. For many years, the shows were performed by white men wearing burnt cork on their faces to make them look black. These men sang black songs that they adapted to popular tastes. They performed black dances and acted out stereotypes of black people. The music and dancing of black people became enormously popular on the American stage. But black people were not allowed there.

This was a kind of black folk music that seems to have come out of the hours slaves spent together entertaining themselves and ridiculing their white masters. The lyrics were satirical, and the music was strongly influenced by Africa. At the same time, it was usually played on European instruments by people who had been exposed to, and often played professionally, European music.

Much of the music that was later taken by white musicians and adapted for the minstrel shows was used by slaves to accompany their dancing. Various men and women would "pat juba" (or "juber"), making music by tapping their feet to keep the strong rhythm and adding variations by clapping their hands and slapping their thighs. One person, the "juber rhymer," would create verses and recite, not sing, them. The description that has come down to us from historical reports makes the juber rhymer sound much like a rap artist.

On one Maryland plantation, the main juber rhymer was a young woman named Clotilda. From a book by James Hungerford called *The Old Plantation, and What I Gathered There in an Autumn Month*, published in 1859, we have the actual words to some of Clotilda's juba songs. The words tell the dancers what steps to do, and make gentle fun of the people in the community. Hungerford's notes indicate that the people answered back in short shouts, reproaching Clotilda for her impudence. Most of the juba songs are lost, however.

There was also instrumental music for dancing, called "fiddle-sings," "jig-tunes," and "devil songs." These, too, are mostly lost. They often had nonsense lyrics that must not have seemed worth recording.

This kind of group dancing was adopted by the minstrel show. Chairs were placed in a semicircle on the stage, where the entertainers sat for the length of the show. The person who in the slave quarters would have been the dance ringleader was now called the interlocutor, or master of ceremonies. There was usually a banjo player. The chorus sang for the dancers, and the rest of the entertainers clapped their hands or shook tambourines to accompany the singers and dancers. At some point, each person in the company would perform a solo. Both the music and the dancing in these shows were derived directly from black culture.

After the Civil War, black minstrel companies began to be formed. They performed the same dances and songs and acted out the same stereotypes as the white ministrels. Many of them even wore burnt cork over their own black faces. And, like the white minstrel shows, they did not include women. There was usually a female character, called "the wench," but she was played by a black man in bustle and wig.

It was not until 1890 that *The Creole Show* introduced African-American women to the stage as dancers. The basic structure was that of a minstrel show. The star was Sam Lucas, a great star of the black minstrel shows. But now there were black women onstage. They were only in the chorus, but still they were there. The show was instantly and enormously popular.

A few years later, the concert singer Sissieretta Jones, barred from a career in opera and the concert stage because of her race, went on tour with her own variation on the minstrel show, the Black Patti Troubadours. The Troubadours performed a kind of variety show at first, later moving toward musical comedy. The women in these shows were often caricatured themselves, as they sang and danced, becoming objects of pleasure and even ridicule. Still, they drew from their cultural traditions. While they made fun of themselves in order to survive, their movements told another story, the real story, and provided a moving juxtaposition of different realities—theirs and white people's.

The dance steps of the minstrel shows bespoke past legacies and cultural traditions and the shows themselves gave African-American dancers an opportunity to be recognized and to evolve. The traditional dances of the American South were no longer "ring shout," "juba," and "bambouche." Instead, black women would shimmy and shake, "ball the jack," and sashay from side to side as they grew in confidence. The images of free-wheeling, sensuous black women at first transfixed America and ultimately transformed American dance.

THE MUSICAL THEATER GENERATION

The musical theater, the fourth generation, emerged within the decade of the 1890s. A big step was taken in 1898 when Bob Cole, having gained experience with Sissieretta Jones's Black Patti Troubadours, wrote, directed, and produced *A Trip to Coontown*. One of the first American musical comedies, black or white, it had a plot and characters, and it was an entirely black production. Still, the stars were men. Only occasionally did a talented black woman move up from the chorus.

One of the first to do so was Aida Overton. A talented dancer, she had toured with the Black Patti Troubadours. When she married dancer and comedian George Walker, who worked with Bert Williams, she immediately became part of the team. Not only did she sing, dance, and act, but she was also their choreographer.

Aida Overton Walker appeared in all of the many Williams and Walker musicals over the next decade. Then George Walker became ill. When he was no longer able to perform, Aida Walker helped Bert Williams meet their last bookings by dressing in men's clothes and performing her husband's biggest dance hits in every show. She went on

to perform in vaudeville and later became a producer.

Ida Forsyne, one of the most famous of the early black women dancers, got her first real start with the Black Patti Troubadours as well. From there, in 1902, she went on to the cast of *Smart Set* and, two years later, appeared in Will Marion Cook's *Southerners*. In London, in 1906, she was billed as "Topsy, the Famous Negro Dancer" and was wildly successful. After a second London appearance, she went on to a year at the famous Moulin Rouge in Paris. For the next several years, Forsyne toured Europe, taking Moscow by storm with her own version of the *kazotzky*, the traditional Russian dance that is done in a squatting position with the arms folded across the chest.

The outbreak of World War I in Europe forced Forsyne to return to the United States, where her career suffered badly. Accustomed to being a headliner, she found that she had trouble getting any work at all. She believed that was because she was unwilling to enact the stereotypes that audiences demanded. In *Jazz Dance*, by Marshall and Jean Stearns, Forsyne is quoted as saying "I wanted to be a little different from the average colored performer. Perhaps my success in Europe made me feel that way."

But American audiences did not want to see a black woman doing Russian dances. When she did the *kazotzky* in Cleveland, she was booed. After appearing in vaudeville and in small parts in a number of shows from 1914 to 1920, Forsyne took a job with the white singer Sophie Tucker. For two years, she was Tucker's maid and also danced while Tucker was taking her bows, to encourage applause. Difficult as it was, she managed to work in black vaudeville, theater, and films until 1936. At that point, her career as a dancer was over.

Forsyne remains, however, an important figure in the history of black women in dance, in part because of her failure. She was undeniably talented and, when performing in countries where color was of less consequence, she was a highly successful entertainer. In her own country, her refusal to bend to the demands of stereotyping kept her from success. And yet, in spite of that, her fierce determination led her to piece together a career for almost forty years.

Most black women dancers of that time never had the opportunity to escape from the chorus and become solo performers. But the simple fact that they appeared on-stage at all changed musical theater. Then, just as black musicals were hitting Broadway, the United States went into one of its most terrible times, in terms of race relations. From about 1910 to 1920, anti-black feeling among the white population reached its height. The Ku Klux Klan terrorized the South. Laws were passed segregating accommodations, transportation, and schools. A large migration of black workers from southern to northern states threatened white workers and increased racial animosity.

In *On with the Show*, Robert C. Toll reports that in this atmosphere, the success of the black musicals triggered racist anger, and that there were fears of a race war when Williams and Walker's *In Dahomey* opened. But, Toll continues, "violence did not drive Negroes off Broadway. . . . Bias, insidious invisible bias and middle-class financiers and producers did. Although the exclusion was not a single, sudden event, 1910 can be pinpointed as the critical date."

Not until the 1920s would black musicals return to Broadway. In the meantime, black dancers turned to vaudeville. Vaudeville shows could, and did, present just about every kind of entertainment you could imagine. A three-hour program might feature acrobats, dog trainers, singers, dancers, comedians, magicians, and ventriloquists.

Vaudeville also featured the most popular entertainers from Broadway musicals, the legitimate stage, and the concert halls. Among these were black performers. Williams and Walker came to Broadway from vaudeville. Sam Lucas and his wife, Carrie Melvin Lucas, performed extensively in vaudeville, as did Bill "Bojangles" Robinson.

Before 1910, there was only one form of vaudeville, and the audiences were almost entirely white. Both Dora Dean, the great cakewalk dancer, and Aida Overton Walker performed on this circuit. Then, in the 1910s, at about the time black performers began to disappear from white stages, black vaudeville developed. In 1909, Anselmo Barrasso organized the Theatre Owners Booking Association (TOBA). TOBA booked black performers into theaters with black audiences. Among these performers were hundreds of black dancers.

As America came out of World War I, black musicals, with their chorus lines intact, moved back to Broadway. In 1920, two teams of vaudeville heavyweights—the singing and piano-playing Noble Sissle and Eubie Blake and the comedy-dancing act of Flournoy E. Miller and Aubrey Lyles—got together to write the musical *Shuffle Along*. After a considerable struggle, it reached Broadway. New York was dazzled. At that point there had been only a handful of successful musical comedies on Broadway—*Adonis, A Trip to*

Chinatown, Florodora, Irene—and there had never been anything like this new all-black musical.

Shuffle Along had a silly plot and stereotyped black characters, but it had fabulous music written by Eubie Blake. And it had dancing such as Broadway had never seen before. Also, following the lead set by Williams and Walker, it featured a female character. Though the four male writers of the show were undeniably its stars, there was an ingenue. This role was first played by Gertrude Saunders. Later, she was replaced by a young woman who was about to become the first real black female superstar: **Florence Mills**, a cakewalk dance champion who had won many dancing competitions.

Although Mills was only twenty-five years old at the time, she was already an experienced performer. As a child, she had been part of a "pickaninny chorus," one of the many groups of black children who were used by white vaudeville stars to bolster their acts—for very little money.

At eight, Mills was singing in the background of a Williams and Walker show. In her teens, she went on tour on the TOBA circuit in a sister act. She later performed in white vaudeville with her husband, U.S. "Slow Kid" Thompson.

In *Shuffle Along*, Mills was a sensation. She quickly became as big a star as any black man on Broadway, as big as most performers of any color. She went from *Shuffle Along* to *The Plantation Revue*, which had a long run at the Plantation Club in New York City before moving to Broadway in 1922. She turned down a major role in Ziegfeld's *Follies* to star in *From Dover to Dixie*, an all-black revue that played in Paris and London before it came to Broadway as *From Dixie to Broadway*. She became the first black woman to play the Palace, the ambition of all vaudeville performers. She starred in *Blackbirds of 1926*, which opened at the Alhambra Theater in Harlem and then went on to London.

While in London, Mills became ill; she returned to the United States, and soon died. Florence Mills' death at the age of thirty-two was a great blow to the progress of black women in the theater. It was also a great blow to her admirers. At her funeral in Harlem, 150,000 people lined the streets.

Another woman stepped directly out of the chorus of *Shuffle Along* into theatrical history. When she first auditioned, she was turned down as too young, too thin, and too dark. But she went back armored in light face powder and managed to snag a job as a dresser. She then proceeded to learn all the songs and all the dances in the show. Sometime, the ambitious teenager figured, one of the chorus girls would drop out. She was right. Someone got pregnant, and the young dresser was ready to take her place.

When **Josephine Baker** went onstage that first night, however, she did not simply sing the songs and dance the dances. She mugged, she shimmied, she crossed her eyes. In short, she made everyone in the theater notice the sixth girl from the right in the chorus. The audience loved her.

In the next Sissle and Blake production, *Chocolate Dandies*, Baker was center stage, a featured performer. Baker's greatest success, however, came when she went to Europe in *La Revue Nègre*. She startled and enthralled Paris with her near-nude dancing. She became a European superstar and saw no reason to return to race-conscious America. However, from her base in Paris, she became an international star, in whom African Americans could and did take pride.

Social dances were still being created at this time, and Cora La Redd did much to popularize a social dance called "trucking." Other dances moved from black parties and clubs to the Broadway stage and then back.

A transitional performer, **Ethel Waters** bridged the gap between the musical theater generation and the "heritage generation." In 1928, she danced and sang in the musical revue *Africana*. This revue reflected black Americans' need to make an artistic connection between themselves and Africa. It was the beginning of many such expressions as other generations of black women dancers emerged.

THE HERITAGE GENERATION

The fifth, or heritage, generation marked a conscious change for black women. The Harlem Renaissance, World War I, and the Garvey Pan-African movement dramatically combined to alter opportunities for women in dance.

In 1931, Edna Guy cofounded the New Negro Art Theater Dance Company with Hemsley Winfield and was featured with him in what was known as "the First Negro Dance Recital in America." In that same year, **Katherine Dunham** founded the Negro Dance Group in Chicago. In 1932, anthropologist, writer, and folklorist **Zora Neale Hurston** wrote a play that featured Bahamian dancers.

Once new opportunities appeared, black women began to emerge as a dynamic force in concert dance. Katherine Dunham starred in the ballet *La Guiablesse* by Ruth Page in 1934. Edna Guy continued to have recitals, and in 1938, an unknown actor named Esther Rolle appeared as a dancer in *Kunguru*, choreographed by Sierra Leonean Asadata Dafora.

In the meantime, Katherine Dunham began studying anthropology at the University of Chicago and went to the Caribbean to do fieldwork. There she studied African-based ritual dance. Not long after, she received a Guggenheim fellowship to study in Haiti, Jamaica, Martinique, and Trinidad. After completing her Ph.D., Dunham formed a professional dance company, supported largely by the Federal Theater Project (FTP) of the Works Projects Administration (WPA). In 1939, she choreographed and produced *L'Ag'Ya*, which was based on the martial arts of Martinique. Then, the company found a new way to support itself.

Cabin in the Sky, produced in 1940, was a white-owned-and-operated "black musical" that tried to interpret black religion, folklore, music, and mythology. It was extremely successful commercially and critically, in large part because of the talents of its black cast, which included Katherine Dunham and her troupe, along with Ethel Waters.

The Broadway show made one major contribution to the American theater — Dunham herself. The great dancer, because of her role in *Cabin in the Sky*, was in a position to develop her dance company. In the years that followed *Cabin in the Sky*, Dunham and her company presented the most entertaining and genuine Caribbean dancing on a Broadway that seemed to have gone wild for the West Indies. Her troupe appeared in *Tropical Revue*, *Bal Nègre*, *Blue Holiday*, and *Caribbean Carnival*. Dunham choreographed and performed in *Carib Song*.

In 1943, she opened the Katherine Dunham School of Arts and Research in New York and strengthened her artistic and intellectual vision in a war-weary country. The school was a home for her dance company and a training ground in theater arts, dance, literature, and world culture for artists. Among the dancers who studied there were Talley Beatty, **Eartha Kitt,** and Archie Savage. Lavinia Williams, who was born in Philadelphia and danced with the Katherine Dunham Company, devoted her career to Haitian dance and went on to found and direct the Haiti Academy of Classic and Folklore Dance in 1954.

From 1939 to 1950, Katherine Dunham and **Pearl Primus** dominated the African-American dance scene, creating dances that decried oppression and racism. Primus came to the United States from Trinidad at an early age. Her first choreographed work, *African Ceremonial,* appeared in 1943 at the Ninety-second Street Young Women's Hebrew Association. By the fall of 1944, she was presenting a solo concert at the Belasco Theater on Broadway.

Primus studied with some of the finest modern dancers, and she also traveled the South, getting to know the lives of other black people. Then she created a series of powerful dances filled with protest. *Strange Fruit*, choreographed to a poem set to music and sung by **Billie Holiday,** expressed Primus' outrage and pain at lynching.

Like Dunham, Primus worked on Broadway, dancing in and choreographing such shows as *Show Boat* (1945), *Caribbean Carnival* (1947), *The Emperor Jones* (1947), and *Mister Johnson* (1956). Also like Dunham, she traveled to Africa to study various regional dances.

Both Dunham and Primus inspired white choreographers to explore African and African-American dances. Examples of this appear in Jerome Robbins' choreography for *On the Town* in 1944, Helen Tamiris' choreography for *Inside U.S.A.* and *Show Boat* also in the 1940s, and Michael Kidd's choreography for *Finian's Rainbow* in 1947. From that time to this, American theatrical dance has been strongly influenced by the dance of African Americans.

THE CONCERT DANCE GENERATION

The sixth generation of African-American women dancers—the concert dance generation of the post–World War II period—introduced **Janet Collins** and **Carmen DeLavallade** to the world. Both dancers hailed from California and had studied with Lester Horton. They represented a new wave of black female dancers in that they were oriented exclusively to ballet and modern dance.

Collins performed in vaudeville while she was still a teenager and then became a principal dancer for Los Angeles Musical Productions, appearing in such black musicals as *Run Little Chillun, Mikado in Swing,* and *Cabin in the Sky*. Then, in 1941, she joined the Katherine Dunham dance troupe, where she remained for two years. Eventually, Collins moved to New York, where she performed regularly in theater and television while continuing to study ballet and modern dance.

In 1951, Collins made dance history when she was hired as the first black prima ballerina at the Metropolitan Opera. She remained there for three years and, in the meantime, made a number of solo concert dance tours. Then, in 1955, she began to devote her energies to choreography and teaching.

Carmen DeLavallade began dancing with Horton in 1950. During the 1950s, she danced in a number of films, including *The Egyptian* in 1954 and *Carmen Jones* in 1955, and on Broadway in *House of Flowers* in 1954. From 1956 to 1958, DeLavallade followed in Collins' footsteps as a prima ballerina with the Metropolitan Opera Ballet. She, too, became a teacher and choreographer.

Collins and DeLavallade did not necessarily consider themselves specifically black dancers, although both had opportunities to work in the traditional genre. They were proudly African Americans, but they participated in a wide range of dance forms, many of which did not relate directly to their black identity.

Also among this first wave of concert dancers were **Mary Hinkson** and **Matt Turney**, both graduates of the University of Wisconsin. They joined the Martha Graham Dance Company in 1951, the year that Collins debuted at the Metropolitan Opera.

In the meantime, Primus and Dunham continued their work, both having trained in modern dance and ballet, and both took their shows on international tours, including long stays in Africa and Haiti.

In 1961, John Butler choreographed *Portrait of Billie* for Carmen DeLavallade. This was the first of many collaborations between white choreographers and black dancers in the concert dance genre. Agnes de Mille followed soon after when she choreographed *The Four Marys*, using newcomer **Judith Jamison** in 1964. The following year, Jamison joined Alvin Ailey's company. In no

time, the great black choreographer and the great black dancer catapulted to international fame.

Judith Jamison started studying dance when she was six years old. As an adult, she trained with Marion Cuyget, Nadia Chilkovsky, and Joan Kerr in her hometown of Philadelphia. In 1964, Agnes de Mille was teaching a master class at the Philadelphia Dance Academy and saw Jamison. De Mille invited her to perform in the Lincoln Center production of her ballet. An audition the next year for an upcoming Harry Belafonte special brought Jamison to Ailey's attention.

From the time she joined the Alvin Ailey American Dance Theater, Jamison worked closely with Ailey. Then, in 1980, she left to perform on Broadway and with several other companies. She began to choreograph, and Ailey encouraged her, producing her first piece, *Divining*, in 1984. Jamison formed her own company, the Jamison Project, in 1988.

Ailey died in 1989. Before his death, however, Ailey had selected Jamison as his successor. She thus became artistic director of one of the largest, most popular, and most prestigious dance companies in America. Jamison's image symbolized for a generation of black women that black people could indeed be beautiful and talented. In her characterizations of black women in such ballets as *Cry* and *Revelations,* choreographed by Ailey, she danced the history of black women in America. As artistic director of the Alvin Ailey American Dance Theater, she is continuing to serve that history.

In 1969, the great black dancer Arthur Mitchell founded the Dance Theater of Harlem after the death of Dr. Martin Luther King, Jr. Its purpose was to give black young people an opportunity to learn and express themselves through concert dance. The company gave us another prima ballerina, **Virginia Johnson**, who redefined the image of a black ballerina and helped to shape black ballet.

Johnson joined the company only six months after it was founded. Since that time she has performed roles that range from Giselle in the classic ballet of that name to Blanche DuBois in a dance adaptation of Tennessee Williams' *A Streetcar Named Desire*. She sees ballet as a natural form for African Americans to explore. "It's not alien because we're black," she told *Dance Magazine* in a 1990 interview. "There is something that classical dance says to human beings. It exhilarates you, it gives you courage to keep going, because it's more than just the physical experience of being. It's that we're not bound by our physical limitations."

Johnson also reminds us of the many black women who were not allowed the opportunity to participate in this art. Several of the women she studied with were dancers of excellence who loved ballet and were rejected by that part of the dance world. Even that rejection, however, taught them something that they were able to pass on to her. In speaking of Doris W. Jones and Claire H. Haywood, cofounders of the Capitol Ballet Company, Johnson said, "Miss Jones was probably a very fine classical dancer, who was not allowed to study in the same room with white students in the twenties. They were pretty militant about being black people and doing ballet. They gave me a sense of a black body moving through space and a sense of heritage."

Another prominent member of this generation is **Sara Yarborough**. She was signed by the Harkness Ballet in 1958 and went on

to dance with the Alvin Ailey American Dance Theater in the reconstruction of Pearl Primus' works *Fanga* and *Wedding Dance*, in which Yarborough played the bride. Yarborough distinguished herself in Donald McKayle's ballet *Rainbow 'Round My Shoulder* and in a work by Alvin Ailey, *A Lark Ascending*.

The concert dance generation has contributed greatly to the recognition of black artists in the American mainstream. These dancers have also helped to synthesize different forms and strains of dance to create a characteristically American art.

THE BLACK RENAISSANCE GENERATION

The seventh generation, the "Black Renaissance generation" was affected by and affected the 1960s cultural revolution. This generation—an extension of the heritage generation with the skills and savvy of the concert dance generation—sought to make statements that were bold, sometimes inflammatory, and always expressively and unapologetically black.

In 1995, *Dance Magazine* stated that America's "most renowned African American repertoire dance companies are Alvin Ailey American Dance Theater, Dance Theatre of Harlem, and Dayton Contemporary Dance Company, and Philadelphia Dance Company (Philadanco)." The first two were founded by men in the late 1950s and early 1960s. In 1995, one of them, the Ailey company, was under the direction of three remarkable women. The other two companies in this group of four were founded by women. They reflect the increasing visibility of black women in dance.

Although the Dayton Contemporary Dance Company (DCDC) was founded in 1968, its story actually begins in 1949. In that year, the founder of the Dayton Ballet, Josephine Schwartz, decided that dance training should be made available to the youth of Dayton, Ohio. So, she started dance classes at the Linden Community Center. One of the early students was eight-year-old **Jeraldyne Blunden**. The little girl went on, as she grew up, to study with Martha Graham, José Limón, and James Truitte.

By 1960, at the age of nineteen, Blunden was director of dance classes at the center. Gradually, she put together a remarkable group of young dancers and, in 1968, formed the DCDC. This young dance troupe was so good that some of the best choreographers in the country, including Alvin Ailey and Talley Beatty, created dances for them. Indeed, when the American Dance Festival sponsored a program to preserve fourteen classic dance works by African-American choreographers, DCDC was chosen to work with more often than any other company by the choreographers. The company has toured nationally and internationally, impressing audiences everywhere with its excellence. Blunden remained at its head well into the 1990s. In 1994, she received, for her work with the company, a MacArthur Fellowship.

Joan Myers Brown founded her Philadelphia School of Dance Arts, out of which Philadanco grew, after spending nine years as a nightclub dancer in package shows headlined by **Pearl Bailey**, Ray Charles, Cab Calloway, and others. All the time she was touring, she took classes at any school she could get into along the way.

The dance company itself came into being in 1970, ten years after the school. Under Brown's direction, Philadanco gave the dance world such prominent dancers as Deborah Chase and Danielle Gee, both of whom subsequently danced with the Alvin Ailey American Dance Theater. Joan Myers Brown's high technical standards and commitment to keeping black dancers and choreographers employed made her company a haven for aspiring and professional black dancers and choreographers. Brown's school, training company, and professional company all attest to her vision of a viable and self-supporting black dance company. In fact, of the four dance companies mentioned by *Dance Magazine*, as of the mid-1990s Philadanco was the only one that was deficit-free.

Many other black women have taken their fate into their own hands in the world of dance. They have founded and served as artistic directors of companies all over the country.

Ella Moore is a former Ailey dancer and codirector (with her husband, Charles Moore) of the Charles Moore Dance Theater, founded in 1974. After the death of her husband in 1985, Moore took over the artistic directorship of the company. Moore has directed the company to new artistic visions and challenges, and the company has maintained a healthy and viable existence under her artistic stewardship.

Dianne McIntyre was born in Cleveland, Ohio, in 1946 and studied dance at the Karamu House in Cleveland. In 1972 she founded Sounds in Motion, a dance company she serves as artistic director. McIntyre has choreographed for other companies, as well as Broadway and off-Broadway shows, including the Alvin Ailey American Dance Theater and Avery Brooks' one-man show *Paul Robeson*. McIntyre has also collaborated with playwright **Ntozake Shange** on *Spell #7, Boogie Woogie Landscapes,* and *The Great McDaddy*. Sounds in Motion exemplifies McIntyre's personal vision of the fusion and interrelatedness of music and movement in black dance.

Amania Payne of Muntu Dance Company in Chicago, Illinois, and Ferne Caulker Bronson, artistic director of Kho-Thi Dance Company in Milwaukee, Wisconsin, are two prominent artistic directors of their own African dance companies. Both women have helped to document, choreograph, and institutionalize the art of African dance in America for the concert stage and in the dance studio.

In the Black Renaissance period, many other women who were empowered by the self-determination of the era used regional arenas to make a national impact. Cleo Parker founded the Cleo Parker Dance Company of Denver, Colorado, and Lulu Washington founded the L.A. Contemporary Dance Theater in Los Angeles, California. **Kariamu Welsh Asante** started the Black Dance Workshop, later to become known as Kariamu and Company, in Buffalo, New York, in 1970. Nanette Bearden (wife of the late artist Romare Bearden) formed the Nanette Bearden Contemporary Dance Theater, headquartered in New York City.

These companies funneled dancers to the national companies, most notably the Alvin Ailey American Dance Theater and the Dance Theater of Harlem. The acceptance of dancers from the regional dance companies into the national companies was an affirmation of the skills and artistic visions of these artistic directors.

Sylvia Waters, Consuelo Atlas and Carole Johnson all emerged in this generation to dance and to lay new artistic and aesthetic foundations. Dyane Harvey, Mickey Davidson, Frances Hare, Yvonne James, Loretta Abbott, Donna Woods, Thea Nerissa Barnes, and Bernadette Jennings were all dancers making a statement about themselves as black women in America.

In the tradition of Mary Hinkson and Matt Turney, Thea Barnes danced with the Martha Graham Company after leaving the Alvin Ailey American Dance Theater. Donna Woods inherited the legacy of Judith Jamison as dancer in the Ailey company. And so the tradition continued.

THE GENERATION OF CONTINUITY AND INNOVATION

When Judith Jamison became choreographer and artistic director of the Alvin Ailey American Dance Theater, a transition began to the eighth generation, the generation of continuity and innovation. The women of this generation dance all the styles—mixing, matching, and synthesizing them into whatever speaks for the dancer. This generation's dancers are unafraid either to be themselves or to draw on the traditions of the past and antiquity. They are Africans, they are black, they are women, and they are human, and that composition can look like anything in the dance.

Jamison is not the only woman in a position of power and responsibility in the Ailey. There are three elements of the company, and women head all three. The thirty-one-member main dance troupe is, of course, the best known. The Alvin Ailey American Dance Center is a school where children can learn the basics and professional dancers can hone their skills. And the Alvin Ailey Repertory Ensemble is a link between the two, giving the most talented students from the school an opportunity to perform and, perhaps, eventually become part of the main troupe.

Denise Jefferson is director of the Dance Center, working to present excellent training to three thousand students a year. In addition to ballet, the school offers modern and jazz dancing. There are also classes in acting and voice for potential Broadway dancers and classes in dance and music history to expand the dancers' minds.

Sylvia Waters is director of the Repertory Ensemble. She works with dancers who are usually between seventeen and twenty-three years old. They are potentially the future members of the most renowned African-American repertoire dance company in the country.

All three of these women have participated in making the Ailey a star of the generation of continuity and innovation. When Jamison introduced into the repertoire *Shelter*, by choreographer **Jawole Willa Jo Zollar**, "people's reaction was 'You're taking such a chance. Isn't that too different?'" says Jamison. "No! What is typically Ailey is just that diversity. . . . Sometimes it's forgotten that this is a repertory company that tried to embrace as many ways of moving as possible."

Zollar, artistic director of Urban Bush Women, leads an all-woman dance company committed to the performance of African and African-American dance forms in a holistic context. Zollar received her B.A.

degree in dance from the University of Missouri and her M.F.A. degree from Florida State University. She studied with Diane McIntyre and went on to create her now famous *Lifeforce I, Girlfriends,* and *The Magician.* Like McIntyre, Zollar collaborates with poets, drummers, and folk artists. She is a powerful, often confrontational choreographer who gives the dance of black women another way to move.

More and more, the choreography of black women expresses who they are as African Americans and as women. Blondell Cummings, in her *Chicken Soup,* invokes the image and memory of grandmothers and evokes warmth and laughter. Judith Jamison, in her work *Ancestral Divinations,* makes a point about who she and her sisters are. Eva Golson is lyrical, fragile in her strength, and so full of music that all her works sing.

BeBe Miller, artistic director of the BeBe Miller Dance Company, is an African American who leads a predominantly white dance company. Miller has been daring in her expressions of her sensibility and sensitivity as a feminist and humanist. Her vision is complementary to the vision of her colleagues who share her commitment to justice and equality for all women. Blondell Cummings is the artistic director of Blondell Cummings, an essentially solo enterprise. Cummings is not only a dance soloist but also an improvisation and performance artist.

Dianne McIntyre, alone or with her company, continues to make her connections, whether they be in the historical ballet *Up North* or in her opera about the writer Zora Neale Hurston. McIntyre closes the circle for black women in dance because, as she moves forward, she looks back at the classic and traditional African-American dance forms that the silent and anonymous generations helped to bring to the fore. She unabashedly weaves those movements into her work, creating a tapestry of voices—some loud, some quiet, some fighting, some singing a sacred song in a strange land.

All of the artistic directors mentioned have distinguished themselves first as dancers, then as choreographers, and finally as artistic directors of companies in a continuity of traditions. Katherine Dunham and Pearl Primus continue to have an impact on dance in America. Their dynamic and fluid legacies have yet to be completed and remain a challenge for dancers, choreographers, and artistic directors who want to continue the legacy into the twenty-first century.

Eight generations of black women in dance have already come, and there are many more yet to come. They come daring to be, daring to confront, willing to share, willing to expose, and they keep coming. They dance the rituals of young women, they know the secret dances of mature women, and they dance the dances of birth, death, enslavement, celebration, and victory.

Since antiquity, dance has been a part of who black women are. Black women danced the "ring shout" dance and kept the spirit. They danced the cakewalk, Charleston, and Lindy hop and changed the rhythms of America. They danced "A Luta Continua" and "A Change Is Gonna Come I Know." When Malcolm X and Martin Luther King, Jr., were killed, they danced a slow mournful dance that threatened to raise Nzingha, ancient warrior dancer. Keepers of the dance, of the culture, and ultimately of the people, black women in their movement bear witness to a life force that is diverse, dynamic, fluid, and spiritual.

[This introduction is based on the article "Dance," by Kariamu Welsh Asante, from *Black Women in America: An Historical Encyclopedia*]

A

Asante, Kariamu Welsh (1949–)

In her dances and in her writing, Kariamu Welsh Asante helps to define the dance of black women today. Asante was born on September 22, 1949, in Tomasville, North Carolina, but she grew up in New York City. "My mother," she says, "loved the arts, and we went to anything free that was presented in Prospect and Central Parks." Those performances included opera, musicals, and the plays of Shakespeare and laid the foundation of Asante's lifelong interest in music and dance.

She attended Franklin K. Lane High School, on the border of Brooklyn and Queens. The school had a notable dance program under the leadership of Ida Waranoff, once a Martha Graham dancer. Waranoff made a strong impression on Asante, who recalls: "When I wasn't selected for a part and I went to her disappointed . . . she said to me, 'If you really want to dance and be in dances, then you need to choreograph.'" The young student, already a writer of poetry and short stories, immediately adopted this new form of expression.

After graduation, Asante went to the State University of New York, where she trained as a dancer and choreographer and received a master's degree in humanities in 1975. Her earliest works—*Revolution: A Change Is Gonna Come I Know*, *Coretta*, *Like It Is and Like It Was*—reflect the concerns of the late sixties and early seventies.

While she was working at the university with a series of noted teachers and choreographers, she was also active in the Buffalo African-American community. She founded Kariamu and Company in 1971, gathering around her a group of skilled and committed dancers. She remains director and choreographer of the troupe more than two decades later.

With her company, she began to develop what she named the Umfundalai technique. It is, in her words, "the essence of traditional African movements and styles that I incorporate into contemporary dance technique to empower myself and others to express ourselves." She was also artistic director and resident choreographer of the Center for Positive Thought, formerly known as the Black Dance Workshop.

In 1981, Asante received a Fulbright Senior Artistic Award that allowed her to go to Zimbabwe. There, she founded the National Dance Company of Zimbabwe. Two additional Fulbrights allowed her to return to that country in 1982 and 1990.

In addition to choreographing dozens of works over the years, dancing, and directing her troupe, Asante is associate professor in the African Studies department and director of the Institute for African Dance Research and Performance at Temple University. She is the founding editor of the *International Journal of African Dance*, a member of the editorial advisory board for *Black Women in America: An Historical Encyclopedia*, and author of books on the Umfundalai technique and on African dance.

KATHLEEN THOMPSON

B

Baker, Josephine (1906–1975)

Josephine Baker was the first and greatest black dancer to emerge in the genre now called performance art. She epitomized through dance what freedom of expression and artistic expression really meant for generations of artists worldwide. Baker was one of the few artists in the world acclaimed and awarded for being themselves. Her genius resided in her conception of music, dance, and comedy. She had a musician's sense of timing, a dancer's instinct for cutting a phrase, and a comedian's ability to deliver the punchline even when it was in the song or gesture. Not merely an entertainer, Baker was in every sense of the word an artist, and it was as an artist that she made her mark on the world.

Baker was also a humanitarian who, in her own unique and eccentric way, tried to live by example. She symbolized beauty, elegance, grace, and, most important, intelligence. Baker helped usher in a new era for black and white Americans that furthered and fostered mutual understanding between the races. Dance was not only the vehicle for her own transformation into racial awareness, it was also the connector for thousands of her admirers.

Born Josephine Freda MacDonald on June 3, 1906, in St. Louis, Missouri, she was the daughter of Eddie Carson and Carrie MacDonald. She made a name for herself as a singer and dancer in Noble Sissle and Eubie Blake's all-black musical *Shuffle Along* in 1921. This revue was seen as the black musical theatrical event of its day and helped to usher in the Harlem Renaissance. It was also a major attraction for white Americans seeking the exotic, which they found in Baker (the surname of her second husband), a fifteen-year-old chorus girl who became the surprise hit of the show.

Baker also toured with **Bessie Smith**, the "Empress of the Blues," and in 1924 she was featured dancing the Charleston and the Black Bottom at the Old Plantation Club in New York. Baker continued to work with composers Sissle and Blake and returned to Broadway in 1924 in their new revue, *Chocolate Dandies*.

In 1925, she went to Paris and became a sensation in the American production *La Revue Nègre,* symbolizing the quintessential exotic black woman. She usually performed as an exotic dancer at the Folies-Bergère and the Casino de Paris. She appeared in two films, *La Revue des Revues* and *La Sirène des Tropiques,* in 1927. In the film *ZouZou* (1934), her first talkie, she sang and danced; one song from *ZouZou,* "C'est lui," stayed in her repertoire for years. In 1934, Baker starred in a remake of Offenbach's 1875 comic opera *The Créole,* in which she had one of her greatest artistic successes. *Princess Tam Tam,* her second talkie, made in 1935, was shot on location in North Africa and told the story of an African beauty who is presented to Parisian society as a princess. Baker appeared in

New York in the Ziegfeld Follies in 1936 and 1938.

Baker introduced the Charleston and Black Bottom dances to Europe. The influx of black talent in the chorus line, including Baker and **Florence Mills**, helped to change dance and fashion in America and Europe. The chorus line was now a precision vehicle performed by women dancing closely together to a swinging rhythm. The poet Langston Hughes said of Baker, "There was something about her rhythm, her warmth, her smile, and her impudent grace that made her stand out" from others in the chorus line.

Starting from a poor community in St. Louis, Missouri, "La Baker," as she was called in France and abroad, came to be feted and toasted in her adult life by European royalty, including Princess Grace of Monaco and Queen Elizabeth of England. Baker also became a friend to many other contemporaries who went on to make national and international contributions. Alexander Calder, an American sculptor and mobile artist, sketched Baker. Novelist Ernest Hemingway proclaimed her the most beautiful woman he had ever seen. She became friends with anthropologist and choreographer **Katherine Dunham** after seeing her company perform at the Théâtre des Champs-Elysées. Baker said that Dunham should be called "Katherine the Great," evidence of her admiration for a fellow artist and black American. George Balanchine, the great choreographer, created a dance for Baker in a Ziegfeld revue. Legendary boxer Joe Louis was another admirer and friend and often called on Baker when he was in Paris. Poet e. e. cummings wrote of Baker's performances: "She resembled some tall, vital, incomparably fluid nightmare which

crossed its eyes and warped its limbs in a purely unearthly manner—some vision which opened new avenues of fear, which suggested nothing but itself and which consequently was strictly aesthetic."

It was an irony of the times that Baker's performances were considered aesthetic and artistic. Black dance forms lagged behind the other art disciplines in gaining acceptance from the white artistic community, but Baker was instrumental in helping to make that transition. Although she was initially regarded as primitive and exotic, she quickly and skillfully redefined those terms as much as she redefined dance.

In Paris, clothing, perfumes, and hairstyles were all promoted under her name. Baker was known for her spectacular costumes and elaborate headdresses. Dior, Lanvin, Poiret, and Balenciaga, the great European designers, designed clothes especially for her. She was known to make as many as seven costume changes in one performance. Baker wore a shorter dress to accommodate the high kicks and freewheeling movements of the Charleston and the Black Bottom. The shorter fashions that she helped make popular freed women from a Victorian and puritanical look. Baker's influence also contributed to the elimination of the corset. Inspired by Baker, designer Paul Poiret revolutionized the fashion world by discarding the corset in order to permit women to dance more freely. Baker's costumes, especially the fan and banana costumes, became part of French iconography. A banana flan was named after her in honor of the banana outfit.

Baker's ability to sing in six languages (Hebrew, Spanish, German, Portuguese, French, and English) combined with her influence in dance and fashion to remove her

A legend to several generations who found her performances irresistible, Josephine Baker is shown here in one of her trademark spectacular gowns. She made headlines during her 1951 American tour when she protested discrimination against her at the Stork Club. (MOORLAND-SPINGARN)

from the realm of the savage, in the minds of Europeans, and raise her into the realm of the citizen extraordinaire. She fulfilled the role that had become embedded in the European psyche: the super-sexy black woman who had a completely free spirit and danced with wild exuberance.

André Levinson, the Russian who became France's first modern dance critic, described Baker and her dancing as "a sinuous idol that enslaves and incites mankind." He also said, "Thanks to her carnal magnificence, her exhibition comes close to pathos. It was she who led the spellbound drummer and the fascinated saxophonist in the harsh rhythm of the blues. It was as though the jazz, catching on the wing the vibrations of this mad body, were interpreting, word by word, its fantastic monologue. The music is born from the dance, and what a dance!"

The long-legged, cocoa-colored beauty was known for her comedic abilities as well as for her sensuous dancing, which often involved dancing topless. This image of "Le Savage" dancing with a string of bananas around her hips tantalized a Europe that had only recently emerged from the ravages of World War I and fulfilled fantasies and philosophies alike for the masses, the literati, and the intelligentsia. Baker was able to appeal to them all. Sadly, despite all her fame abroad, she was unable to capture the same sort of critical adoration and adulation in America.

Although she made repeated trips to America in the early part of her stay in France, in 1937 she chose to become a French citizen because there she did not face the same level of racial discrimination and prejudice. The indignity of performing before segregated or abusive audiences prevented her from ever seriously considering a return to the

United States. Unlike her contemporaries, singers **Bessie Smith** and **Billie Holiday**, Baker refused to suffer the habitual and pervasive abuse meted out to black female entertainers in America. In addition, she resisted what she considered to be the stereotyped image of the black female performer. When asked about returning to America she said, "They would make me sing mammy songs and I cannot feel mammy songs, so I cannot sing them." On a tour of southern states with musician Artie Shaw, she had a confrontation with a racist who appreciated her music but referred to her as a "nigger wench." Baker insisted on retaliation, but her speaking out often got her in trouble with a nation of audiences accustomed to black entertainers who always smiled and stayed silent, regardless of the verbal and physical abuse heaped upon them.

The "Black Venus" of France, as she was also known, entertained Allied soldiers in North Africa during World War II. As a Red Cross volunteer, she worked as an ambulance driver on the Belgian front. After the German invasion of France in 1940, she became involved in underground intelligence activities and made numerous trips throughout Europe and North Africa for the Free French Resistance; for her efforts, Charles De Gaulle later awarded her the Legion of Honor and Rosette of Resistance decorations. After the liberation of Paris in 1944, Baker resumed her performing career at the Théâtre aux Armées, and after the war, she performed at the Folies-Bergère.

Baker's life was not without political controversy. While on tour in Italy, she heard Mussolini advocating the takeover of Ethiopia. She was misquoted or misinterpreted as supporting Mussolini and was roundly condemned by the black press in the United States. In Argentina, she made anti-American statements that were denounced by Congressman Adam Clayton Powell, Jr., who accused her of letting herself be manipulated by foreign interests. Her tendency to disparage American audiences further distanced her from Americans, including black Americans; this distance was bridged only when she began to support civil rights issues in subsequent visits to the United States.

Baker was married four times and divorced three times. About her first husband, Willie Wells, little is known, and Baker rarely spoke of him. The greatest contribution of her second marriage, to Will Baker, was his surname. Her third husband, Count Pepito Abatino, orchestrated a disastrous Ziegfeld Follies tour. After Baker got out of her contract with the Follies, the marriage broke up, even though Abatino was then dying of cancer. Later, she married musician and bandleader Jo Bouillon, but they separated some time before her death.

Well known as an animal lover—and owner of a menagerie that included snakes, cheetahs, monkeys, and a pig named Albert—Baker also loved children. In the 1950s, she embarked on what she called her "experiment in humanity": She began to adopt orphaned children of different races and nationalities to make a point about humanity and racism. With husband Jo Bouillon, she adopted twelve children and settled into a fifteenth-century chateau, Les Milandes, in France's Dordogne Valley. In 1956, she retired from show business to take care of the children full time. It was a noble experiment, but it was ill-fated; with no income from performing, the expense of keeping such a large, unique family in the extravagant style to which she was accustomed grew prohibitive and strained her marriage.

Forced to return to show business, Baker made her second Paris debut in 1959, at the Olympia de Paris in *Paris, Mes Amours,* a revue based loosely on her own life. Baker and her "Rainbow Tribe," as she called her children, moved into a house in Roquebrune, France, provided by Princess Grace as a testament to Baker's belief in racial harmony and equality.

On a visit to the United States in 1951, Baker said, "My greatest desire will always be to see my people happier in this country." In 1963, she demonstrated her activism and her faith in the civil rights movement by flying in for the march on Washington, D.C., and a Carnegie Hall civil rights benefit at which she performed. In 1964, her appearances at the Brooks Atkinson and Henry Miller theaters in New York were favorably received by both critics and audiences, who marveled at the preservation of her voice and body.

Trying to support her children, the sixty-seven-year-old Baker returned to the United States again in 1974 and 1975 on a tour of major cities that ended in a sold-out performance at Carnegie Hall. The response was the unadulterated appreciation of a living legend. Many Americans had only heard of her and found it a special treat to see and hear the real star. There was ambivalence, however, from the black community. Although Baker was appreciated for her legacy and stature in the world community, her expressed intolerance of the Black Power movement—a movement based solely on race—made many feel that she was of little help to the cause of black Americans.

Baker died in Paris on April 12, 1975, after a performance and a dinner party in her honor. She was still adored by millions of fans throughout the world, and she was given a twenty-one-gun salute, the only such honor to be given by France to an American-born woman citizen. At a memorial service in New York, Rosetta LeNoire, the African-American stage and television actress, eulogized Baker this way: "She died in triumph, a woman nearing seventy seemingly transformed to her youth in voice, figure, and vitality, joining her damaged heart with the hearts of cheering audiences which welcomed her back to her beloved Paris."

Baker herself may have said it best in 1927. When a reporter asked about her future, she answered, "I shall dance all my life, I was born to dance, just for that. To live is to dance, I would like to die, breathless, spent, at the end of a dance."

A major biography, *Josephine: The Hungry Heart*, by Jean-Claude Baker and Chris Chase, was published in 1993.

KARIAMU WELSH ASANTE

Blunden, Jeraldyne   (1941?–)

The founder of the renowned Dayton Contemporary Dance Company, Jeraldyne Blunden has been at the forefront of regional American dance from the late 1960s into the 1990s. Her company is known for its talent and its "astonishing conviction," as well its ability to make New York critics sit up and take notice.

Blunden grew up in Dayton, Ohio. In 1949, when she was eight years old, Josephine Schwartz started dance classes for urban youth there, at the Linden Community Center. Schwartz was a well-regarded dance teacher who had founded the Dayton

Ballet. Blunden fell in love with dance, and studied under both Josephine and Hermene Schwartz. Seeking out the great contemporary dancers of her time, Blunden studied under Martha Graham, José Limón, and James Truitte.

Blunden went on as a concert dancer, performing largely in the Ohio region. She danced with the Dayton Theater Dance Company (descended from Schwartz's Dayton Ballet), the Karamu Dancers at the Antioch Summer Theater, and the Connecticut College Dance Theater Workshop. Blunden also performed with her own Dayton Contemporary Dance Company.

In 1968 Blunden founded the Dayton Contemporary Dance Company (DCDC). Through her vision the troupe first gained renown as a remarkable regional company, then as a national presence in the American dance community. The company has toured widely, both in the United States and abroad.

Blunden is also committed to dance education, especially in the Ohio region. She has taught at Wright State College, Ohio State University, Miami University, Toledo University, Wilberforce University, and Sinclair Community College.

As a guiding spirit in American dance, Blunden has sat on the boards of many prominent dance organizations, at both the national and regional level. She is currently a board member of Dance U.S.A., where she helps both to influence the direction of dance across America and to promote the art's responsibilities to the general public. She has also served on the boards of the National Association for Regional Dance, Ohio Dance, and the Northeast Regional Ballet Association.

Blunden won the prestigious MacArthur Fellowship in 1994, and has been honored with many other awards as well. In 1990 she was given an honorary doctorate in fine arts from the University of Dayton, and was awarded the Regional Dance America Award in 1991. In 1988 she was given the Ohio Dance Award for Outstanding Achievement, and she became the first woman to receive the Kuzaliwa Award for contributions to the African-American community.

While the Dayton Contemporary Dance Company faced a financial struggle in the 1990s, Blunden's vision carried on. In spite of the difficulties, Blunden insisted that it is important that "we still maintain our identity as a culturally diverse organization and continue expanding our educational programs. It is my dream to see the Dayton Contemporary Dance Company rise and take their place among the leading dance companies of the world!"

KATHLEEN THOMPSON

Brown, Joan Myers (19??–)

Head of one of the most renowned regional dance companies in the United States, Joan Belle Myers Brown is a gifted artistic director and advocate of black dance in America. As founder and chief of the Philadelphia Dance Company (otherwise known as "Philadanco"), she has developed her trademark combination of high-energy and highly disciplined dance. She has also shown that excellent dance can thrive outside of New York City, and that black dance can thrive outside of white limitations.

Born in Philadelphia, Brown was the only child of Thomas and Nellie Myers. She grew up when all the color bars were still in place

in Philadelphia. In black dance performances, light-skinned children got the leading
roles, while Brown was relegated to the chorus. When she went home she made up her
own programs on the porch, where she was
the lead.

She studied for six months under a skilled
black instructor, Essie Marie Dorsey, one of
the pioneers of black dance in that part of
the country. Brown performed at the Philadelphia Cotillions, black debutante balls
that staged elaborate production numbers.
Brown danced in several of these, and
learned a great deal about production from
Marion Cuyjet, another Philadelphia pioneer in black dance training. Along the way
Brown won a precious $100 scholarship

Joan Myers Brown is head of the Philadelphia
Dance Company, and one of the most gifted
artistic directors in the country. She is a strong
advocate of black dance in America. (PHILA-
DELPHIA DANCE COMPANY)

that enabled her to study ballet in New York
once a week for a summer.

During this period the acclaimed English
dancer and choreographer Anthony Tudor
was brought to Philadelphia to teach every
Sunday. He held integrated classes, though
it distressed the organization that brought
him. Tudor quickly recognized Brown's talent and had her dance the lead in "Les
Sylphides." However, he warned Brown
that there was little hope for her future in
white concert dance.

By the early 1950s Brown had given up
ballet in favor of nightclub dancing, where
she could get a job. She went on tour with
such stars as Cab Calloway, **Pearl Bailey**,
and Sammy Davis, Jr. By 1960 she was
performing in Atlantic City and had also
opened her own dance school in Philadelphia, commuting between the two cities.
Her school, the Philadelphia School of
Dance Arts, recently celebrated its thirty-
fifth anniversary. In 1970, Brown founded
the equally long-lived Philadanco.

Although an integrated company,
Philadanco has upheld the tradition of black
dance, even while combining it with ballet
or dance forms from other cultures. Known
for its high energy and polished talent, one
of the hazards the Philadanco company has
faced is that its dancers are so good that they
are often pirated away by larger companies
in New York.

Brown has also proven to be an exceptionally able arts administrator. Philadanco
is not only one of the finest black repertoire
dance companies in the nation, it is one of
the few that is financially solvent. This is
credited to Brown herself, who, despite being artistic director, at times can be seen
washing out the dancers' costumes. While
salaries are not high, Brown has built a

company that offered its dancers a paid, 52-week contract, which is quite a rarity in the dance world. Philadanco owns its own building, a renovated factory, and provides subsidized housing for its dancers in nearby apartments. One apartment is reserved for visiting choreographers.

Because Philadelphia has few performance spaces suitable for dance, Philadanco has toured widely and has built a national reputation from these tours. The company has appeared to critical acclaim in New York, Italy, and at traditionally black colleges around the country.

Wishing to encourage black performance art beyond Philadelphia, in 1988 Brown initiated the International Conference of Blacks in Dance. This gathering has continued as an annual event, now encompassing more than 400 dance professionals from 80 groups around the nation. In 1990 Brown went on to help found the International Association of Blacks in Dance.

Brown has received many awards over the years. Most recently she was awarded an honorary doctorate from the University of the Arts, where she also teaches as a Distinguished Professor.

After so many accomplishments Brown is still creating new ventures for black dance. She is now involved in a real estate project called Avenue of the Arts, Inc. This will create an arts hub involving several organizations, centered along Broad Street in Philadelphia near the venerable Academy of Music. Philadanco will be the only dance company in the complex.

One of the great spirits of black American dance, Joan Myers Brown has enhanced a great arts tradition outside of the world of formal New York dance, and often without mainstream funding. She credits Philadanco's strengths to her performers, whom she regards as family. As she talks about her company she says "I think the ability to work together in a situation without stress and the close relationships the dancers have with one another is also a strength. The competitiveness of New York is not here."

KATHLEEN THOMPSON

C

Collins, Janet (1923–)

Janet Collins is known as the first black prima ballerina in America to perform in a

Years before she became the first black prima ballerina in the Metropolitan Opera, Janet Collins was offered a position with the Ballets Russes de Monte Carlo on the condition that she paint her skin white. To her eternal credit, she refused. (MOORLAND-SPINGARN)

major ballet company. Collins was born in 1923 in New Orleans and moved to Los Angeles, California, as a young girl. She attended Los Angeles City College and the Los Angeles Art Center School. Collins was also an accomplished painter, which helped her finance her move to New York to pursue her dance career.

Collins was in the initial tour of the **Katherine Dunham** dance troupe in Los Angeles. She auditioned for the Ballets Russes de Monte Carlo but was rejected on the basis of her skin color. However, she was offered a chance to perform with the company if she would paint her skin white; she refused. Collins received a Rosenwald Fellowship to study classic, Hebrew, and Negro dances. In 1949, she made her New York City debut in a solo concert. In 1950–51, Collins was lead dancer in Cole Porter's musical *Out of This World,* for which she won the Donaldson Award. She then joined the corps de ballet of the Metropolitan Opera in 1951. The following year she went on to become prima ballerina. Collins also taught as a professor at the School of American Ballet in New York. Following her retirement she moved to Seattle, Washington, where she pursued her painting.

KARIAMU WELSH ASANTE

D

DeLavallade, Carmen (1931–)

Carmen DeLavallade was born in Los Angeles, California, on March 6, 1931. A protégé of the late modern dance pioneer Lester Horton, she came to be known as a "total" dancer who was equally at home in ballet, modern, or theatrical dancing. DeLavallade could also sing and act, which contributed to her reputation as a well-rounded performer.

DeLavallade began her dancing career with the Horton Dance Theater in 1950 in the role of Salome in Horton's ballet *The Face of Violence*. Subsequently, she was featured with the Metropolitan Opera Ballet, the Boston Ballet, the Alvin Ailey American Dance Theater, and her own company. DeLavallade is best known for her interpretation of West Indian dances choreographed by her husband, Geoffrey Holder, a renowned dancer, choreographer, and artist. Carmen DeLavallade is also known for her work with choreographers John Butler and Glen Tetley.

She danced in four films, *Lydia Bailey* (1952), *Demetrius and the Gladiators* (1954), *The Egyptian* (1954), and *Carmen Jones* (1955). The choreographer for *Carmen Jones* was Herbert Ross, who cast DeLavallade in *House of Flowers* (1954), a Broadway production that also featured Alvin Ailey and Geoffrey Holder. DeLavallade also starred in several television productions, including Duke Ellington's *A Drum Is a Woman* and Gian Carlo Menotti's Christmas opera *Amahl and the Night Visitors*. From 1956 to 1958, DeLavallade appeared as a prima ballerina with the Metropolitan Opera Ballet in several productions, including *Aida* and *Samson*

Best known for her interpretation of West Indian dances by her husband, Geoffrey Holder, Carmen DeLavallade has had a wide-ranging career, appearing in films such as the acclaimed Carmen Jones, *on television in Duke Ellington's* A Drum Is a Woman *and Gian Carlo Menotti's* Amahl and the Night Visitors, *on Broadway in* House of Flowers, *and at the Metropolitan Opera as a prima ballerina in* Aida *and* Samson et Dalila. (SCHOMBURG CENTER)

25

et Dalila. The film *Odds Against Tomorrow* (1959), starring Harry Belafonte, featured DeLavallade danced the role of Bess in a ten-minuet ballet sequence adapted from *Porgy and Bess* and presented on CBS on January 15, 1961. Carmen DeLavallade has also taught at the Yale School of Drama in New Haven, Connecticut, and has choreographed several of the school's theater productions.

KARIAMU WELSH ASANTE

Dunham, Katherine (1909–)

Katherine Dunham, an artist of many talents, is best known as a popular and widely acclaimed dancer who, with her troupe, per-

A scholar as well as a performer, Katherine Dunham wrote a Ph.D. thesis on the dances of Haiti that was published in Spanish, French, and English. (MOORLAND-SPINGARN)

formed on stages throughout the world in the 1940s and 1950s, choreographing Caribbean, African, and African-American movement for diverse audiences. Her concerts were visually and kinesthetically exciting and appealing; they were also based on a profound understanding of the peoples and cultures represented as well as on a keen knowledge of social values and human psychology. Dunham's achievements as anthropologist, teacher, and social activist are less well known.

By her own account, in her autobiography, *A Touch of Innocence* (1959), Dunham was born in Chicago on June 22, 1909. The family lived in Glen Ellyn, a white suburb of Chicago. Katherine's mother, Fanny June (Taylor), was an accomplished woman of French-Canadian and Native American ancestry who died when Katherine was young. Katherine's father, Albert, Sr., of Malagasy and West African descent, left Katherine and Albert, Jr., her brother, with aunts in Chicago while he traveled as a salesman.

Katherine's father subsequently remarried and his family moved to Joliet, Illinois, where he ran a dry-cleaning business. Albert, Sr., was an embittered man, and conflicts among her father, brother, and stepmother caused the young Katherine to seek solace in her own life of imagination. She attended Joliet High School, where she was active in athletics and joined the Terpsichorean (dance) club. She continued her education at Joliet Junior College, where she took lessons in dance. Her brother persuaded her to apply for admission to the University of Chicago where he was studying philosophy. She was accepted, and she was able to support her education by giving dance lessons and by working as an assistant librarian.

In Chicago, Dunham studied modern dance and ballet and joined with a member of the Chicago Civic Opera Company to establish a black dance group, later the Chicago Negro School of Ballet. Her troupe performed at the Chicago Beaux Arts Ball in 1931 and Ruth Page invited her to appear as a solo lead in *La Guiablesse* (1934), based on Martinique folklore, at the Chicago Civic Opera Theater. Dunham also appeared in one of the productions of the Cube Theater, cofounded by her brother. There she met poet Langston Hughes, historian St. Clair Drake, jazz composer W. C. Handy, and dramatists Ruth Attaway and Canada Lee.

At the University of Chicago, she was attracted to anthropology through a course with Robert Redfield, who stressed the importance of dance as a part of social and ceremonial life. She chose to do fieldwork in the Caribbean, where she could study the forms and functions of African-based ritual dance as well as the role of dance in popular culture. She prepared for her fieldwork with Melville Herskovits, who had published numerous works on African and Haitian societies.

Dunham impressed psychologist Erich Fromm and sociologist Charles Johnson with her accomplishments. They recommended that she be invited to present her fieldwork plans before the board of the Julius Rosenwald Foundation. During her presentation, she startled the board members by demonstrating the different dance styles she planned to investigate. Moved by her resolve and enthusiasm, they decided to support her research. She received a Guggenheim Award in 1937 to pursue her investigation of dance in Haiti, Jamaica, Martinique, and Trinidad.

When the great dancer, choreographer, and teacher Katherine Dunham researched the dances of the Maroon peoples of Jamaica, she so won their trust that they accepted her as one of the "lost peoples" of Africa. Her work with the Children's Workshop in East St. Louis inspired a former gang member to credit her with saving his life. This charismatic figure has incalculably enriched the world of dance, opened communication between cultures, and served the black community of the present and future. (SCHOMBURG CENTER)

Journeying to Jamaica, she visited the Maroon peoples of Accompong. She succeeded in viewing the Koromantee, a war dance with sacred and political meaning. The Maroon peoples' decision to allow her to see the dance signaled their acceptance of her as one of the "lost peoples" of Africa, whose mission was to instruct her people in their heritage. Her abilities were further demonstrated in Haiti, where she was initiated into the Vaudun religion and performed in the public dance after the secret ritual. She subsequently maintained a lifelong relationship with the people and culture of Haiti and participated in the Vaudun up to the highest level, that of "seer." An avowed mystic, Dunham demonstrated the ability of dance and an open spirit to heal and transform lives.

To complete her Ph.D., Dunham wrote a thesis, "Dances of Haiti," which was later published in Spanish, French, and English (1947, 1957, 1983). Subsequently, she chose to present her cultural knowledge through dance, although she continued in her relationship to the academic world, giving lecture-demonstrations at Yale, University of Chicago, the Royal Anthropological Society of London, and the Anthropological Societies of Paris and Rio de Janeiro. She also held academic positions, as visiting professor at Case Western Reserve University and artist in residence at Southern Illinois University at Carbondale and the University of California at Berkeley, as well as university professor and professor emerita at Southern Illinois University at Edwardsville.

Dunham's social conscience and political awareness were heightened through her association with political and cultural leaders in Haiti, such as Dumarsais Estimé, president of the republic (1946-50), and Dr. Jean Price-Mars, an anthropologist and cultural nationalist; but she had challenged racism even as a child. She and her family had encountered discrimination in the white community of Glen Ellyn, where in grade school she had refused to sing a song that was degrading to African Americans, and where she had faced the "color barrier" when she worked as a librarian. She felt that

her brother, a brilliant philosophy student of Alfred North Whitehead, never received recognition commensurate with his abilities. Dunham saw these aspects of her personal history as part of a heritage of colonialism and slavery, in which Africans and peoples of African descent were oppressed and exploited for purposes of power and profit. In her career, she expressed her social convictions through her art, promoting understanding and respect for African-based cultural expression as well as fostering self-esteem and creativity among her students.

Throughout her career, Dunham took controversial stands, working with the National Association for the Advancement of Colored People and the Urban League to end segregation in accommodations and audiences in the cities in which the Dunham troupe performed. In one city she announced after a performance that she would not return until the audience was integrated. In Brazil, the strong criticism and embarrassment that occurred when the Dunham troupe was not allowed to stay at a certain hotel led to the first public accommodations act in that country. While on an international tour she presented the ballet *Southland* (which dramatized a lynching) during the sensitive period following the lynching of Emmett Till in Mississippi, despite pressure by the U.S. State Department to stop the performance.

Dunham founded her first professional dance company in 1939, performing in Chicago and New York; at first, she subsidized her company through federal support projects that were a part of President Roosevelt's New Deal program; she produced and choreographed the ballet *L'Ag'Ya*, based on the martial arts of

Martinique, for the Federal Theater Project. Later the company appeared at the Windsor Theater in New York and in the Broadway production *Cabin in the Sky* (1940), in which Dunham worked with George Balanchine on choreography. They went on tour with the musical in 1940-41, closing in Los Angeles. In 1942, Dunham appeared in *Star-Spangled Rhythm*, a wartime film to raise morale. She choreographed and appeared with her troupe in several other movies during 1942-43, then, with impresario Sol Hurok, toured the United States in her *Tropical Revue*. During a Boston appearance, the troupe's performance of "Rites de Passage," a serious treatment of sexuality in a non-Western context, was censored.

While working for the Federal Theater Project, Dunham met and married John Pratt, a costume and set designer, who continued to design her productions until his death in 1986. Their daughter, Marie Christine, was adopted in 1951. A designer, she resides in Rome.

In 1943, the Katherine Dunham School of Arts and Research opened in New York. Students studied theater arts, dance, literature, and world cultures as a part of their training as artists. In addition to members of the Dunham troupe, other well-known artists such as the actors Marlon Brando, Arthur Mitchell, and James Dean studied there. Some members of her dance troupe, including Talley Beatty, **Eartha Kitt**, and Archie Savage, went on to establish international reputations in their own right. The Katherine Dunham troupe appeared in concerts, touring the United States, Canada, Europe, Asia, and Latin America between 1940 and 1963. Dunham continued to conduct anthropological investigations throughout this time, taking dancers into the villages and neighborhoods where she obtained her choreographic movements and ideas, so that the dancers could become knowledgeable about the cultural and social contexts of the dances they performed.

After its early years, the Katherine Dunham troupe was entirely self-supporting. Audiences were transported by performances; psychiatrists sent patients to them as a part of therapy, and people often came to her dressing room with tears in their eyes. During a postwar London performance of *Shango* (Haitian war god), the audience screamed in empathetic response to the presentation. The last performance of the Dunham company was at the Apollo Theater in 1965.

Although she considered herself a teacher and choreographer rather than a dancer and favored ensemble over solo dancing, Katherine Dunham was an extremely popular and critically acclaimed performer. In Europe, hat styles and spring fashion collections were named the "Dunham line" and "Caribbean Rhapsody"; the Chiroteque Française made a bronze cast of her feet. Alvin Ailey commented that the interior meaning of his work *Masekela Language* is that all of the women are Katherine Dunham in some aspect of her performance.

From 1965 to 1967, Dunham was in Senegal, representing the United States at the Festival of Black Arts in Dakar and training the National Ballet of Senegal. When she returned to the United States, she moved to East St. Louis to develop the Performing Arts Training Center of Southern Illinois University. Through the center, Dunham has encouraged an appreciation for cultural heritage by bringing in artists and scholars from Haiti, Brazil, Senegal, and elsewhere. In the Children's Workshop, students learn

Creole, African languages, and folk arts including music, stories, and dance from representatives of African, Latin American, and Caribbean cultures. Through Dunham technique, the children learn discipline and develop balance and grace; they develop respect for themselves and for others. Nearby is the Katherine Dunham Museum, which houses artifacts and art objects from Dunham's world travels.

Katherine Dunham has published a number of works in addition to those already mentioned. *Island Possessed* (1969) is an account of her ongoing relationship with the people of Haiti; *Kasamance* is a fictional work set in Senegal. She has published many articles on her philosophy of dance and of life; and is writing her memoirs. She has won many awards, including the Kennedy Center Award (1983), the Albert Schweitzer Music Award (1979), the *Dance Magazine* Award (1968), and the University of Chicago Alumni Professional Achievement Award (1968), as well as numerous honorary degrees. In 1986 she received the Distinguished Service Award of the American Anthropological Society. She has received numerous medals and citations from the government of Haiti. In 1987 Dunham directed the reconstruction of several of her works by the Alvin Ailey American Dance Theater, and *The Magic of Katherine Dunham* opened Ailey's 1987–1988 season.

JOYCE ASCHENBRENNER

F

Forsyne, Ida (1883–?)

One of the most famous of black dancers in the early twentieth century, Ida Forsyne lived a life marked by great triumphs and even greater frustrations. Her unwillingness to remain within stereotypical roles and images eventually led to her rejection by audiences but make her now an inspiring figure in the history of black women in dance.

Ida Forsyne was born in Chicago in 1883 to a mother who was a domestic worker and a father who left them when Forsyne was two. She began dancing early in her life. By the age of ten, she was a professional, dancing first for pennies in the street and then working with a ragtime band at Chicago's 1893 Columbian Exposition. When she was fourteen, she ran away from home with a show called *The Black Bostonians*. When the show went broke in Montana, she made her way back to Chicago by train, dancing and singing in the aisles to make her fare.

Forsyne's first real break came when she was hired by Black Patti's Troubadours, a troupe that was the training ground for many black musicians and dancers of the time. She remained with the show for a number of years. When the show was not on tour, she worked at Atlantic City or Coney Island. In 1899, she ruined her singing voice while trying to shout her songs over a band that was playing too loudly. From that time on, she was a dancer.

In 1902, Forsyne began to appear in musical comedy. She was in the original cast of *Smart Set* and then performed in Will Marion Cook's *Southerners* at the New York Roof Garden. In 1906, she went to London with a troupe of New York musicians who called themselves The Tennessee Students. The group included, along with Forsyne, the legendary Abbie Mitchell. Billed as "Topsy, the Famous Negro Dancer," Forsyne was a huge hit.

After London came Paris and the Moulin Rouge, then all of Europe. She was successful everywhere, particularly in Moscow. There, she performed the *kazotsky*, a Russian dance done in a squatting position, arms folded, kicking out one leg and then another. However, when World War I broke out, she was forced to return to the United States. From that time on, her career went downhill.

The years Forsyne spent in Europe had unsuited her to dance within the minstrel show stereotypes that were still demanded of African Americans in the states. When she tried to do the *kazotsky* in Cleveland, she was booed off the stage. For the next several years, she performed in a few shows and tried to travel the Theater Owners Booking Association (TOBA) circuit with her own act. Finally, she ended up working for Sophie Tucker as a maid. To encourage applause for Tucker, she also danced onstage while Tucker took her curtain calls.

In 1924, Forsyne returned to the TOBA circuit as a backup dancer for blues singer Mamie Smith. She also had small parts in a few films and plays in the decade that followed. However, her career was essentially over by 1936. She returned briefly to consult on the choreography for *Cake Walk* with the New York City Ballet.

KATHLEEN THOMPSON

H

Hinkson, Mary (1930–)

Mary Hinkson, dancer, teacher, and choreographer, was born in Philadelphia, Pennsylvania, in 1930. She attended the University of Wisconsin, which had a budding dance program. After graduation, Hinkson moved to New York to study with Martha Graham, the modern dance pioneer and visionary. Hinkson danced with the Martha Graham Dance Company in many roles that Graham created specifically for her, such as *Ardent Song* (1955), *Acrobats of God* (1960), *Samson Agonistes* (1962), and *Phaedra* (1969). Hinkson is best remembered for her role as Circe in the dance of the same name in 1963.

Hinkson has worked as a guest artist with many dance companies in the United States and in Europe. Some of the other choreographers she worked with were Pearl Lang (*Chosen People*, 1952), Donald McKayle (*Rainbow 'Round My Shoulder*, 1959, in which she created the female lead), John Butler (*Carmina Burana*, 1966), George Balanchine (*Figure in the Carpet*, 1960), and Anna Sokolow (*Seven Deadly Sins*, 1975, in which Hinkson danced in "The Dance of Anna.)"

Hinkson remains known for her long and outstanding work with Graham, which began in 1951. She has taught the Graham technique at the Martha Graham School in New York. Although Hinkson is known primarily as a dancer and a teacher, she has choreographed several dances. She performed her most notable dance, *Make the Heart Show*, in 1951. Hinkson also has taught at the Dance Theater of Harlem's school, the Juilliard School, and at the High School of Performing Arts, all in New York City.

KARIAMU WELSH ASANTE

J

Jamison, Judith (1943–)

Judith Jamison was appointed artistic director of the Alvin Ailey American Dance Theater in 1990 and has been a vital force in the dance community since the early 1970s. Although her early training was in ballet, she went on to become an international symbol of American modern dance and provided inspiration for generations of aspiring young African-American female dancers.

A striking six-foot-tall, cocoa-colored woman with a short-cropped natural hair style, Jamison was an appropriate image to emerge from the 1960s and 1970s cultural revolution. She helped to redefine the image

An international symbol of American modern dance, Judith Jamison has been an inspiration for generations of aspiring young African-American women dancers. Here she performs in Nubian Lady. (SCHOMBURG CENTER)

of a dancer with her African appearance and carriage. In the tradition of **Katherine Dunham** and **Pearl Primus**, she proudly acknowledged her heritage through her own choreography with works like *Divination* and *Ancestral Rites. Cry*, the magnum opus created by the late choreographer Alvin Ailey for Jamison, epitomized the struggle of black women in America and symbolized for the world the dignity and strength of black women through four hundred years of oppression and victory. In the 1980s she starred in the Broadway hit *Sophisticated Ladies* (with music by Duke Ellington) with actor-dancer Gregory Hines.

After a distinguished career as a dancer, Jamison went on to establish her own company, the Jamison Project, in 1987, before becoming the artistic director of the Alvin Ailey American Dance Theater. Jamison is the first African-American woman to direct a major modern dance company. She and her contemporaries, choreographers Dianne McIntyre (Sounds in Motion), **Kariamu Welsh Asante** (National Dance Company of Zimbabwe), and **Jawole Willa Jo Zollar** (Urban Bush Women), have extended the lineage of Katherine Dunham and Pearl Primus to ensure the artistic legacy of African Americans.

KARIAMU WELSH ASANTE

Johnson, Virginia (1950–)

Virginia Johnson was born January 25, 1950, in Washington, D.C. She attended New York University and the Washington

School of Ballet. Johnson made her debut with the Washington Ballet in 1965 and the Capitol Ballet in 1968. She is known best for her work with the Dance Theater of Harlem, for which she has danced since 1971. Johnson, a lyrical dancer, is a premier black ballerina. Her versatility as a dancer has allowed her to move successfully from classical ballet roles like the *Don Quixote* pas de deux to contemporary dramatic ballets like Valerie Bettis' *A Streetcar Named Desire*. Johnson also created the role of Giselle in Arthur Mitchell's reinterpretation of the romantic ballet *Giselle*. As Giselle, she plays the sheltered, half-caste daughter of a recently freed African slave. The ballet is set in the bayous of Louisiana. Deborah Jowitt, dance critic for the *Village Voice*, applauded Johnson's representation of Giselle as a "triumph of intelligence, sensitivity, and good taste."

Johnson found her niche in dramatic ballets, and she mastered many of the classics, including Agnes De Mille's "The Accused" in *Fall River Legend*, a dramatic rendition of the celebrated case of Lizzie Borden. Anna Kisselgoff of the *New York Times* lauded Johnson's performance and pronounced the production "a sheer triumph." Johnson continues to dance the technical, emotional, and dramatic spectrum of ballets and continuously extends her artistic range from historic classical to contemporary experimental ballets.

Johnson received the Young Achiever Award of 1985 from the National Council of Women of the United States for her work with young dancers, in master classes, and in lecture demonstrations.

KARIAMU WELSH ASANTE

P

Primus, Pearl (1919–1994)

Pearl Primus was born in Trinidad in 1919 and moved to New York at an early age. She attended Hunter College and graduated in 1940 majoring in biology and premedicine. Primus received a dance scholarship to the New School for Social Research and began to study what were called at the time "primitive dances." Her first choreographed work, *African Ceremonial*, premiered at the Ninety-second Street Young Women's Hebrew Association on February 14, 1943. This was considered her professional debut, and the work received positive reviews. After a ten-month engagement at a club called Café Society Downtown, she left to prepare her first solo concert. This performance took place at the Belasco Theater on Broadway in the fall of 1944. This was an extraordinary achievement for a young black woman in that period. Primus went on to study with some of the great modern dance teachers of that time including Martha Graham, Doris Humphrey, Charles Weidman, Hanya Holm, and Sophie Maslow.

Primus traveled the South observing the lifestyles of the common people, living with sharecroppers, and visiting black churches. It was that experience that inspired much of her subsequent choreography. Dances such as *Strange Fruit* became classics, because of her bold statement of social protest. Some of the other works choreographed by Pearl Primus are *Shango* (1947), *Impinyuza* (1951), *Naffi Tombo* (1960), the legendary *The Negro Speaks of Rivers* (1943), choreographed to a poem by Langston Hughes, and *Michael Row Your Boat Ashore* (1979), which was about the horror of the Birmingham, Alabama, church bombings. Primus' choreography chronicled the black experience in the United States and the traditional dances of Africa and the Caribbean. Primus also worked on

Whether traveling the American South, living with sharecroppers, or working with the National Dance Company of Liberia, Pearl Primus always used her exceptional talents as a choreographer and dancer to explore the lives of her people. (MOORLAND-SPINGARN)

Broadway dancing in and choreographing such shows as *Show Boat* (1945), *Caribbean Carnival* (1947), *The Emp*eror Jones (1947), and *Mister Johnson* (1956).

Like her predecessor **Katherine Dunham**, Primus received a Rosenwald Fellowship to finance her travel to Africa for eighteen months. In 1949, she was able to visit what was then known as the Gold Coast (Ghana), Angola, the Cameroons, Liberia, Senegal, and the Belgian Congo (Zaire). Later, on another trip to Africa with her husband, Percival Borde, she was named "Omowale"—which means "the child returns home" in Yoruba—by the Nigerians. In 1959, on her second major trip to Africa, Primus was named director of Liberia's Performing Arts Center. Her work with the National Dance Company of Liberia and her stylization of the Liberian dance "Fanga" earned her that country's highest award, the Order of the Star of Africa, which was bestowed on Primus by President William V. S. Tubman.

Primus' husband was also a dancer and choreographer. After their two-year stay in Liberia, they returned to the States and formed the Earth Dance Company in the 1970s. In 1976, two of Primus' dances, *Fanga*, a dance of welcome, and the *Wedding Dance*, were performed by the Alvin Ailey American Dance Theater. The American Dance Festival in Durham, North Carolina, reconstructed Primus' *The Negro Speaks of Rivers* and presented the dance in its black dance classic series.

Primus has taught dance and anthropology at Hunter College, the State University of New York at Buffalo, New York University (where she received her Ph.D. in dance education), and at Smith College (where she was a Five College Professor of Humanities). She was honored by President George Bush for her contributions to dance and received the National Medal of Arts at the White House on July 9, 1991. She died at her home in New Rochelle, New York, on October 29, 1994.

KARIAMU WELSH ASANTE

T

Turney, Matt (1930–)

Matt Turney was born in Americus, Georgia, in 1930. She studied at the University of Wisconsin and at the Martha Graham School in New York. Known as a "dancer's dancer," she was suited to Martha Graham's myth-oriented, highly technical choreography. She joined the Martha Graham Dance Company in 1951 and continued to perform in the company until 1972. Among the many Graham-choreographed dances in which she created roles were *Ardent Song* (1954), *Seraphic Dialogue* (1955), *Clytemnestra* (1958), *Embattled Garden* (1958), *Visionary Recital* (1961), and *Phaedra* (1969).

Turney also danced with the companies of Donald McKayle, Alvin Ailey, Paul Taylor, and Pearl Lang. In a 1960 recital by her colleagues Bertram Ross and Robert Cohan, Turney performed *Praises*, *The Pass*, and *Quest*.

KARIAMU WELSH ASANTE

W

Waters, Sylvia (1940–)

Sylvia Waters was born in New York City on January 22, 1940. While she was in junior high school, she began studying modern dance. Her studies continued at the New Dance Group of New York City and later in the dance department of the Juilliard School. She graduated from Juilliard in 1962 and began her career as a professional dancer. She performed with the dance company of Donald McKayle and, on scholarship, studied at the Martha Graham School of Contemporary Dance.

Waters' life changed dramatically when she was cast in the musical *Black Nativity*, written by Langston Hughes. The show toured Europe for seven months; when the tour ended, Waters remained in Paris. For three years she performed with the Paris Opera Ballet and appeared on French television. However, ballet was not her first love. In 1968, after dancing with Maurice Bejart's Ballet of the Twentieth Century at the Olympic Games in Mexico City, she returned to the United States and modern dance.

That same year, Waters joined the Alvin Ailey American Dance Theater in New York. For her first seven years there, she was part of the performance ensemble. Then, in 1975, she became director of the Alvin Ailey Repertory Ensemble, a training ground for young dancers. Through lectures and master classes, as well as performances, students are prepared to take their place either in the senior Ailey company or in any of a number of other major dance companies around the country. The ensemble also performs experimental works by major choreographers.

After the death of the legendary Ailey, Sylvia Waters was a part of the team that continued Ailey's work and made the Ailey company a name to conjure with in modern dance.

KATHLEEN THOMPSON

Y

Yarborough, Sara (1950–)

In a famous description of Sara Yarborough's dancing, Alvin Ailey said it came as close to flight as humanly possible. It is certainly true that, since the late 1960s, she has soared in the world of American dance.

Sara Yarborough was born in New York City in 1950. She grew up in Haiti, where her mother, Lavinia Williams, established a school of dance. From an early age, the daughter was trained to follow in the mother's footsteps. At age six, she began studying all varieties of dancing, from ballet to jazz to tap, at her mother's academy of dance. She showed a remarkable aptitude for and interest in ballet.

At the age of eleven, Yarborough came to the United States. She studied for two years at George Balanchine's School of American Ballet. A few years later, in 1967, she came to the attention of Benjamin Harkarvy at the Harkness School. Soon she was a member of the Harkness Ballet. Still in her teens, she began performing difficult and demanding roles with great elegance. Among her earliest appearances were roles in *Firebird and Time Out of Mind*.

Yarborough performed a number of other important roles at the Harkness before Alvin Ailey spotted her while he was rehearsing *Feast of Ashes* at the Harkness.

The next year, when the company closed, Ailey invited Yarborough to work with the Alvin Ailey Dance Company.

For the next four years, Yarborough was a star in the Ailey constellation, performing with grace and beauty in such works as *The Lark Ascending* (1972) and *Hidden Rites* (1973). From 1975 to 1976, she danced with the Joffrey Ballet, but she returned to the Ailey in 1977.

Sara Yarborough is a tremendous inspiration to young dancers who aspire to the heights of excellence in performance without ever forgetting their heritage.

KATHLEEN THOMPSON

Z

Zollar, Jawole Willa Jo (1950–)

Born in 1950 in Kansas City, Missouri, Jawole Willa Jo Zollar attended the University of Missouri in her hometown and then went on to earn a master's degree from Florida State University. At Florida State, she studied traditional ballet and modern dance, but she felt unsatisfied. "What was lacking was who I was," she told *People* magazine in 1990. "It was someone else's vision." Zollar completed her studies and received an M.F.A. degree. Then, in 1980, she moved to New York City.

In New York, she studied with noted dancer and choreographer Diane McIntyre, artistic director of Sounds in Motion. Then, in 1984, Zollar formed her own company, Urban Bush Women. The company combines modern and jazz choreography with Caribbean and African rhythms. Also into the mix go tribal chants, gospel testifying, and the moves of the urban black ghetto. The themes of the dances come out of the urban black experience. The Urban Bush Women spend about thirty weeks each year on tour. The rest of the time they perform in New York City.

Playwright **Ntozake Shange** says of Zollar's work, "The ensemble that Jawole Willa Jo Zollar has assembled and sustained takes women's bodies, racist myths, sexist stereotypes, postmodern conventions, and the 'science' of hip-hop and catapults them over the rainbow, so they come tumbling out of the grin of the man in the moon."

Jawole Willa Jo Zollar formed her company, Urban Bush Women, in 1984. Ntozake Shange says of the ensemble that it "takes women's bodies, racist myths, sexist stereotypes, post-modern conventions, and the 'science' of hip-hop and catapults them over the rainbow, so they come tumbling out of the grin of the man in the moon."

One of Zollar's works, *Anarchy, Wild Women and Dinah*, is based on South Carolina Sea Islands folk culture. In reviewing it, *Dance Magazine* said, "Company director Jawole Willa Jo Zollar is a sensational performer who sums up cosmic concepts in a few words or gestures, or conversely transforms everyday annoyances into homilies of universal significance."

Many of Zollar's pieces bridge the space between dance and theater with monologues, dialogues, and stories. *Shelter*, which the *Christian Science Monitor* calls "an intense work about the plight of the homeless," has been added to the repertoire of the Alvin Ailey Dance Theater.

KATHLEEN THOMPSON

Chronology

1667

The earliest known reference is made to "Pinkster Day" (Pentecost Sunday), in a sermon book written by Adrian Fischer. This slave festival features traditional African singing and dancing in which both men and women participate.

1741

The earliest known "'Lection Day" festival is held by slaves in Salem, Massachusetts.

1818

Dances that occur in New Orleans every Sunday in the Place Congo are historically noted for the first time. The circular dances, performed by both men and women after Sunday services, are thought to be African dances directly transplanted to the southern United States.

1859

James Hungerford publishes *The Old Plantation, and What I Gathered There in an Autumn Month*, which contains the first record of the words to juba songs that tell the dancers what steps to do, as sung/spoken by a slave woman named Clotilde.

1888

Concert singer **Sissieretta Jones,** barred from a career in opera and the concert stage because of her race, goes on tour with her own variation on the minstrel show, the Black Patti Troubadours.

1890

The Creole Show introduces African-American women to the stage as dancers.

1898

Bob Cole opens *A Trip to Coontown,* one of the first American musical comedies, black or white. It is an all-black production from beginning to end.

1902

Ida Forsyne joins the cast of *Smart Set.*

1903

The play *In Dahomey* tours to London, popularizing the cake-walk dance in Europe.

1904

Ida Forsyne performs with Will Marion Cook's *Southerners.*

1905

The Memphis Players, the first modern jazz band, makes its debut in New York, with Abbie Mitchell singing and Ida Forsyne dancing.

1906

Ida Forsyne performs in London, and at the Moulin Rouge in Paris billed as "Topsy, the Famous Negro Dancer."

1909

Anselmo Barrasso organizes the Theater Owners Booking Association (TOBA) which books male and female black performers into theaters with black audiences.

1916

In Los Angeles, California, Lauretta Green founds the Butler Dance Studio, the first black-owned dance school for children. The school trains both blacks and whites.

1921

The musical comedy *Shuffle Along* becomes the first all-black musical to be produced on Broadway. The show launches the careers of Gertrude Saunders, **Florence Mills**, Caterina Jarboro and **Josephine Baker**.

1922

The Plantation Revue moves to Broadway with its star Florence Mills.

1923

Runnin' Wild is performed on Broadway, choreographed by the first-known African American choreographer, Elida Webb.

1926

Florence Mills stars in *Blackbirds of 1926*, which opens at the Alhambra Theater in Harlem and then moves on to London.

Josephine Baker stars at the Folies-Bergere in Paris, performing her famous 'banana dance.'

1927

Florence Mills dies in London at the age of thirty-two. At her funeral in Harlem, 150,000 people line the streets.

1928

Ethel Waters dances and sings in the musical revue *Africana*, the first musical revue that reflects black Americans' need to make an artistic connection between themselves and Africa.

1931

Edna Guy cofounds the New Negro Art Theater Dance Company with Hemsley Winfield and is featured with him in what is known as "the First Negro Dance Recital in America."

Katherine Dunham founds the Negro Dance Group in Chicago.

1932

Anthropologist, writer, and folklorist **Zora Neale Hurston** writes a play that features Bahamian dancers.

The Cleveland Opera Company produces Shirley Graham's *Tom-Tom: An Epic of Music and the Negro*, with a cast of 500.

1933

The federal government creates the Works Progress Administration (WPA), which provides funding and therefore opportunity and visibility to many young dancers and choreographers.

1934

Katherine Dunham stars in the ballet *La Guiablesse* by Ruth Page.

1937

Katherine Dunham receives a Guggenheim Award to pursue her investigation of dance in Haiti, Jamaica, Trinidad, and Martinique.

1938

Esther Rolle appears as a dancer in *Kunguru*, choreographed by Sierra Leonean Asadata Dafora.

1939

Katherine Dunham choreographs and produces *L'Ag'Ya*, which is based on the martial arts of Martinique.

1940

Katherine Dunham and her troupe, along with Ethel Waters perform in *Cabin in the Sky*, a white-owned-and-operated "black musical" that is a huge success on Broadway.

Katherine Dunham's performances in *Tropics* and *Le Jazz Hot: From Haiti to Harlem* in New York establishes her reputation as a dancer.

1941

Janet Collins joins the Katherine Dunham dance troupe.

1943

Katherine Dunham opens the Katherine Dunham School of Arts and Research in New York. Among the dancers who will study there are Talley Beatty, **Eartha Kitt**, Archie Savage, and Lavinia Williams.

Pearl Primus' first choreographed work, *African Ceremonial*, is premiered at the Ninety-second Street Young Women's Hebrew Association.

1944

Pearl Primus makes her Broadway debut, presenting a solo concert at the Belasco Theater.

1945

Pearl Primus choreographs *Show Boat* on Broadway.

1947

Pearl Primus choreographs both *Caribbean Carnival* and *The Emperor Jones* on Broadway.

1949

Josephine Schwartz (founder of the Dayton Ballet) starts teaching dance classes at the Linden Community Center.

1950

Carmen DeLavallade begins dancing with Lester Horton.

1951

Janet Collins makes history when she is hired as the first black prima ballerina at the Metropolitan Opera, performing in *Aida*. She is the first black person ever to perform on the stage of the Metropolitan Opera House.

Mary Hinkson joins the Martha Graham Dance Company.

1954

Carmen DeLavallade dances in the movie *The Egyptian* and dances on Broadway in *House of Flowers*.

Lavinia Williams founds the Haiti Academy of Classic and Folklore Dance.

1955

Janet Collins begins to choreograph and teach.

Carmen DeLavallade dances in the movie *Carmen Jones*.

1956

Pearl Primus choreographs *Mister Johnson* on Broadway.

Carmen DeLavallade joins the Metropolitan Opera Ballet as a prima ballerina.

1958

Sara Yarborough is signed by the Harkness Ballet.

Alvin Ailey founds his world famous dance company, The Alvin Ailey Dance Theater.

1960

At the age of nineteen, **Jeraldyne Blunden** becomes the director of dance classes at the Linden Community Center.

Joan Myers Brown founds the Philadelphia School of Dance Arts.

1961

John Butler choreographs *Portrait of Billie* for Carmen DeLavallade.

1964

Agnes De Mille choreographs *The Four Marys*, using newcomer **Judith Jamison**.

1965

Judith Jamison joins the Alvin Ailey American Dance Theater and then goes with the company on the most successful European tour ever made by a U.S. dance troupe.

1968

The Dayton Contemporary Dance Company (DCC) is founded by Jeraldyne Blunden.

1969

The Dance Theater of Harlem is founded and **Virginia Johnson** joins the company, giving the world another great black prima ballerina.

1970

Joan Myers Brown founds the Philadelphia Dance Company, later to become famous as Phildanco.

Kariamu Welsh Asante starts the Black Dance Workshop, later to become known as Kariamu and Company, in Buffalo, New York.

1971

Sara Yarborough joins the Alvin Ailey American Dance Company.

1972

Dianne McIntyre founds her dance company Sounds in Motion.

1974

Alvin Ailey founds his 'second company,' the Alvin Ailey Repertory Company, as a training ground for future dancers. **Sylvia Waters** is its artistic director.

Ella Moore founds (with her husband, Charles Moore) the Charles Moore Dance Theater.

1975

Sara Yarborough joins the Joffrey Ballet in New York City for one year.

1984

Judith Jamison produces her first piece, *Divining*.

Jawole Willa Jo Zollar founds Urban Bush Women, a dance company that incorporates new theatrical styles and an enormous variety of dance forms, creating a new style of dance and dance theater.

1985

After the death of her husband, Ella Moore becomes the artistic director of the Charles Moore Dance Theater.

1988

Judith Jamison forms her own company, the Jamison Project.

1989

When Alvin Ailey dies, Jamison (selected by Ailey himself) becomes artistic director of the Alvin Ailey American Dance Theater.

1994

Jeraldyne Blunden receives a MacArthur Fellowship.

SPORTS

Introduction

When **Jackie Joyner-Kersee** ran her victory lap at the 1992 Olympics, millions cheered. Americans felt their hearts swell with pride. Olympic decathlon champion Bruce Jenner walked up to Joyner-Kersee and said, "You're the greatest athlete in the world. Man or woman, the greatest athlete in the world."

For almost fifty years, black women have dominated women's track and field in America. As a group, they are the fastest, strongest, highest-jumping women this country has yet produced. And they're rapidly closing the gap with the men.

And yet, until after World War II, opportunities for black women in sports were practically nonexistent. And still today, there are whole areas of competition that are virtually closed. Why has this terrible inconsistency endured in an area of life that is supposed to be the domain of sportsmanship and fair play? How have black women managed to triumph in the ways and places that they have? The answers to these questions are found in the history of black women in American sports.

THE BEGINNING

In the history of black women, there is always, in every situation, double discrimination. In some areas discrimination on the basis of race is most significant. In other areas, gender may be a larger problem. In sports in the United States, discrimination against women has been so pervasive that there hardly seems room for any other form. And yet, even here, black women have faced added obstacles.

Until recently it was considered completely natural and within a woman's capabilities to haul water, beat clothes against rocks, carry forty-pound children, help plow the fields, chop wood when necessary, and do whatever else was needed to keep the house clean, the children healthy, and the men fed. It was, however, considered unfeminine to run a foot race. Even after women of every color, built the airplanes that helped the Allied powers win the World War II, the International Olympic Committee wouldn't allow women to run more than 200 meters for fear they would collapse from the strain.

The attitudes toward white women applied to black women as well. Before emancipation, of course, the vast majority of black women in America were slaves. But it is important to keep in mind that there was, as far back as the late seventeenth century, a minority of African Americans who were free. Their limitations, as well as their freedoms, were different from those of their slave sisters.

In the early years of this country, women settlers were so busy working that they had little or no time for games of any kind. Black women, who (themselves or their ancestors) were brought to this country to work as slaves, were even less likely to find a spare hour for recreation. However, both groups combined work and play in such activities as corn shucking and quilting bees. Also, on Saturday evenings, when they were allowed to rest from their week's work, black women gathered to participate in simple games, foot races, and, especially, dances.

Later, as the country became more settled and a class developed that had more leisure time, some white women began to be involved in such activities as ice skating, boating, and horseback riding. Free black women of the middle class probably engaged in some of these activities as well, but to a considerably lesser degree, since every aspect of their lives was restricted by society and by law.

However, whatever freedom middle-class women of any color enjoyed was soon to be limited. Early in the reign of Queen Victoria of England, the ideal white woman of the time was seen as, to quote Janet Woolum in *Outstanding Women Athletes,*

> gentle, passive, pure, and moral. Generally, according to the ideal, women stayed inside the home to maintain their purity, rebuffed any strenuous exercise, and wore corsets that cinched the waist to give the appearance of a petite, delicate, and frail body. Many believed that women could not take the strain of any physical exertion and any overt activity would have negative effects on female sexuality and the ability to give birth.

This is the image that was so effectively attacked by **Sojourner Truth** in her famous "Ain't I a Woman?" speech:

> That man over there says that women need to be helped into carriages and lifted over ditches and to have the best place every-where. Nobody ever helps me into carriages or over mudpuddles or gives me any best place. And ain't I a woman? Look at me! Look at my arm! I have ploughed and planted and gathered into barns, and no man could head me! And ain't I a woman? I could work as much and eat as much as a man—when I could get it—and bear the lash as well. And ain't I a woman? I have borne thirteen children and seen most all sold off to slavery, and when I cried out with my mother's grief, none but Jesus heard me. And ain't I a woman?

Truth's impassioned protest lays bare the contradictions in the Victorian ideal. Belief in its standards of physical frailty could be maintained only if you looked at the minority of women who were upper-class and, for the most part, white. For all other women, life included constant labor. And for slaves, few distinctions of any kind were made between men and women. When there was hard work to be done, whoever was available did it—man, woman or child.

And yet, even while the majority of black women were doing harsh physical labor on Southern plantations, there were others who accepted the Victorian ideal for themselves. Respectability was extremely important to free black women who were trying to gain acceptance or at least tolerance from the dominant culture. They would not jeopardize this by defying the definition of ideal womanhood. So, the limitations that applied to white women of their class applied largely to them as well.

Late in the second half of the nineteenth century, social attitudes toward women and physical activity began to change. Doctors started to suggest that exercise might actually be good for women. Again, participation was mainly determined by class. Women from families with a certain level of income were free to spend at least part of their time in archery, bowling, croquet, and other "lady-like" pursuits. It was even acceptable for women to play tennis so long as they didn't get carried away and run to reach a ball. This was true for black women of this class as well.

Tennis was introduced into the United States by a white woman, Mary Ewing Outerbridge, in 1874, on her return from a holiday in Bermuda. By 1890, many black families owned tennis courts. As a result, matches and tournaments began at black colleges in 1895 and in suburban Washington, D.C., by 1910. Women as well as men participated in these games.

In Chicago, Mrs. C. O. "Mother" Seames began teaching tennis on dirt and clay courts in 1906. In 1912, she became a charter member of the Chicago Prairie Tennis Club, a group that is still active today. In 1920, Seames built four courts on the South Side of Chicago that became, for all purposes, the first private black tennis club.

For working-class women of all colors, of course, the situation was very different. There were no public tennis courts or golf courses, no parks with archery ranges or croquet lawns. There were no basketball hoops in vacant lots, and women and girls wouldn't have been allowed to use them if there had been. It was acceptable then, as it is now, for very young girls to run and climb trees and even play ball with their brothers and the other boys in the neighborhood. But at a certain age their freedom ended. They were expected to take on "womanly" roles.

Among the working classes, girls took on responsibilities in the household at a very early age. In addition, in industrial America of the late nineteenth century, most working-class children worked. Among black families, as among immigrant families, the money that children could earn in the factories or in the fields was a critical part of the family income. Girls who picked cotton or worked at looms all day and then helped their mothers cook and clean were not likely to have time to bat a ball around. A time would come for women from families such as these, but not quite yet.

It was not until the last decade of the nineteenth century that middle- and upper-class women began to overcome one of the major obstacles to participation in sports and games. Under the influence of the Victorian ideal, respectable women were expected to wear corsets, starched petticoats, and long skirts. They were weighted down with heavy, restrictive clothing that made it almost impossible to walk fast, much less run. All of this was changed by feminists and bicycles.

The feminists started working for dress reform earlier in the century, but they were not particularly successful. Even Susan B. Anthony could not bring herself to give up her long skirts and appear in public in the "sensible" outfits designed by such women as Amelia Bloomer. She tried. But she was so embarrassed that she wrote in a letter to her friend Elizabeth Cady Stanton that she would simply have to disappoint Bloomer, much as she hated to do so.

However, when the safety bicycle came along in 1888, women couldn't resist it. It offered mobility, freedom, and fun. And they couldn't ride it in their long skirts, which got caught in the spokes. But there, ready to hand, were the "bloomers" that the dress-reforming feminists had been pushing for years. These bloomers were baggy trousers worn under a dress that came down to about the middle of the calf. Other women adopted the split skirt that other dress reformers had suggested. Some bold souls even wore knickerbockers.

Once women were wearing these less restrictive garments, many other forms of physical activity were possible for them. They were even able to run on the tennis court.

At this time, from the last years of the nineteenth century until the First World War, most organized sports activity for women took place in colleges. The popular sports were croquet, bowling, rowing, and baseball. Basketball was invented by James Naismith in the early 1890s.

Basketball in particular seemed, to physical education instructors, to have potential as a sport for women. For one thing, it was not supposed to involve any significant physical contact. (They should have seen the NBA!) Still, the game was not widely accepted for women until Senda Berenson, a teacher at Smith College in Massachusetts, created "girl's rules." These rules, designed to protect girls and women from the roughness of athletic competition, declared that a player could dribble only three times before passing or shooting the ball. This was to protect players from the dangers of running. Another anti-running rule divided the court into three sections, in each of which a certain number of girls from each team remained throughout the game. That way, no one had to run down the entire court. Girls were also forbidden to steal the ball from each other or to hold the ball for more than three seconds.

In 1914, the three-section court gave way to a two-section court. Otherwise, Berenson's rules remained in effect for women in high school and college basketball until the 1960s. They were only one of many ways that women were "protected" against athleticism in both black and white colleges.

The next great development in the world of sports protected women so thoroughly that they weren't even there.

THE OLYMPICS— THE EARLY YEARS

"We feel," said the founders of the modern Olympics, "that the Olympic Games must be reserved for the solemn and periodic exaltation of male athleticism with internationalism as a base, loyalty as a means, arts for its setting, and female applause as reward."

You can't get any clearer than that. The position of women in the Olympic Games was in the bleachers, watching. At that, modern women were doing better than the ancient Greeks. In the original Olympics, a woman caught watching would be taken out of the stadium and thrown off a cliff.

At the first modern Olympic Games, in Athens in 1896, there was one woman who, legend has it, wanted to run in the marathon and was curtly refused permission to do so. This woman, Melpomene, ran unofficially. She finished the last lap running around the outside of the stadium while the official male contestants were running inside.

At the second Olympic Games, in 1900, there were two women's events. That was because the games were held in Paris and, at that time, the hosts were allowed to decide what events were included. The French scheduled women's competitions in golf and lawn tennis. At the third games, in 1904, women had one event: archery.

After the third Olympics, the all-male International Olympic Committee (IOC) decided to reorganize things, taking control of the program of events itself. As a kind of trial run, they held the Interim Games in 1906. Women were allowed to compete in singles and mixed doubles tennis.

At the fourth official Olympics, there were 36 women and 1,999 men. The women competed in tennis, archery and figure skating. None of those women were Americans. It seems that women competitors were not required to wear long skirts, and the all-male American Olympic Committee (AOC) had decided to protect the women of the United States from the corrupting influence of seeing other women in bloomers. In 1912, women also competed in swimming events. At that Olympics, there were 57 women and 2,490 men among the competitors.

The 1916 Olympics were canceled because of World War I. At this point, no African-American women or men had competed in any event in the Olympic Games. But the war and other occurrences of the next few years would change that forever.

A number of forces came together in the years after World War I to move black women to the forefront of American Olympic competition. Some of them were social, some economic. Some, ironically, involved restrictions placed on the freedom of middle-class white women.

First, a lot of the men who showed up to serve in the war were physically unfit. As a result, the federal government instituted a program to encourage sports among the general population. They helped to organize the National Amateur Athletic Foundation (NAAF), with a separate arm for women, called the Women's Division. The stated policy of the Women's Division was to promote physical activity for the mass of women and not to encourage the individual achievement of highly skilled women. It

was, fundamentally, opposed to competition. This philosophy dominated women's athletics in colleges and universities. The result? Middle-class and upper-class women, most of them white, were taught at every turn that it was not nice to try to win. They were also kept out of any form of public competition, leaving the way clear for women who were not so limited—working-class and black women.

In the meantime, there was a huge migration of black workers from the southern United States, where no public facilities were open to them, to the North, where at least some were. In the large cities of the North, there were settlement houses, churches, industrial training schools, and **Young Women's Christian Associations** (YWCAs), as well as public schools and parks. These community resources provided the opportunity for participation in such sports as basketball and track.

Track for black women developed rapidly in the 1920s. Among the city clubs to produce champions of national stature at that time were the New York Mercury Club and the Illinois Women's Athletic Club. Along with the Tuskegee Relays in the South, which began in 1927, such clubs in the North afforded black women an opportunity to showcase their talent.

The first African-American men went to the Olympics in 1924. In that year, DeHart Hubbard and Edward Gourdin won gold and silver medals, respectively, in the long jump. In 1928, African-American men again entered, but none received medals. It wasn't until 1932 that black women first qualified for the U.S. Olympic team. In that year **Louise Stokes**, who got her training in the Malden, Massachusetts, parks, and **Tidye Pickett**, from the parks of Chicago, qualified for the U.S. 400-meter relay team. They were actually in Los Angeles, staying in Olympic Village and training to compete, when U.S. Olympic officials decided to replace them with white runners. The officials claimed that the white runners, whom Stokes and Pickett had beaten in the time trials, were really faster.

The star of that 1932 Olympics was a white working-class woman named Mildred Ella "Babe" Didrikson. She escaped the non-competitive curse of the collegiate woman athlete because she never even finished high school. She entered athletic competition representing the company she worked for. As a member of the U.S. Olympic team in 1932, she won two gold medals and tied for a third. The tie was settled in favor of the other woman on a technicality, and Didrikson won the silver.

After the Olympics, Babe Didrikson had to give up her amateur standing so that she could make money to support her family back in Texas. The Babe established the image for women competitors for decades to come. Unlike the gentleman athlete that the Olympic Games were designed to celebrate, she was poor. She was also bluntly outspoken and successful by virtue of singleminded dedication to her sport. The women track stars who followed her in the decades to come resembled her in almost every way. The difference was that most of them were black.

In the next Olympic Games, held in Berlin in 1936, Tidye Pickett again qualified. Louise Stokes did not. However, she was made a member of the team, perhaps because officials recognized that she had been unfairly treated in the past. But when push came to shove, she was not allowed to compete. She was in Berlin practicing to run in the 400-meter relay when the officials again

decided to replace her with a white woman. Pickett competed in the 80-meter hurdles and struck a hurdle.

Because of World War II, no Olympic Games were held in 1940 or 1944. When they started up again in 1948, the domination of track and field by black women would begin.

OFF THE TRACK

Outside the Olympics, off the running track, black women still had few opportunities for participating in sports. And the main thing that stood in their way continued to be the double burden they carried. Arthur Ashe, Jr., in *A Hard Road to Glory*, described the twenties and thirties this way:

> Most black women spent very little time engaged in competitive, organized sport. They worked in the home with few appliances of convenience. There were no washers and dryers, no dishwashers, no disposable diapers, and the average work day was twelve hours long. In the South, two-thirds of all black women who worked outside their own homes did so as domestics in the homes of whites. The only times for recreation were Saturday and Sunday afternoons.

As late as March 14, 1930, one black paper, the *California Eagle*, reported that

> Colored girls are showing a smaller percentage engaged in regular athletic sports than any other race in the Los Angeles area. . . . In this wonderful climate, where outdoor sports may be played year-round, and there's no color bar set up at the gym door or the playgrounds, is there any reason why our girls have fallen so far behind our boys? The answer was yes, they had work to do.

For the few who were not limited by economics, sports existed in a carefully segregated atmosphere. Excluded by white sporting organizations, such as the U.S. National Lawn Tennis Association (USLTA), black tennis players formed their own governing group, the American Tennis Association (ATA), in 1916. Black women were co-participants in the competitions as early as 1917.

The ATA national championship in 1917 was won by **Lucy Diggs Slowe,** daughter of a prosperous family and later dean of women at **Howard University. Ora Mae Washington** won eight times in the 1930s before turning to basketball.

According to Ashe, basketball was a popular sport among black women at this time, and teams were sponsored by black newspapers, YWCAs, churches, and clubs. For example, the *Philadelphia Tribune* women's basketball squad, founded by Ora Washington, dominated women's basketball from 1931 through 1940. Washington was the player-coach for the basketball team, which traveled all over the country, playing the best black and white teams. After competitions and exhibitions that often were played according to men's rules, the team also offered clinics and coaching to members of local communities.

The YWCAs provided, in addition to basketball courts, swimming pools. Pioneering the surge of athletic talent in this area was Anita Gant, a schoolteacher, YWCA basketball captain, and swimming and tennis champion. Gant trained at the Washington, D.C., YWCA and went on to win the national ATA mixed-doubles championships in 1929 and 1930, as well as numerous swimming prizes.

Similarly, Inez Patterson proved to be Philadelphia's multitalented champion. In high school, Patterson was the only black member of the women's field hockey team. As a member of McCoach Playground she broke swimming records and captained the girls' basketball team. Later, at Temple University, Patterson made all-collegiate teams in hockey, tennis, basketball, track, volleyball, and dancing.

These talented athletes broke ground in sports wherever it was possible for them to do so. However, as women and as African Americans, they still faced serious obstacles. Women were not allowed on golf courses during prime playing hours, for example, and African Americans were not allowed on most golf courses at all. Male sports organizations were largely closed to women, and white sports organizations were closed to African Americans. One of the first black women to break through the latter barriers was tennis player **Althea Gibson**.

Gibson grew up rough in a rough neighborhood in New York City. She was known for ditching school and staying out all night, but she could play basketball, baseball, and anything else that came along. She often played paddle tennis at courts set up by the Police Athletic League (PAL), an organization formed by New York City Police officers to provide opportunities in sports to urban kids.

When a PAL supervisor saw her play, he arranged for her to be admitted to the Cosmopolitan Club, a wealthy black tennis club. Soon, she was regularly winning ATA tournaments. From 1947 to 1957, she won ten consecutive women's national championships. In the meantime, ATA officials started working to get Gibson admitted to USLTA events.

Althea Gibson's autobiography is entitled I Always Wanted to Be Somebody. *She succeeded. The first black woman to reach the top ranks of professional tennis, she has also served as a role model to generations of children and young people. She is shown here giving pointers to an aspiring (and clearly admiring) young tennis player.* (NATIONAL ARCHIVES)

In 1949, Gibson was admitted to the USLTA-sponsored Eastern Indoor Championships and then to the National Indoor Championships. She competed again in 1950 and won the Eastern Indoor. But she wasn't invited to play in the USLTA national tournament, in part because her participation could lead her to Wimbledon, the famous British tennis tournament.

It looked as though Gibson was doomed to remain indoors until former tennis champion Alice Marble wrote an editorial in *American Lawn Tennis* magazine stating, "if Althea Gibson represents a challenge to the present crop of women players, it's only fair that they should meet that challenge on the courts, where tennis is played. . . . If she is refused a chance to succeed or to fail, then there is an ineradicable mark against a game to which I have devoted most of my life, and I would be bitterly ashamed."

After the editorial, the Orange Lawn Tennis Club in New Jersey invited Gibson to play. The barrier was broken, and Gibson played in the 1950 national championships at Forest Hills. In 1951, she played at Wimbledon and reached the quarterfinals. By 1956, she was ranked the second-best woman tennis player in the USLTA.

Then, in 1957, Althea Gibson won Wimbledon. She came back to the United States to be greeted by ticker-tape parades and presidential congratulations. Then she won the U.S. National Championship at Forest Hills. In 1958, she successfully defended both her titles. She was, quite simply, the best woman tennis player in the world. The next year, she retired from amateur competition.

In the early 1960s, Gibson broke another barrier when she earned her Ladies Professional Golf Association (LPGA) player's card. She played on the tour for seven years before retiring from golf as well.

THE GOLDEN ERA

When women athletes gathered from around the country to try out for the 1948 Olympics in London, twelve years had passed since the games had last been held. A great deal had happened in those years. Black men and women had died in World War II. There was a new mood in the country, especially in the black community. The results of those Olympic trials gave the community something to be proud of. When the stopwatches had all been clicked and the measurements all made, eleven women had been chosen to represent the United States in London. Nine of them were black.

Four of those black women—**Alice Coachman**, **Nell Jackson**, Mabel Walker, and Theresa Manual—had been trained at Tuskegee Institute in Alabama. This was by no means a coincidence. The historically black college had become a training ground for the best young black women in the country.

Major Cleveland Abbott was the guiding figure in the development of the Tuskegee program. He started the Tuskegee Relays in 1927, basing them on the interracial Penn Relays at Franklin Field in Philadelphia. In the beginning the Tuskegee Relays included all track and field events for men and two for women—the 100-yard dash and a 440-yard relay. Three years later, he added the 50-yard dash and the discus.

Abbott did not agree with the opinion that women would be harmed by competition. He trained and recruited the best runners, jumpers, and throwers he could find. He even hired a woman coach, Amelia C. Roberts. In 1936, the Tuskegee team entered the American Athletic Association (AAU) Nationals for the first time and came in second. In 1937, it took first, with **Lula Mae Hymes [Glenn]** as its star.

Because of the noncompetition bias, most of the team's competitors were not from other colleges but from athletic clubs. Their main rivals were the Mercury Athletic Club in New York and the Illinois Women's Athletic Club. Virtually all of the women active in competitive track and field at this time had working-class backgrounds, and a great many of them were black. As Michael D. Davis pointed out in *Black American Women in Olympic Track and Field*, "track is one sport which requires no expensive equipment, not tennis rackets, golf clubs, or memberships in exclusive clubs. Sometimes not even a pair of sneakers is needed. In fact, one of the greatest American women sprinters, **Isabel Daniels**, won her first race in competition at Tuskegee Institute running barefoot."

In addition to the Tuskegee women, there were two athletes from Washington Park Playground in Chicago, Bernice Robinson and Lillian Young. The Police Athletic League of New York contributed small and mighty **Mae Faggs**. The other two black women came from a school that would become legendary in the next two decades.

In 1944, a second black university entered the field of women's track. Cleveland Abbott's daughter, Jessie, left her father's school and became track coach at Tennessee A&I, which later became Tennessee State University. In the next two decades the Tennessee Tigerbelles, as the women's track team was called, surpassed even Tuskegee in women's track and field.

The nine black and two white women who were sent off to London in 1948 did not come back with an armload of medals. They were ambushed by one of the greatest woman athletes ever to enter the Olympics—Dutch housewife and mother Fanny Blankers-Koen, who won four gold medals. They may also have been thrown off by the menu they enjoyed on the ship on which they crossed the Atlantic. They were young and poor, and the food was good and rich. Nell Jackson said later, "Sometimes I think we ate ourselves out of some of the races on the boat."

Nonetheless, they did come home with the first and second medals ever won by an African-American woman. **Audrey Patterson**, of Tennessee State, took the bronze in the 200 meters. Alice Coachman took the gold in the high jump. And from that time on, black women have always been a majority of the U.S. women's track and field team at the Olympics.

Coachman became an instant star. London loved her. President Harry S. Truman invited her to the White House to congratulate her

personally. Albany, Georgia, her home town, declared an Alice Coachman Day. Michael D. Davis, in *Black American Women in Olympic Track and Field*, quotes a contemporary account of that celebration, by Marion E. Jackson of the *Atlanta Daily World*:

> Let me write now that until the parade terminated at the auditorium, Georgia had seen democracy in action. It was not a homecoming for a Negro Olympic star, but a champion of champions. As I watched the faces of thousands of Georgians from all over the state it was interesting to note, that all of their prejudices, preferences, passions and hates were momentarily swept from their countenances as if a heavy rainstorm had drenched a mountainous street. They came to applaud, cheer and praise an agile, slim and speedy star whose flying feet had brought her acclaim not only from her home state, but from the forums of the world. And then my dream was shattered. Reality returned and I knew that Georgia would not make Alice's welcome a wholehearted one. Mayor James W. "Taxi" Smith droned on about Georgia's other Olympic champion [Forrest "Spec" Towns, who had won the 110-meter hurdles twelve years earlier, in the 1936 Olympics]. He never shook her hand nor did he look at her. Alice never got a chance to speak.

Davis goes on to point out that Alice Coachman's sorority, **Delta Sigma Theta**, gave her a splendid banquet. And besides, once you've had tea with Lady Astor and visited the White House, you can afford to laugh at Taxi Smith.

In 1952, fifteen-year-old **Barbara Jones** became the youngest person ever to win a gold medal in track and field, as part of the 400-meter relay team. The other members were Mae Faggs, Catherine Hardy, and

Janet Moreau, a white athlete. It was the only medal earned by the track and field women that year, but it was a good one.

Before the race, the American team had not won a single medal. The team, in fact, had accumulated only one point, earned by Mae Faggs' sixth-place finish in the 100-meter finals. The members of the relay team, who came from different parts of the country, had never run together before. Young Barbara Jones had to be blackmailed into practicing by Mae Faggs, who refused to set her hair unless she showed up on the practice field. The critics were saying that the American women were cream puffs.

However, when the dust settled, the four runners had set a new world record of 45.9 seconds and won four gold medals. Davis reports that "in the middle of the stadium three American black girls and one American white girl put their arms around each other and danced jubilantly in a circle. They laughed and screamed until their eyes filled with tears of joy."

The next Olympics, in 1956, was the beginning of the golden years. To fans of track and field, **Wilma Rudolph** is a name to conjure with, and she made her first appearance in the 1956 Olympic Games. On the team with her were other legends of sport, including the massively powerful **Earlene Brown**, a shot-putter who could make the shot soar like a baseball. Mae Faggs was there again, earning her title of Queen of the Sprints as she led the relay team to a bronze. **Willye White** took a silver medal in the long jump in the first of her three Olympic competitions. **Mildred McDaniel** won the gold in the high jump. And then, in 1960, the legend of Wilma Rudolph really took shape.

Rudolph was born in a small town in Tennessee. As a child of four, she had double pneumonia, scarlet fever, and polio. It took years of trips into Nashville, forty-five miles away, for medical treatments, and four daily massages by her parents and her brothers and sisters before she was able to walk with a brace. By the time she was eight, she was walking with a special shoe. At eleven, she started playing basketball with her brothers. In high school, she averaged 32.1 points a game and was undefeated in track.

When she ran on the relay team in the 1956 Olympics, she was only sixteen years old. At seventeen, she went to Tennessee State University to work with Ed Temple, who was now track coach. Three years later, in spite of a number of illnesses in the meantime, she went to Rome on the U.S. team.

Rudolph won the 100-meter dash by three yards. She set a new Olympic record when she won the 200-meter dash. And in the 400-meter relay she and three other Tennessee Tigerbelles—Barbara Jones, **Lucinda Williams**, and **Martha Hudson**—set a new world record of 44.4 seconds. She was the first American woman to win three gold medals at one Olympics.

But Wilma Rudolph was more than that. She awed the world with her grace and beauty, as well as her tremendous athletic skill. French journalists called her "La Gazelle" and "La Perle Noire" (the Black Pearl). After shattering more records in the next two years, she retired from competition and became a teacher. She later headed the Wilma Rudolph Foundation for disadvantaged young people. She proved that she had grace of every kind and captured the imagination of the world.

Rudolph's image was significant not only for black women, but for women athletes of all colors. She seemed to redefine the word *lady* so that there was room in it for strength, energy, and even the desire to win. The result was an enormous boost for women's sports. They became more popular than they had ever been in history.

Picking up the baton from Rudolph was **Wyomia Tyus**, another Tigerbelle. In her first Olympics, in 1964, Tyus took home a gold medal (and a world record) in the 100-meter dash and a silver in the 400-meter relay. In her second, she became the first athlete in the history of the Olympics to win two consecutive 100-meter golds, setting another world record in the process.

Tyus retired after the 1968 Olympics, but came back in 1973 to help the newly formed Professional International Track Association (PITA). In her first year as a pro, she won eight of the eighteen races she entered. In her second year, she won all of the twenty-two she entered. She also gave the cause of professional track for women a huge boost.

Gibson, Rudolph, Tyus, and many other remarkable athletes had transformed women's sports. They had captured the imagination of the American public and become stars of as great a magnitude as any in sports. But there was another step that had to be taken. It was time to level the playing field.

This is a formal portrait of the 1956 Tennessee State University Tigerbelles track team. Front row left is Darlene Scott and to the far right is Willye B. White. (The two women in the middle are unidentified.) In the back row (left to right) are Coach Edward S. Temple, Martha Hudson, Yvonne Macon, Lucinda Williams, Isabelle Daniels, Wilma Rudolph, Charlesetta Reddick, Margaret Matthews, Lorraine Holmes, Ella Ree Turner, and Mae Faggs. (TENNESSEE STATE UNIVERSITY)

TITLE IX AND BEYOND

Prejudice does not have only one way of hurting and limiting people. Stereotyping is one of its many weapons. Shutting the doors of opportunity is another. And one of the most powerful is denying access to positions of power and authority. All of these weapons have been used against black women in sports. And for decades, these athletes had nothing to fight back with except their skills and their determination.

The situation for women, and therefore black women, in sports began to change significantly in 1972, when Congress passed the education amendments to the Civil Rights Act. These amendments included Title IX and did for women in sports what Title VII did for African-American and other women in employment. The wording of the key part of the amendment is clear:

No person shall, on the basis of sex, be excluded from participation in, be denied the benefits of, be treated differently from another person or otherwise be discriminated against in any interscholastic, intercollegiate, club, or intramural athletics offered by a recipient [educational institution receiving federal financial assistance], and no recipient shall provide any such athletics separately on such basis.

Three years after the bill was passed, the regulations for implementing it were in place and it went into effect. The government allowed another three years for high schools and colleges to get their programs in line. And, of course, the process of eliminating discrimination against women athletes in schools is still very much going on.

For one thing, there has been a lot of argument about what equality in this situation means. For another thing, legislating against bias doesn't get rid of it. Still there has been an enormous change. In 1970, women benefitted from only 1 percent of the budgets of athletic departments in American colleges and universities. One percent! By 1982, seven years after Title IX became effective, women were receiving almost 20 percent of the total athletic budget, and the percentage continues to grow.

Title IX had an impact on the historically black colleges as well as those usually associated with whites. In basketball, for example, there were few if any varsity women teams until after the passage of the act. When forced to by legislation, black college athletic directors opened up their programs and, between 1979 and 1988, three black schools won national women's titles in basketball. South Carolina State won the Association for Women's Athletics II title in 1979. Virginia Union won the NCAA II title in 1983. And Hampton University won the NCAA II title in 1988.

In fact, basketball has become a rival to track and field for the participation of black women. Again, it is a sport that requires little in the way of expensive equipment, and basketball courts are not owned by exclusive clubs. Today, the women's basketball teams of most mainstream universities include many, sometimes a majority, of black athletes.

One of the first black women stars in basketball was **Lynette Woodard**. A post-Title IX athlete, she began playing basketball in high school in 1975. In her freshman year at the University of Kansas, she led the nation in rebounds with a 14.8 average and was second in scoring, averaging 25.2 points a game. In her second year, with a 31-point average, she was number one in the nation in scoring. She also set a single-season scoring record of 1,177 points. She was a four-time All-American and set a career college scoring record for women of 3,649 points.

Woodard was captain of the U.S. Olympic women's basketball team in 1984, leading the team to a gold medal. Then, in 1985, she became the first woman member of the Harlem Globetrotters. She played with the team for two years.

One of Woodard's teammates at the 1984 Olympics was **Cheryl Miller**, who had led her University of Southern California team to two consecutive NCAA titles. While still in high school, she once scored 105 points in one game. At the Olympics, she was the lead scorer. Her record over the years has been so remarkable that, in 1991, she was inducted into the Women's Sports Hall of Fame. Former All-American Nancy Lieberman called her "the best thing that could have happened to the game." After a knee injury in the late 1980s, Miller became a television sports commentator.

Another 1984 Olympian was Pam McGee. One of a pair of basketball-playing twins, McGee presented her gold medal to her sister, Paula, who had not made the Olympic cut.

Teresa Edwards led both the 1988 and 1992 Olympic women's basketball teams. From Cairo, Georgia, she is considered one of the greatest players in the history of women's basketball.

Coming up to rival Miller, Woodard, and the others are young women such as Charlotte Smith and Chamique Holdsclaw. As a University of North Carolina forward in 1995, Smith was the first woman in ten years to dunk the basketball in a regular game. Holdsclaw is a three-time AAU All-American, leading her high school team to

number one in the *USA Today* rankings. In 1995, she was considered one of the two best high school women basketball players in the nation.

But basketball and track are not the only sports in which black women now excel. There are stars in such diverse sports as volleyball, fencing, and tae kwon do. Black women are breaking new ground in tennis, figure skating, and gymnastics.

In volleyball, Kim and Elaina Oden are standouts. Kim had a remarkable college career at Stanford University, and Elaina was equally important to the University of the Pacific. In 1992, they were both on the U.S. Olympic team. Fencer Sharon Monplaisir has participated in three Olympic Games. So has **Leora "Sam" Jones**, a team handball player. **Lynette Love** has won ten national heavyweight championships in tae kwon do.

One of the most remarkable of contemporary black women athletes is **Zina Garrison**. In 1990, she was the first black woman to play on Wimbledon's center court since Althea Gibson more than thirty years earlier. One of the few black players ever to break into the upper level of professional tennis, she was ranked among the top ten women players from 1983 to 1991, took home Olympic gold in 1988, and paved the way for such new young players as Venus Williams and Stephanie Adele Johnson.

Still the track and field athletes continue to get the lion's share of public attention. And with **Evelyn Ashford**, Jackie Joyner-Kersee, and **Gail Devers** leading the pack, who can wonder?

THE NEW ATALANTAS

According to legend, the young princess Atalanta was told by her father that she must marry any man who could defeat her in a foot race. She defeated suitor after suitor until one shrewd young man distracted her by throwing golden apples at her feet. Stooping to pick them up, Atalanta lost a few precious seconds, the race, and her independence.

There are certain parallels between that ancient Greek racer and the stars of women's track and field today. First, like Atalanta, they are swift. Second, people are throwing golden apples at them, in the form of contracts to endorse shows, clothing, and even makeup. Third. . . . Well, that's where the analogy breaks down. Today's stars are not being distracted from their goals. And they are certainly winning their races.

Evelyn Ashford's first Olympics was in 1976. She was an unknown nineteen-year-old who surprised everyone by finishing fifth in the 100-meter run. In the next few years, she did so well in world meets that she was seen as the most likely winner of the 1980 gold medal.

But the 1980 Olympics didn't happen for American athletes. President Jimmy Carter declared a boycott to protest the Soviet Union's invasion of Afghanistan. So Ashford had to keep training, winning world meets, and looking forward to 1984. It turned out to be worth the wait. She won first place in the 100-meter run and set a new Olympic record of 10.97 seconds. She also won a contract to endorse the American Express card. But she wasn't finished.

In 1988, Ashford was back at the Olympics. She had, in the meantime, had a baby. She was also thirty-one years old. But she won two more medals. This time she took a silver in her specialty, but she shared a gold in the 400-meter relay.

Ashford's last Olympics was the second for the Queen of the Golden Apples. **Florence Griffith Joyner,** or "Flo Jo" as she came to be known, has earned more than four million dollars since she first sprinted into the public consciousness, hair flying and long, long fingernails sparkling in the sun.

Her commercial success sometimes overshadows her extraordinary achievements on the track. In her first Olympic appearance, Griffith Joyner won a modest silver medal in the 200-meter run. Four years later, in 1988, she stunned the world when she won three gold medals—in the 100-meter and 200-meter runs and the 400-meter relay—and then, topping Wilma Rudolph's record, added a silver medal in the 1600-meter relay.

What no one could ever have predicted was that Griffith Joyner's sister-in-law would not only rival but actually surpass her, not in number of medals but in sheer athletic virtuosity.

Jackie Joyner-Kersee, whose brother married Florence Griffith in 1987, was a winner at the 1984 Olympics in spite of a hamstring injury. She took home a silver medal in her specialty, the heptathlon. It was the first time an American woman had won a multievent medal. In 1988, she won the gold, along with another for the long jump. In 1992, she won a gold medal in the heptathlon for the second time. No woman had ever done it before.

The heptathlon consists of seven separate events that test an athlete's all-round skills. It is not enough to go fast: you must go high. It is not enough to go high: you must go far. It is not enough to run: you must also throw. With amazingly hard work, Joyner-Kersee has come to do these things better than just about anyone. Of the top six women's heptathlon scores of all time, she has six. No one else is even near her.

INTO THE FUTURE

Shifts in attitude, along with Title IX, have changed things dramatically for black women in sports. But there is still a long way to go before women in general and black women in particular have gained true equality in this area.

The authors of a 1978 text, *Sociology of American Sport*, felt it necessary to argue against the following three myths concerning women in sports. 1) Athletic participation masculinizes females. 2) Sports participation is harmful to the health of females. 3) Women are not interested in sports, and they do not play well enough to be taken seriously.

It is difficult today, less than two decades later, to believe that people actually thought these things were true. We look at Jackie Joyner-Kersee, for example, and we see a beautiful, amazingly healthy woman who is one of the greatest athletes who ever lived. We look at Florence Griffith Joyner, **Debi Thomas**, Cheryl Miller, and hundreds of other remarkable athletic figures, and the objections raised in the past to women in sports seem absurd.

However, the prejudices of today may seem more reasonable. They are, after all, *our* prejudices. The first and most significant of these prejudices is probably that men and women cannot, or should not, play together on the same teams or compete against each other.

This is not clearly the case. In the first place, women are closing the sports gap at a remarkable rate. "It's as if Woman and Man are running a race," writes Mariah Burton Nelson, in *Are We Winning Yet?* "He has a head start, but over the years her speed increases and his stays relatively constant. To look at a chart marking the decrease in men's and women's world-record times in many sports is to see one fairly flat line tilting gradually downhill and another plummeting as dramatically as a ski slope."

In 1988, for example, Florence Griffith Joyner's 100-meter world record of 10.64 seconds was only .72 seconds slower than the record set by Carl Lewis. The 1988 world records that Janet Evans set in the 800-meter and 1500-meter freestyle in swimming would have been world records for men as recently as 1972. Evans' coach believes that, if Evans had been allowed to compete in her best event, the 1500-meter freestyle, "she would have beat everyone by twenty-five seconds." By everyone, he meant men as well. But the 1500-meter freestyle is not a women's event.

Recently, a number of women have finished first overall in longer marathons. In 1989, Ann Trason won a national championship 24-hour race. In this kind of competition, the runners keep going for exactly twenty-four hours, and then the distances they covered are compared. Trason ran 143 miles. The second-place winner, a man, ran 139. A woman also came in fourth.

The current world record for swimming the English Channel is held by a woman who was thirteen when she did it. In the triathlon, it is predicted that a woman will soon be finishing in the top ten, with the men.

None of this is to say that there are no differences in the physical potential of men and women. But it is possible that we are far enough from realizing our full potential as human beings that certain women can compete with men in certain areas . . . and should be allowed to do so.

The second prejudice we have, and it is a strong one, is that women cannot be leaders in sports. Nelson points out that before Title IX told us that we had to take women's sports seriously by providing scholarships and equipment and paying coaches reasonable salaries, 90 percent of all college coaches of women's athletics were women. By 1990, 53 percent of the coaches of high school and college women were men. More than 30 percent of the women's athletic programs in universities had no women in the administration at all.

And we really don't think women can coach men. More than 99 percent of all college men's teams are coached by men. "Nor do women have equal representation in other sport-related jobs," Nelson writes. In a recent survey of the Olympic movement, sports media, and intercollegiate and major professional sports in the United States, the Amateur Athletic Foundation of Los Angeles found that at the end of 1988, only 5 percent of the 12,735 positions available were held by women.

Up-to-date statistics are not available to show how many of the few women in coaching and administration are black. However, in a 1979 study by Margaret Diane Murphy, only 4 percent of all head coaches in women's college athletics were black women. The same percentage were assistant coaches. Clearly, the position of black women is even worse than that of white women.

Still, in the wake of Title IX, black women have begun to assume positions of some authority in the athletic world. For example, Dr. Dorothy Richey became the first woman athletic director for both men's and women's sports when, in 1974, she rose to that position at Chicago State University. Nell Jackson became assistant athletic director at Michigan State University in 1973. In addition she was a member of the board of directors of the U.S. Olympic Committee and vice president of The Athletic Congress. **Willye White**, a member of five Olympic teams, also was a member of the committee.

C. Vivian Stringer made sports history in 1995 when she was hired as the coach of

In 1995 C. Vivian Stringer was hired as coach of women's basketball at Rutgers University at a salary higher than that of both the men's basketball coach and the football coach. (UNIVERSITY OF IOWA)

women's basketball at Rutgers University at a salary higher than that of both the men's basketball coach and the football coach. She deserved it. She took an unknown Cheyney State College basketball team to a second-place finish in the national championships in 1982 and, when she moved to the University of Iowa, she compiled a won/lost record of 269-84.

Today, attorney **Anita DeFrantz** is a member of the International Olympic Committee. Wendy Hilliard is president of the Women's Sports Foundation. And there are many other black women in positions of authority in state and local organizations.

The world of sports must come to terms with both of these prejudices before black women can take their rightful place in that world. And there are other obstacles. In the past, there were few women in team sports. When Robert J. Condon wrote *Great Women Athletes of the 20th Century* in 1991, he included fifty women. Of those women, only one—softball player Joan Joyce—had made her reputation in team sports. Today, that is changing, at least in collegiate sports. But volleyball is still the only successful professional team sport for women.

In addition, outside tennis and golf—in which there are very few black players—most women athletes who make a living at what

Anita DeFrantz is the first black woman to be a member of the International Olympic Committee. (AMATEUR ATHLETIC FOUNDATION OF LOS ANGELES)

they do are able to do so only because of commercial endorsements.

Still, it is almost impossible not to be optimistic when you see Venus Williams serve a tennis ball. Or Charlotte Smith dunk a basketball. Sports are changing. Black women are changing sports.

[This introduction incorporates material from the article on "Sports," by D. Margaret Costa and Jane A. Adair in *Black Women in America: An Historical Encyclopedia*]

A

Ashford, Evelyn (1957–)

She was one of the gold medal winners and media favorites of the 1984 Los Angeles Olympics. Personable, disciplined, and a dauntless competitor, Evelyn Ashford recovered from racing setbacks and cold war politics to win recognition as a sprinting great in women's track.

Born on April 15, 1957, in Shreveport, Louisiana, Ashford was the oldest of five children. Her father was a sergeant in the U.S. Air Force, and the family moved often. Even as a little girl, she dreamed about winning a gold medal in the Olympics.

By the time Ashford entered high school, her father was stationed at McClellan Air Force Base in California. She went to Roseville High School in the town of the same name, near Sacramento. One day the football coach noticed her running down the field and asked if she would like to race his fastest football player. She agreed and beat him in a 50-yard run.

Soon Ashford was running with the boys' track team: There was no track team for the girls. A club coach spotted her racing against boys and arranged for her to enter the Amateur Athletic Union's women's finals. As her reputation spread, she was offered one of the first women's track scholarships at UCLA. Better yet, she had the chance to work with Pat Connolly, a former Olympic runner and one of the top women's track coaches in the country.

On the first day of practice in 1975, Connolly had Ashford run the 100-meters. Ashford was so fast that Connolly thought she must have misread the time. So Ashford ran it again—and Connolly suggested she try out for the Olympics.

Ashford made the team for the 1976 Olympics in Montreal. She finished fifth in the 100-meter run, ahead of experienced American runner **Chandra Cheeseborough** and well ahead of her future rival, Mariles Gohr of East Germany. As a racer, Ashford was just beginning to mature, so she set her sights on the 1980 Olympics.

Connolly coached Ashford through her track years at UCLA, until financial pressure and other interests caused Ashford to leave college in 1979. That same year she married Ray Washington, a professional basketball player. It was a great competitive year for Ashford. She won the 100-meter and 200-meter runs in the World Cup competitions in Montreal. Connolly continued to coach her on a volunteer basis, looking forward to the 1980 Olympics in Moscow.

But Ashford never went to the Moscow Olympics. President Jimmy Carter ordered an American boycott of the games in protest of the Soviet Union's invasion of Afghanistan, and the hopes of the racer were dashed, along with those of many other American athletes.

Ashford was deeply disappointed after so many years of hard work. She was considered at her prime as a runner and the favorite for winning in the 100-meter ran. In 1979, she had defeated her closest rival, Gohr, in the Montreal World Cup. Now an Olympic medal was out of reach for another four years, if she could maintain her form that long. She and her husband had postponed starting a family until after the 1980 Olympics, so the boycott meant a further postponement as well. In a race at UCLA after Montreal, Ashford pulled a muscle and fell into the cinder track. She managed to finish the race, but she was well and truly discouraged.

Ashford seriously thought about quitting track and field completely. She spent that summer traveling around the country with her husband, trying to think what she should do. She finally decided to go back and have her try at an Olympic gold medal. Her husband agreed. "I figured if running was going to keep her happy," he said, "we should try to stay with that." Ashford went back to work for another four years.

Ashford came back to race well, winning the sprints in another World Cup meet in 1981. In 1983, she beat Gohr once again. That same year she set another world record in the 100-meter run, with a time of 10.79 in Colorado Springs.

Ashford was ready to race against the East Germans again at the World Championship races in Helsinki, but she strained a muscle. She lost to Gohr, her old rival. In the upcoming Olympics, she said, "it's going to be me or Gohr, and it's going to be me."

It was indeed Ashford in the 1984 Olympics. Those Olympics were held in her native Los Angeles, and that year the Communist-bloc countries boycotted the games. She won gold in the 100-meter run, with an Olympic record time of 10.97 seconds. She followed that victory with an-

other gold medal with her teammates in the 4 x 400 meter relay, clocking a total time of 41.65 seconds.

Still, without the Soviet-bloc athletes in competition, the championship was never really hers, not until she raced against them again. Her chance came less than a month later in Zurich, when Ashford beat the East Germans and broke her own Olympic time with a new world record of 10.76 seconds in the 100-meter run. Now the title was truly hers.

Now, at last, Ashford could take time off to have her baby. Nine months after the Olympics she had a baby girl, Raina. She immediately went back to training. There was some question about the ability of women to come back to racing form after a pregnancy. After shedding the extra pounds, Ashford came back stronger than ever, with better endurance. Still sprinting at remarkable speeds, at the Vitalis Olympic Invitational in 1986, she won the 55 meter run in 6.6 seconds.

Ashford won a place in the Olympic finals yet again for the team that would go to Seoul in 1988. In the 400-meter relay she recovered from a weak pass-off to help her team to a gold medal, with a total time of 41.98 seconds. She took a silver in the 100-meter run, losing to her Olympic teammate **Florence Griffith Joyner**. However, she won the 100-meter shortly afterwards, with a time of 11.05 seconds, at the Chuhei Nambu meet in Sapporo, Japan.

In 1992, at the age of thirty-five, Ashford competed in the Barcelona Olympics, where she won her fourth Olympic gold medal as the lead-off runner in the 400-meter relay. In June 1993 she retired from competition.

After long years of effort, the victories at the Los Angeles Olympics brought fame and financial security to Ashford. She became a reporter on cable television for "World Class Women," a series on female athletes. Then she won a four-year contract with Mazda to race with and represent their newly organized track club. She also was a public representative for Puma shoes.

A competitor who has come back stronger after any number of setbacks that would have ended the career of a lesser woman, Ashford has proven herself to be a true champion and a sprinter in for the long haul.

ANDRA MEDEA

B

Bolden, Jeanette (1960–)

Runner Jeanette Bolden is a prime example of how much a person can achieve with determination and spirit. She was born on January 26, 1960 in Los Angeles, California, with club feet and severe asthma. She began running when she was twelve years old, while attending the Sunair School for Asthmatics. She attended Centennial High School in Compton, California, graduating in 1978. Moving on to UCLA after graduation, she continued her track career and joined the World Class Athletic Club, where she was coached by Bob Kersee.

In 1982, Bolden set the world indoor record in the 60-yard run with a time of 6.6 seconds. Then, in 1986, she beat her own time by running the event in 6.54 seconds. She has defeated both Marlies Gohr and **Alice Brown**, two of the best starters in the world, in the 60 yards. Running other distances, she established five indoor American records and, in 1981, placed second in the 100-meters at the U.S. Nationals. As a member of the 1984 Olympic team, Jeanette came in third during the 100-meter trials and won a gold medal as a member of the 400-meter relay team, along with Alice Brown, **Chandra Cheeseborough**, and **Evelyn Ashford**.

HILARY MAC AUSTIN

Brisco-Hooks, Valerie (1960–)

She was one of the stars of the 1984 Los Angeles Olympics. Winning three gold medals in track, and setting three Olympic records in the process, Valerie Brisco-Hooks went from being a little-known outsider to an instant celebrity.

Born in Greenwood, Mississippi, on July 6, 1960, Brisco-Hooks was the daughter of Arguster and Guitherea Brisco. She was one of ten children. Her parents moved the family to Los Angeles when she was five years old. She went to Locke High School, where, in 1974, her older brother Robert was shot and killed by a stray bullet while running on the track. Her brother remained an inspiration to her.

While a strong sprinter on her high school track team, Brisco-Hooks only managed haphazard training. Nonetheless, in 1979, while still a teenager, she ran a 400-meter race in 52.08 seconds. That time remained her personal best until she shattered it preparing for the Olympics.

This same year Brisco-Hooks joined the World Class Track Team, coached by Bob Kersee. She trained with some of the best runners in America, such as **Florence Griffith Joyner** and **Jackie Joyner-Kersee**. She learned about training with a vengeance. Workouts were seven hours each day, five days per week, with an additional two to three hours of weight training. This was topped by a standard 1,000 sit-ups and 250 push-ups. Brisco-Hooks called Kersee "a slave-driver with no mercy," but she developed the stamina that made her a star.

Brisco-Hooks was attending California State at Northridge when she met Alvin

Hooks, whom she subsequently married. His career as a football wide receiver took him to Philadelphia in 1981, and Brisco-Hooks went with him. The following year he was sidelined with a knee injury, and Brisco-Hooks was sidelined by the birth of her son.

Brisco-Hooks had gained forty pounds with her pregnancy, far too much extra weight for a runner. She worked fiercely under Coach Kersee to get back into shape. By 1983, she was back on track, stronger than ever.

In 1984, the Athletic Congress track meet was held just a week before the Olympic trials. Most top athletes did not go, not wishing to risk an injury just before the Olympic trials. Brisco-Hooks went and appeared in top form. She set an American record for the 400-meters at 49.83 seconds. At the Olympic trials she won the 200-meters and came in second in the 400-meters. Brisco-Hooks improved her time to 49.79 seconds, but her Olympic teammate **Chandra Cheeseborough** won with a new record of 49.28 seconds.

The Los Angeles Olympics was a hometown affair to Brisco-Hooks. The competition was impaired by a boycott by most of the Communist-bloc athletes, but Brisco-Hooks brought in wins so strong as to silence doubters. She not only won her events, but she also set new Olympic records each time. She won gold medals in the 200-meter and 400-meter runs and the 4 x 400 meter relay. She set Olympic and American records in all of these: 21.81 in the 200-meter, 48.83 in the 400-meter, and 49.23 in her third leg of the 1600-meter runs. At Los Angeles Brisco-Hooks became an instant star.

However, Brisco-Hooks still had doubters to satisfy. The famed East German sprinters were not at the Olympics that year, and her title was not safe until she had bested them. In the next major meet in Europe, she ran against the East Germans in the 200-meter run and lost. However, she raced against them again in 1985 in Zurich, and there she won against the best of the East Germans, reaffirming her title. Four years later, at the Seoul Olympics, Brisco-Hooks won a silver medal for her part in the American 1600-meter relay team.

A warm, personable athlete, Brisco-Hooks was very much in demand for public appearances. While keeping a clear head, she received her share of fame and fortune after her Olympic wins. She and her husband had been living at her mother's home before the Olympics. Now they could afford a place of their own. Along with her many speaking engagements and corporate contracts, Brisco-Hooks has also appeared in drug-prevention films for young people.

Described by one writer as a "thoroughbred of a sprinter who runs with raw power and with artful grace," Brisco-Hooks has a heart as big as her talent. After one of her Olympic wins, she was asked by a visually and hearing-impaired young man to pose for a photograph. She placed her gold medal around his neck for the photo, then walked away and let him keep it. She was the kind of winner anyone could admire.

ANDRA MEDEA

Brown, Alice (1960–)

"Alice is always there," said Bob Kersee, legendary coach of the World Class Athletic Club. Alice Brown was born on September 20, 1960, in Jackson, Mississippi. When she was a child, her family moved to Pasadena, California, where she attended Muir High School. Graduating in 1978, she went on to attend California State University at Northridge.

While at Cal State, Brown joined the World Class Athletic Club and began to be coached by Bob Kersee. In 1980, she won both the TAC and AIAW titles and became the eighth-ranked runner in the world. She also tied for sixth place in the All-Time U.S. list in the 100-meter run. At the 1984 Olympics in Los Angeles, she won a silver medal in the 100-meter run and was a member of the gold medal-winning 400-meter relay team, which also included Jeanette Bolden, **Chandra Cheeseborough**, and **Evelyn Ashford**. In Seoul, South Korea, in 1988, Bolden was again a member of the gold medal-winning 400-meter relay team. This time she was joined by Evelyn Ashford, Sheila Echols, and **Florence Griffith Joyner**. Bob Kersee called Alice Brown "America's most durable sprinter." She is also one of America's great team players.

HILARY MAC AUSTIN

Brown, Earlene (1935–1983)

She was an Amazon of a woman. At 5′9″ and 250 pounds, she was the foremost American woman of her time at shot put and discus throwing. Working without the basics of training and support that any modern athlete could count on, Brown hardly entered competition until she was twenty-one, married, and a mother. Then she went on to set a series of American records and join three Olympic teams. Motherly, good-natured, and yet powerfully competitive, Brown came back time and again against overwhelming odds to make her mark on Olympic and American sports history.

Brown was born on July 11, 1935, in Latero, Texas. When she was three years old, her mother left her father, who had once been a semiprofessional baseball player in Texas. Brown grew up with her mother in Southern California, where she spent her free time playing softball and volleyball with the boys. Always large, at the age of ten she was playing outfield in a local softball game when she made a spectacular one-handed catch. Within a week she was in Oregon as a member of a softball team, playing in the northwestern U.S. and in Canada. She stayed with that team for six years.

Brown's mother was supportive of everything she did. There wasn't a lot of money, but her mother sent her to dance classes where Brown learned the grace that helped her become a great athlete. She was remarkably agile. She could not remember when she weighed less than 180 pounds, yet she started out as a sprinter, doing the 100-yard run in 12.8 seconds. She was anchor on the relay team, but she also learned the basketball throw, which put her large hands and great strength to good use.

Seeing the potential in this teenager, her gym teacher, Addie Valdez, taught her discus. Her history teacher taught her shot put, using an old-fashioned cross-over step. Brown won national championships with this outmoded style, until her Olympic coach taught her the modern way.

Despite her great athletic talent and affection for people, Brown was not a team athlete. She did not bother to join the standard American sports organization, the Amateur Athletic Union until 1956, at the age of twenty-one. By then she was married and already had a son. At her first AAU national championships in August 1956, she won her event with a shot put throw of 45 feet, setting a new American record. In this, her first national tournament, she came in second in the discus.

A week later she was trying out for the Olympics. In a disappointing performance, Brown came in third in the morning's shot-put competition. A rival broke Brown's new record by six inches. "It really hurt to lose that record," Brown later said. During the lunch period she went behind a barn to practice. She came back that afternoon and set a new American record at 46 feet, 9½ inches. She followed it with a record discus throw at 145´6´´, a full five feet over the previous record.

Brown's success at track was quickly matched by discord at home. After having won the Olympic tryouts, Brown tried to be a proper wife and asked her husband if she could attend the 1956 Melbourne Olympics. He said no. She realized she never should have asked him and went anyway.

Melbourne was her first Olympics. Although Brown did not earn a medal, she improved her personal best and proved to be an enormously popular goodwill ambassador. She taught Russians how to dance rock 'n' roll and charmed the Australian press. Unexpectedly, Brown had found her place in life, as an international athlete.

A string of national and international victories followed. Brown still had no formal training, so her victories were uneven. A gifted natural athlete, she was competing in spite of a raft of obstacles. Track and field athletes were rarely supported in those days. There were no corporate sponsors with deep pockets. Brown had to work long hours in her beauty shop to make ends meet, standing on her feet all day and breathing chemicals.

She could only get together training time in bits and pieces. Still, she was able to beat people with twice the backing.

In July 1958, Brown went to the AAU outdoor nationals in Monmouth, New Jersey, where she appeared in top form. She had been able to work out prior to the event, and the training showed. She began her performance with a shot-put throw of 47 feet, 5½ inches. This won first place and broke her own American record. She followed this with a gold-medal showing in discus, with a throw of 152 feet, 5½ inches.

This remarkable performance put her on the American team that would tour Europe.

Known primarily as a shot-put champion, this photo shows Earlene Brown as the winner of the discus throw at the third Pan-American games. She set a new games record of 161 feet, 9½ inches. (NATIONAL ARCHIVES)

She took first place against the best of the Russian athletes in Moscow, with a shot-put throw of 54 feet, 3½ inches. This was over a foot and a half beyond the throw of her closest rival. At the Warsaw games, she won gold medals in both shot put and discus.

Later in that tour, the American team was competing against the Greek team in Panathenian Stadium, where the first modern Olympics were held. Astoundingly, Brown threw the discus out of the stadium and into the stands. It hit two people. She ran into the stands to see if anyone was hurt. One of the women who was hit said, "That's all right; it doesn't hurt much; but could I have your autograph?" She won a gold medal in that match, too. Then she took gold in the discus.

Brown returned from Europe with seven gold medals and one silver. Still in training, in 1958 she attended a track and field event where she competed in the basketball throw. She set a new record, heaving the basketball *30 feet* over the old record of 105 feet, 9 ½ inches. Sports officials were dumbfounded.

Still no one thought about Brown's training. She was so successful, everyone thought she could do this indefinitely. However, without adequate training, Brown's performance began to fade. In 1959, Brown did break her own record in discus with a throw of 153 feet, 8 inches. She set new records in discus and shot put at the Pan-American Games that year. But in the 1959 meet against the USSR in Philadelphia, she only took second in shot put and third in discus.

Brown managed to bring herself back into shape yet again, and when she entered the Olympic trials for the 1960 Olympics, she set yet another American record for discus at 176 feet, 10½ inches. At the Rome Olympics, Brown was popular as ever, the mother of all the young athletes. She took only a bronze in shot put, but just three weeks later she improved her performance mightily at a competition in Frankfurt. She set yet another American record in the shot put, beating the woman who had just won the gold medal in Rome.

Brown went on to win shot put and discus at the British Commonwealth Games. But by 1961 the financial strain on Brown had become unmanageable and she could no longer afford to compete in Europe. She won the qualifying trials for the touring 1961 American team, but she could not afford to go. She had to stay in America and earn a living.

In 1962, the AAU outdoor nationals were held in Los Angeles, Brown's hometown. This time Brown dashed back and forth between her beauty shop and the stadium, working on customers' hair one moment and competing the next. Brown was losing the match when, on her last throw, she hurled the shot put 48′ 10½″, winning the event.

In 1964, Brown again won a place on the Olympic team, but had to struggle financially to get to Tokyo, Japan, where the 1964 games were held. One story reveals the kind of financial pressure she was under. Having been notified that she made the team, Brown cleaned out her checking account, which contained all of $4.30. She paid $2 in gas to get to a passport photographer, where passport photos cost another $2. This left her thirty cents. She made two phone calls to friends to borrow the money to pay for her passport. This left her with a dime, and she still had to wait for the money. Someone else lent her the money, and she finally got her passport two days later. Then she rushed to rejoin the team for training. She had barely enough time to limber up. Not only were Brown's throws miraculous. It was miraculous that she was willing to compete at all.

With the 1964 Tokyo Olympics, Brown became the only athlete in existence to have reached the shot-put finals in three consecutive Olympics. She improved mightily within the short training time that she had, but there was not enough time for her to make up the difference. While Brown did not win a medal at Tokyo, at British Commonwealth Games in Osaka that followed she brought down a gold medal in shot put and a silver in discus.

Later, Brown described what it was like to be a black woman competing in the Olympics. "I'm just wondering if this isn't the story of the Negro girls in the Olympics: They pulled themselves up beyond where they really were supposed to be. None of them were supposed to be at London, Helsinki, Melbourne, Rome or Tokyo; or riding first class on a jet plane, eating a five-course dinner and drinking champagne. They are all Cinderella girls. They come back home and at 12 o'clock their carriage turns to a pumpkin and they have bills, bills, bills. They are the ones who are holding up the high standards of American athletics, the ones all America cheers. But how many people realize just how it really is?"

Very few Americans realized how truly amazing Earlene Brown was. After leaving amateur sports, Brown returned to her beauty shop, and later became a superstar with the roller derby.

ANDRA MEDEA

C

Cheeseborough, Chandra (1959–)

Chandra Cheeseborough was born on January 10, 1959 in Jacksonville, Florida. Running on the track team at Ribault High School in Jacksonville, she soon surpassed her peers and was competing nationally. At the age of sixteen, she shone at the Pan-American Games. The times she established there are still Florida records.

In 1976, when Cheeseborough was just seventeen years old, she was ranked tenth in the world in the 100-meter run, won The Athletics Congress 100-meter title and participated in her first Olympics. By the 1984 Olympics—the 1980 Olympics were boycotted by the United States—Chandra was one of the best 400-meter runners in the world. She followed **Valerie Brisco-Hooks** to the finish line to win a silver medal, and together they established United States dominance in the event. She added two gold medals to her silver by running with **Alice Brown**, Jeanette Bolden, and **Evelyn Ashford** in the 400-meter relay and with Valerie Brisco-Hooks, Lilli Leatherwood, and Sheri Howard in the 1600-meter relay, which established a new Olympic record.

HILARY MAC AUSTIN

Coachman, Alice (1921–)

Alice Coachman's reign over high jump competition in the United States began in 1939 when she won her first national championship. The first black woman Olympic champion demonstrated exemplary determination, and her dominance of the high bar was unparalleled. For nearly a decade, her opponents knew they would finish no better than second.

Alice Coachman (Davis) was born on November 9, 1921, in Albany, Georgia, to Fred and Evelyn Jackson Coachman. In an era when few girls entered high-performance sport, Coachman's interest in the high jump began when she attended a boys' track and field meet. Intrigued with the sport, she began jumping over ropes. She left Albany for the first time at age sixteen to enter a meet at Tuskegee Institute in Alabama. Officials began rewriting the record books when Coachman, without shoes, broke the high school and collegiate high jump records. Coach Cleve Abbott of Tuskegee invited her to train with his team during the summer of 1939. Preparatory school students and collegians comprised Tuskegee's track and field teams. After lengthy family debate, Coachman gained the approval of her parents and enrolled at Tuskegee Preparatory School.

Coachman's stellar performance at national Amateur Athletic Union meets contributed to Tuskegee Institute's reputation as a power in women's track and field. From 1941 to 1948, she won three 100-meter dash titles, finished second in that event three times, ran on two championship relay teams, and won five 50-meter dash titles. On four occasions she won the national individual high-point title. While competing for

Tuskegee and in her senior year at Albany State College, Coachman won a dozen national indoor and outdoor high jump titles and was named to five All-American teams. She also excelled in basketball at both schools and was an All-American guard at Tuskegee.

During the 1948 Olympic trials at the Brown University stadium, Coachman eclipsed the American high jump record by an inch and a half. In spite of back pain, she cleared the bar at 5 feet 4¾ inches and secured a place on the Olympic team. On the eve of the Olympic high jump competition at the London Olympics, Coach Catherine Meyer reminded Coachman that she was the only American woman who had a chance of winning a medal. Upon entering the stadium, Coachman concentrated more on Meyer's words than on the 65,000 spectators. During the final moments of the high jump, all other events ceased and the crowd was enthralled with the duel between Coachman and Dorothy Tyler of Great Britain. Both jumpers were credited with a new Olympic record of 5 feet 6 inches, but

Coachman had fewer misses and was awarded the gold medal. The first black woman Olympic champion concluded her sterling competitive career.

After graduating from Albany State College with a major in home economics and a minor in science, Coachman began teaching physical education. Her background in nutrition, science, and sports was put to use at South Carolina State College, Albany State College, and Tuskegee High School. Her son, Richmond, and her daughter, Evelyn, were both versatile athletes. After retiring, she resided with her second husband, Frank Davis, in Tuskegee, Alabama.

Coachman competed when society at large did not embrace sportswomen and excelled in international sports during an era of limited fanfare. She was a pioneer who competed because she loved sports. She has been inducted into eight halls of fame, including the National Track and Field Hall of Fame, the Georgia Sports Hall of Fame, and the Albany Sports Hall of Fame.

PAULA WELCH

D

Daniels, Isabel (1937–)

She was a power sprinter with the Tiger-belles, the world-class track team from Tennessee State. Racing relay, she helped the Tigerbelles sweep national competition in women's track for five years straight. In the short sprints she was nearly unbeatable, hitting the ground so hard that sparks jumped from the spikes of her track shoes. Isabel Daniels was one of the best.

Born at Jakin, Georgia, on July 31, 1937, Daniels was the daughter of a fairly prosperous cotton farmer. She was the youngest of the family, with eight older brothers and sisters. She didn't have to pick much cotton. By the time she was old enough to help, her father had machines to bring in the crop. Growing up, Daniels rode horses and ran barefoot, like other farm children in the South. Her first race was won barefoot at the Tuskegee relays, a famous racing event at Tuskegee University. Ed Temple, the track coach from Tennessee State, saw this talented youngster and asked her to join the newly forming track team that already included Olympic sprinter **Mae Faggs**.

An explosive runner, Daniels was sheer power in motion. She sprang off the blocks and charged down the track with memorable force. But she got real competition both from Faggs, who was a few years older and experienced in international competition, and from **Lucinda Williams**, who was another freshman at Tennessee State. National sprinting championships went from one to another of this remarkable team. Put the three together, and add a fourth for relays, and the combination swept away the competition.

Daniels joined the Tennessee State team in 1954. That same year, her relay team won the Amateur Athletic Union (AAU) outdoor nationals and set a new record in the 800-meter relay. The following year at the indoor nationals in 1955, Daniels beat Faggs in the 60-yard run. Later, at the Pan-American Games in Mexico City, Daniels came in second in the 60-meter run, then helped the American team win in the 400-meter relay.

Daniels was with the Tennessee State team when it won both girls' and women's divisions at the AAU outdoor nationals in 1955. She won the 100-yard run, then the 50-yard run in a record-breaking 5.8 seconds. At the AAU indoor nationals the following year, Daniels once again beat Faggs in the 100-yard race. Daniels matched the indoor world record and followed that with a win in the 50-yard run, where she tied her own outdoor record. Then Daniels and her team captain Faggs fought back from a ten yard deficit in the relays and won the race with five yards to spare.

Next came the AAU 1956 outdoor nationals, raced in 95° heat in Philadelphia. This time Daniels came in second to Faggs in the 100-yard run, but won a gold medal in the 50-yard.

The Olympic trials were held the following week in Washington, D.C. Daniels this time beat Faggs in the 100-meter run, and won a spot on the team to Melbourne. Her teammates Faggs and Williams were sent to Melbourne with her.

Daniels had a difficult time at the Melbourne Olympics. Facing cold, rainy weather (it was winter in Melbourne), Daniels placed fourth in the 100-meter race. However, she and her American teammates took the bronze in the 400-meter relay.

Daniels maintained her indoor championship at 50 yards in 1957, 1958, and 1959, the last year she raced competitively. In 1957 in Cleveland she set an indoor world record in the 50-yard run at 5.7 seconds. This record lasted nine years and was then broken by another Tigerbelle, **Wyomia Tyus**, in 1966.

Daniels won a place on the American track team that competed in Europe in 1958. This remarkable relay team won gold medals in Moscow, Warsaw, Budapest, and Athens. In 1959, her last year at Tennessee State, she maintained her supremacy in the 50-yard run at the indoor AAU nationals, and went on to win a gold medal with the relay team at the Pan-American Games.

ANDRA MEDEA

Dawes, Dominique (1977–)

In many areas of life, fame and achievement do not come until late in life. In athletics, it can come to those who have not yet even reached adulthood. But, as gymnast Dominique Dawes could testify, it does not come easily or without effort.

Dominique Dawes was born in 1977 to Don Dawes, a Maryland health-product salesman, and Loretta Dawes. She began training in gymnastics early in life, encouraged by parents who wanted a way for her

to channel her energy. She was quickly successful, in part because of her remarkable spirit. Her father told *People* magazine that, when she was nine, Dawes prepared for meets by writing the word *determination* on her mirror with a crayon over and over. "I was amazed that she even knew how to spell it," he said, "but it worked."

It certainly did. When Dawes was only fifteen, she was on the United States gymnastics team that went to the 1992 Olympics in Barcelona, winning a bronze medal. Two years later, she competed at the National Gymnastics Championships in Nashville and took gold medals in all four events: the vault, uneven bars, balance beam, and floor exercise. It was the first time that feat had been accomplished in almost three decades, since 1969. Even the legendary Mary Lou Retton had not accomplished it.

The fourth-ranked gymnast in the world, Dawes then had a decision to make, whether to compete in the 1996 Olympics or to begin her schooling at Stanford University, where she has a scholarship, and compete intercollegiately. She participated in the 1996 Olympics in Atlanta, Georgia, winning the bronze medal in the floor exercise and taking a share of the gold in the women's team competition.

KATHLEEN THOMPSON

DeFrantz, Anita (1952–)

An outspoken advocate of social reform through athletics, Anita DeFrantz has been among the most powerful women in the area of sports organization. A bronze medalist in the Olympics of 1976, she was born in Philadelphia in October 1952. Shortly thereafter, her family moved to Indianapolis, where her father ran a local Young Men's Christian

An advocate of athletes' rights, Anita DeFrantz was the first black woman to serve on the ninety-member International Olympic Committee. At the 1976 Summer Olympics in Montreal, she and her teammates won the bronze medal in the first eight-member women's rowing competition ever included in the games. (AMATEUR ATHLETIC FOUNDATION, LOS ANGELES)

Association. She had undertaken little in the way of athletic training prior to becoming a student at Connecticut College, where she was first introduced to the sport of rowing. DeFrantz competed officially for the first time in 1975, the same year she began law school at the University of Pennsylvania, located near Vesper Boat Club, an outstanding location for women's rowing. Already determined to prepare for Olympic competition, she maintained a six-day-a-week training schedule, and at the Montreal Olympics in 1976 received a third-place award in the first eight-member women's rowing competition ever to be included in the games. She went on to become U.S. national champion in eight-member competition, two-time national

champion in two-member competition, and three-time national champion in the four-member category.

Receiving her law degree in 1977 from the University of Pennsylvania, she devoted herself to training in preparation for the 1980 Olympics. When President Jimmy Carter called for a U.S. boycott of the Moscow competition in response to the Soviet invasion of Afghanistan, DeFrantz quickly voiced opposition. After filing a suit against the U.S. Olympic Committee (USOC) in response to the boycott, she retired from competition in 1981. She received the 1980 Olympic Order medal for lifetime contributions to the sport, given by the International Olympic Committee. Bearing the torch in the 1984 Los Angeles Olympics, DeFrantz was second-in-charge of the USOC Olympic village. She also served on the Athletes' Advisory Council, the President's Council on Physical Fitness, the Los Angeles Organizing Committee on Physical Fitness, and the Los Angeles Organizing Committee for the 1984 competition. An advocate of athletes' rights and other reforms, DeFrantz in 1988 became the first black woman to serve on the ninety-member International Olympic Committee, and she subsequently served as president of the Amateur Athletic Foundation of Los Angeles. In 1992, DeFrantz was elected to serve on the IOC's eleven-member executive board.

JOHN L. GODWIN

Devers, Gail   (1967?–)

By 1991, Gail Devers had lost the vision in one eye and was unable to walk because of the sores on her feet, caused by Graves' Disease. In 1992, Gail Devers won a gold medal in the closest sprint in the history of the Olympic games. The story of Devers' remarkable triumph over her physical ailments is the story of a champion.

Devers excelled at track at the University of California at Los Angeles, where she trained under the famous track and field coach Bob Kersee. While a senior, she won the 100-meter run at the national collegiate championships and set a new American record in the 100-meter hurdles. She graduated in 1988 and married her college sweetheart, Ron Roberts. They bought a house in nearby Palmdale, California, and Devers continued to train for the 1988 Olympics.

The Olympics were held in Seoul that year, and Kersee worked with the cream of American runners. Devers qualified for the American team, along with her best friend, **Jackie Joyner-Kersee.** But soon Devers had the feeling something was wrong. She had become too tired to finish her workouts. Her racing was slow, and she was getting pulled muscles and other injuries from fatigue. She was also suffering from severe headaches. Once she arrived at the Olympics, she ran the slowest hurdle heat she had run since high school and did not even make the finals.

Thoroughly discouraged, Devers returned to training in Los Angeles. By now her hair was falling out and she was rapidly losing weight. By the beginning of 1989, she weighed only 97 pounds and had to buy her clothes in the children's department. She would sometimes lose the vision in one eye. But in spite of these symptoms, the doctors could not find out what was wrong. They thought perhaps she was overtraining.

In reality, Devers had slowed down so badly she had to give up competing, even though she was determined to stay at the training program. In the fall of 1990, she happened to be noticed by a team physician at UCLA, who noticed a swelling on her throat. The doctor sent her for thyroid tests, where it was discovered that Devers had Graves' Disease.

Devers began radiation treatments soon afterward and begun to feel better. Then she started having serious reactions to the radiation. She developed blood blisters all over her feet, which put her on crutches until the doctors discontinued the radiation. By March of 1991, Devers had begun to work out once again, starting by just limping around the track in her socks. By May of 1991, she was competing again.

Devers wasn't strong enough to win at first, but her time in the hurdles was good enough for her to qualify for The Athlete's

Congress (TAC) national meet, which was to be held the next month, in June. TAC, in turn, was the qualifying meet for the World Championships that were to be held in Japan in August of 1991. On sheer determination Devers won the hurdles, finishing in 12.83 seconds. It was as good a time as any an American had run that season.

Devers took a second-place silver medal at the World Championships and, two weeks later in Berlin, she ran even better in the hurdles. In February of 1992, Devers won the 60-meter hurdles at the Millrose meet at Madison Square Garden in New York, with a time of 7.93 seconds. When she tried out for the Olympic team that June, Devers made the team in both the 100-meter run and the hurdles.

Devers was still having trouble from the Graves' Disease, and one leg was numb as it hit the track. Still, she took the 100-meter run in a photo-finish contest. Five of the eight sprinters were within a few hundredths of a second of each other. It was the closest race in the history of the Olympics. After judges studied photos from a variety of directions, Devers was awarded the gold medal with a time of 10.82 seconds, one of the fastest ever run.

Devers' luck did not hold up in the hurdles. She was in the lead when she hit the last hurdle with her leg and ended up finishing fifth. Like a champion, she hugged the winner, Parasakevi Patoulidou of Greece.

Devers won again by an eyelash at the world outdoor track and field championships held in Stuttgart, Germany, in 1989. She ran the 100-meters in a time of 10.81 seconds, although the official posting was later changed to 10.82 seconds after officials had to study video footage for two hours to determine the exact winner.

In 1993, Devers was chosen Athlete of the Year by the U.S. Olympic Committee. In 1994, she had to withdraw from the USA/Mobil Indoor Championships because of an aggravated hamstring, but she kept her place as a role model of the classic competitor. In the 1996 summer Olympics in Atlanta, Devers became only the second woman in Olympic history to defend her 100-meters title successfully. She ran the race in 10.94 seconds, edging out the second-place runner in a dramatic photo finish. As she said after the 1992 Olympics, "Use me as an example. When the walls are closing in, when someone doesn't know where to turn, tell people I was there. I kept going. So can others. Sounds like a sermon, doesn't it?" Then she laughed. That's Gail Devers, solid gold.

ANDRA MEDEA

E

Edwards, Teresa (1964–)

One of the best of the modern women basketball players and the holder of two Olympic gold medals, Teresa Edwards has been called "the Michael Jordan of women's basketball." Although she had to go abroad in order to continue basketball on a professional level, Edwards has made an indelible mark on the American game.

Born in Cairo, Georgia on July 7, 1964, Edwards was the daughter of Leroy Copeland and Mildred Edwards. Her mother was only 16 when she became pregnant with Edwards, and had to drop out of high school and work in the vegetable fields to make ends meet. Later her mother became a machine operator at a local factory.

Edwards grew up close to her mother. She was the oldest daughter, with four younger brothers. As a child she played tackle football and softball with the local boys, and shot baskets through the rim of a bicycle tire nailed to a tree. When Edwards wanted to join the seventh grade team at Washington Middle School, her mother said no. Instead, Edwards kept staying at school later and later. Her mother never knew about practice until Edwards had already made the team.

Edwards went on to play at Cairo High School. During her junior and senior years her team had 53 wins and only 8 losses, and won a state championship. She graduated in 1982 and went on to the University of Georgia.

In her freshman year Edwards was voted most valuable player in the Southeastern Conference. That same year she set a school record with 189 assists. In 1984 she took All-Tournament honors at the regional championship. She capped her year as a member of the gold-medal women's basketball team at the 1984 Los Angeles Olympics.

In both 1986 and 1990 Edwards was part of gold-medal winning teams at the world championships and the Goodwill Games. In 1987 she helped the U.S. team win a gold medal at the Pan-American Games. At the Pan-American meet she averaged 16.8 points per game.

In 1988 Edwards matched her gold medal performance by helping the American team to a victory at the Seoul Olympics. She scored 18 points in the final game, a 77–70 match against Yugoslavia.

In 1989 Edwards became the first in her family to graduate college, with a B.S. in recreation from the University of Georgia. With her degree in hand, she had her mother's blessing to turn pro. Because there are no real avenues for professional women basketball players in the United States, Edwards went to Italy. She played two seasons there for approximately $50,000 per year, and then played the next three seasons in Japan, where she quadrupled her salary. She didn't spend the money on herself. She spent it on her mother.

Edwards came back to play for the American team in the 1992 Barcelona Olympics.

Most of the press focused on the men's "Dream Team" that played that year, but the women's team won gold medals as well. The women's team had an offer to stay at the expensive hotel that housed the male basketball players, but the women turned down the offer in order to stay at the Olympic village, the traditional home for Olympic athletes.

The only player, male or female, to play on three Olympic gold-medal basketball teams, Edwards has proved how well American women can play basketball—even if she had to go abroad to do it.

ANDRA MEDEA

F

Faggs, Mae (1934–)

Just 5′2″ and weighing around one hundred pounds, this small powerhouse defined a new generation in women's track. Known as "Little Mae," Faggs outraced track-and-field stars who towered above her, becoming one of the few women to win a place on three Olympic track-and-field teams. This great athlete first went to the Olympics at the age of fourteen. She raced competitively for another ten years. The winner of five Amateur Athletic Union (AAU) titles and a gold medal in the Helsinki Olympics, Faggs held every American sprinting record, indoors or out, and led the way for the dynasty of championship runners of Tennessee State.

Aeriwentha Mae Faggs was born on April 10, 1934 (1932 by some accounts) in Mays Landing, New Jersey, not far from Atlantic City. She grew up in Bayside, Long Island, and went to the public schools. When she was in the seventh or eighth grade, a policeman came around looking for boys to run in the Police Athletic League's (PAL) track and field team. Faggs assured the policeman she could outrun any boy there. When she did, he signed her up for the girls' team.

At PAL Faggs met her coach, friend, and mentor, Sergeant John Brennan, a big Irish cop. She was fourteen years old when he told her she was ready to try out for the Olympics at the national trials in Providence, Rhode Island. Faggs barely came in third after two outstanding, nationally experienced athletes. But third meant she made the team. She was going to London.

Faggs traveled first class to the 1948 London Olympics, on the USS *America*. She was disqualified in the trial heats, but she showed amazing confidence even then. As she later said: "I had a little green hat I put on top of my head and I stood there in this big, big doorway and looked around the stadium. I said to myself 'I'll be back.' The other girls thought I was someplace crying, but I was sitting at a little stand drinking hot chocolate and eating some cookies. I wasn't a bit concerned that I didn't make it. I just knew I'd be back."

The next year, at fifteen, Faggs competed for the first time in an AAU national meet. She ran in the 220-yard race, against Stella Walsh, a famous runner whose gender was later called into question. Walsh had held the race record since 1930. Another competitor, **Audrey Patterson**, was the bronze medal winner in the 1948 Olympics. They were both much bigger and taller than "Little Mae," but Faggs beat them and broke Walsh's long-standing record with a time of 25.8 seconds. She was still in high school.

For the next three years Faggs set the pace on women's sprints at the AAU national meets, even though she was only a teenager. She beat all contenders at the 220-yard run, and was the anchor of the victorious PAL 440-yard relay team. After defeats in 1951, she came back to win the Olympic trials in the 100-meters, then placed second in the

200-meters. She became the only member of the 1948 Olympics team to earn a place on the 1952 team.

The Helsinki Olympics did not go well. The American track-and-field team lost time and again, often failing even to qualify for the finals. The only chance remaining was the relay race, but relay was a matter of split-second timing, and most of the team had never worked together before. Young **Barbara Jones**, who later became a racing star, refused even to practice. Faggs' sheer determination saved the team from disgrace. She took the team in hand, worked on their timing every day, and coerced Jones into practice by refusing to set her hair if she didn't cooperate. It worked. Facing a field of tough competitors, Faggs' team won the gold medal and set a new world's record at 45.9 seconds.

After the 1952 Olympics Faggs went to Tennessee State University, where she received a work scholarship. Tennessee was to become the country's foremost training ground for women's track, but when Faggs got there there wasn't even a women's team. There was only one other woman interested in track, and no funds whatever to go to track meets. Faggs couldn't even travel to the 1953 AAU meet to defend her own championship in the 220-yard race. By 1954 more students joined the team, including future Olympic competitors Isabel Daniels and **Lucinda Williams**.

Coach Ed Temple was a great coach for Tennessee State, but Faggs was the catalyst. She nurtured, inspired and competed with those girls. By 1954, Faggs and the others were at the AAU nationals, where she took back her title for the 220-yard run. Faggs and the relay team set a new American record.

By now, sprinting competition was getting tougher, and Faggs was encountering occasional losses in national meets. She just trained harder and came back stronger. She set new records in the trial heats at the Pan-American Games in Mexico City and then lost in the final races. But then Faggs and the American team won the 400-meter relay.

By 1955 Faggs, was back at the top of her form. At the AAU outdoor nationals at Ponca City, Oklahoma, Faggs and the Tennessee State team changed the direction of American racing. Tuskegee Institute used to have the best racers and the best program. Now that reputation was going to Tennessee and their track team, the Tigerbelles.

At Ponca City, Faggs set a new record in the 100-yard run, with a time of 10.7 seconds. She broke one of Walsh's records, which had lasted 25 years. Then she set a new meet record in the 200-yard run, wiping out another of Walsh's records. Next, her team ran the 440-yard relay in 49.1 seconds, leveling another record that had stood for 25 years. The Tennessee State Tigerbelles had come into their own. More young runners came to Nashville to train with that talented corps, and women's track in America was never the same again.

In 1956, Faggs was chosen by the State Department to be the only woman athlete among six male athletes on a goodwill tour of Africa. She raced and coached in Liberia, Ghana, and Nigeria. When Faggs returned to the States she faced even tougher competition. A rising star from Tennessee State, Isabel Daniels, beat her in the 100-yard run. Together on the relay team, the two came from behind and brought the team to victory with a five-yard margin.

The next AAU women's track meet, in Philadelphia, was held in miserable heat. Never one to be discouraged, Faggs made a splendid showing. She won in the 100-yard and 220-yard races, and anchored the winning 440-relay race.

The next week was the Olympic trials for 1956 in Melbourne. **Wilma Rudolph**, who later became a famous runner from the Tennessee State team, came in neck-and-neck with Faggs for the 200-meters. It was Faggs who steadied Rudolph's nerves enough to keep her in the race. They both set a new American record at 24.1 seconds, though Faggs won by a hair. Daniels beat Faggs in the 100-meter once again. Together the team from Tennessee State went on to the Olympics at Melbourne under **Nell Jackson**, the first black woman to coach an Olympic track-and-field team.

Rudolph was a bundle of nerves on this trip, and Faggs was on hand to soothe her rival. In Melbourne, however, the American team ran into difficulties. After a string of losses, Faggs pulled the team together for the relay race. She told them in no uncertain terms that she was not about to go home without a medal. Together the Tennessee team came in third, winning a bronze.

This was the end of the road for Faggs' track career, but by then she had securely launched the Tigerbelles, who were to go on to many victories. Over her years in track, Faggs set records in the 60-yard, 100-yard, and 200-yard sprints, as well as in 400-meter, 440-meter, and 880-meter relays. She had been a champion through good times and bad and helped her own competitors on to victories greater than her own. Rudolph, who went on to win a landmark three gold medals at the next Olympics, credited her career to Faggs' kind influence.

Faggs later became a school teacher and married a principal. She was active in promoting youth programs in Cincinnati, Ohio. She was elected to the Helms Hall of Fame in 1965, and the New York Track and Field Hall of Fame in 1995.

ANDRA MEDEA

Ferrell, Barbara Ann   (1947–)

Born on July 28, 1947 in Hattiesburg, Mississippi, Barbara Ferrell moved to Chicago when she was very young. There she was a member of the Girls Athletic Association and attended Harrison Technical High School. While at Harrison she was the state champion in the 60-meter run.

Upon graduation, Ferrell moved to Los Angeles where she entered California State University and joined the L.A. Mercurettes track team, coached by Fred Jones. In 1967, she was the Amateur Athletic Union (AAU) 100-meter champion and the gold medalist at the Pan-American Games for the same distance. In 1968, Barbara Ferrell set a new world record in the 100-meter run and at the 1968 Olympics she set the American 200-meter record, won a silver medal in the 100-meters and was a member of the gold medal-winning 400-meter relay team. In 1969, she won the AAU 100-meters and 220-meters. At the Olympic trials in 1972, Barbara Ferrell was first in the 100 meters and second in the 220 meters.

A member of the International Track Association in the mid-1990s, Barbara Ferrell was married with two children, working in the field of education, and living in the Los Angeles area. In 1988, Barbara Ferrell's contribution to the world of sport was recognized when she was inducted into the Women's Track and Field Hall of Fame. She once told an Olympic Panel, "Let kids see what you're doing. . . .What did you do?" For herself, her sport, and women of all races, Barbara Ferrell can be proud of the answer to her own question.

HILARY MAC AUSTIN

Franke, Nikki (19??–)

"Our youth must not only be told," Nikki Franke once wrote, "but must truly be made to feel that they can excel at any sport they choose to pursue." Nikki Franke chose to pursue fencing and was one of the first black women on an Olympic Fencing team.

Born in New York City, Franke attended Brooklyn College, where she graduated *cum laude* in 1972. Her graduate degrees—an M.S. and an Ed.D.—were earned at Temple University. Her first large fencing competition was in 1973 when she was a member of the World University Games fencing team. The following year she joined the U.S. national fencing squad.

In 1975, Nikki Franke not only was a silver and bronze medalist as a member of the U.S. Pan American fencing team, she also became the National Woman's Foil Champion, a title she won again in 1980. She was on the fencing teams representing the United States at both the 1976 and 1980 Olympics. In 1980, she was ranked the number one women's foil fencer and was named the Top U.S. Female Fencer by the United States Olympic Committee. From 1978 to 1980, she was the captain and a member of the championship women's foil team.

Franke subsequently taught at Temple as a fencing coach, assistant professor of health education, and an administrative advisor. Remaining active in fencing, she also helped create the first Black Women in Sport Conference at Temple. She has testified at the Pennsylvania Commission for Women's Hearings on Equal Opportunity for Girls in Athletics and co-authored the book *Black Women in Sport*. Active on numerous committees and boards, she felt that "it's imperative that young minority women have as many role models to identify with and emulate as possible." Nikki Franke has certainly practiced what she preaches, serving as a powerful role model herself.

HILARY MAC AUSTIN

G

Gallagher, Kim (1964–)

Some people believe that on the track field, black women are only successful as sprinters. Like so many stereotypes, this one has been shattered, first by Madeline Manning, who won a gold medal in the 800-meter run during the 1968 Olympics in Mexico City, and then by Kim Gallagher, who won a silver in 1984 in Los Angeles and a bronze in Seoul in 1988.

Born in Philadelphia, Pennsylvania, on June 11, 1964, Kim Gallagher grew up in suburban Fort Washington. She attended Upper Dublin High School, where she started long distance running. During those years she held the high school record for the 5000-meter run. After graduation, Kim moved on to the University of Arizona and began to concentrate on the 1500 and 800-meters. In 1984, she won The Athletics Congress Championships in the 1500-meters and finished first in the 800-meters at the Olympic trials.

Kim Gallagher's career on the track field faced a new challenge after the 1984 Olympics. She had to battle a problem with anemia. The condition, which leaves those who suffer it more than usually tired and physically sapped, didn't stop Kim Gallagher from winning the 800-meter run at the 1988 Olympic trials with her best time ever, or from winning the bronze medal in the finals.

The authors of *Black Olympic Medalists* declare that, during her years in track and field, "at her best Gallagher [was] probably the most respected U.S. distance runner after, perhaps, Mary Dekker-Slaney." If you look at lists of Olympic medalists in the 800-meter races from 1928 through 1988, you will find that only two American women won medals in that sixty year span: Madeline Manning, in 1968 and Kim Gallagher, in 1984 and 1988.

HILARY MAC AUSTIN

Garrison, Zina (1963–)

It was a historic moment. In the 1990 Wimbledon women's singles final, Martina Navratilova won her ninth singles title, a record held by no other person, when she defeated Zina Garrison, the first black woman to play on Wimbledon's center court since 1958, when **Althea Gibson** won her second of two Wimbledon crowns. Making history, or being first, has been a rather common occurrence for professional tennis player Zina Garrison.

Zina Garrison, the youngest of seven children, was born on November 16, 1963, in Houston, Texas, to Mary and Ulysses Garrison. Her father died before she was a year old, and she was raised by her mother, who worked as an aide in a nursing home. When Zina was ten, she began playing tennis at the local public park courts where she received instruction from the coach. After a few months he was impressed with her talent and entered her in local tournaments; she did well. By the time she was sixteen, she was playing in national tournaments. She and Lori McNeal, another black player from the Houston public courts, won the 1979 National Hard Court doubles championship for ages sixteen and under. The next year, 1980, Garrison won the National Girls Sixteen singles championship and, with McNeal, three national junior doubles titles. In 1981, at seventeen, she was the first black player to win the junior singles championship at Wimbledon. She also won the junior singles title at the U.S. Open. As a result of these wins, the U.S. Olympic Committee named her top female amateur athlete in tennis, she received the Junior of the Year Award from the International Tennis Federation, and she was awarded the Girl's Sportsmanship Trophy by the U.S. Tennis Association. Washington, D.C., proclaimed January 6, 1982, Zina Garrison Day. She turned professional and was ranked sixteenth in the world at the end of 1982.

In the following years, as a professional tennis player Garrison won many championships and millions of dollars in prize money. She has been a member of the Federation Cup team and captain of the Wightman Cup team (1988). Zina Garrison was a member of the 1988 U.S. Olympic tennis team—the first team since 1924 to compete in the Olympic Games. At the games, held in Seoul, Korea, she won the gold medal with Pam Shriver in doubles and a bronze medal in singles.

Another historic moment for Garrison occurred at the U.S. Open in 1989, when she defeated Chris Evert 7–6, 6–2, during the last tournament of Evert's career. Garrison has also had big wins over Martina Navratilova and Steffi Graf, both champion players. Ranked among the top ten women tennis players 1983–91, at one time she was ranked number four in the world.

Zina Garrison married Willard Jackson, a Houston businessman, in 1989. In 1993 they founded the All Court Tennis Academy for the youth of Houston's inner city. She is a role model for black youngsters and often gives clinics and talks in inner city areas.

Zina Garrison is one of the top professional tennis players in the world—the best African-American woman in the sport since Althea Gibson. Popular among the professionals, she is said to be one of the few players who applaud their opponents when they make a good shot. A determined competitor, her ultimate goal is to win a Grand Slam title.

JOANNA DAVENPORT

Gibson, Althea   (1927–)

Althea Gibson was the first person to break the color barrier in professional tennis. Gibson's 1950 integration of tennis occurred within the same time frame as baseball's inclusion of Jackie Robinson into major league baseball. Perhaps Gibson's achievements are even more remarkable than Robinson's since they occurred in an upper-class sport, seldom played by African Americans, and also since her pursuit of athletic excellence was unconventional for black women and women in general during this era. It was Gibson's driving desire to excel, described in her biography, *I Always Wanted to Be Somebody* (1958), that cast her in the fateful position as the first black woman in modern professional sports.

Althea Gibson was born on August 25, 1927, in Silver, South Carolina, the oldest of five children of Daniel and Annie Gibson. When Althea was three, her father pulled up his sharecropper roots and moved the family to New York City. In Harlem, Gibson developed a "tough kid on the block" image, which would manifest itself in adulthood in the competitive qualities of mental toughness and determination. Truancy from school and her flight from home and relatives brought Gibson into contact with the Society for the Prevention of Cruelty to Children. She then acquired a license to work, but after moving from job to job she lapsed into welfare dependence. Gibson's athletic ability stood out among other youth, and she drew attention to her aptitude by winning the Police Athletic League and Parks Department paddle tennis competitions.

Musician Buddy Walker recognized her talent, purchased rackets, and took her to the Harlem River Tennis Courts. Shortly thereafter, the prestigious Harlem Cosmopolitan Tennis Club took up a collection to provide her with membership and tennis lessons. Gibson got her start in 1942 by winning the girls' singles New York State tournament sponsored by the all-black American Tennis Association (ATA). The Cosmopolitan Club then sent her on to the ATA nationals, where she lost in the girls' singles finals. Gibson consecutively won the 1944 and 1945 girls' tournaments. At age eighteen she played in the women's 1946 ATA nationals and lost to Roumania Peters in the finals.

Friends played an important role in the direction of Gibson's life. Boxer Sugar Ray Robinson was one of her most supportive friends. Gibson's big break was to occur when Hubert A. Eaton of Wilmington, North Carolina, and Robert W. Johnson of Lynchburg, Virginia, offered her a home, secondary schooling, tennis instruction, and the encouragement and support to realize her potential. As a consequence of their interest in her, she graduated from Williston Industrial High School in Wilmington, learned to get along in a variety of social settings, acquired self-discipline and self-respect, and won the ATA women's singles ten years in a row (1947–56), thus establishing herself as the best black woman tennis player.

In 1949, Gibson was invited to play in the desegregated National Indoor Championships, where she lost in the quarterfinals. In 1950, while in her freshman year at Florida Agricultural and Mechanical University, she reached the finals before being defeated. It then appeared that political intervention would keep Gibson out of the segregated grass court invitationals, but her break came in July 1950 when tennis champion Alice Marble declared in the magazine *American*

Althea Gibson rose from childhood brawling in the streets of New York to the fabled courts of Wimbledon, integrating the women's singles tennis tournament in 1951. In 1957, she won the singles title. (NATIONAL ARCHIVES)

Lawn Tennis, "She is not being judged by the yardstick of ability but by the fact that her pigmentation is somewhat different." Largely due to Marble's influence, the Orange Lawn Tennis Club in New Jersey issued Gibson an invitation. This led to a long-awaited invitation to the 1950 national championships at Forest Hills, where she lost to Louise Brough in the second round. Gibson entered Wimbledon in 1951 and thus became the first African American to play in this exclusive international tournament. After disappointing tournament performances in 1951, 1952, and 1953 and a two-year stint as a physical education teacher at Lincoln University in Missouri, she accepted an invitation from the State Department to represent U.S. tennis on a team tour of Southeast Asia. The tour instilled self-confidence in Gibson, and the quality of her tennis improved. She proceeded to win the Indian and Asiatic women's singles titles and other European tournaments at the conclusion of the Asian tour. In 1956, although the Wimbledon singles title was to elude Gibson, who lost in the first round to Shirley Fry, she went on to win the Wimbledon doubles championship with her partner, Angela Buxton.

Ranked second in the United States after Shirley Fry, Gibson again faltered before Fry at Forest Hills in 1956. Gibson then won pre-tournament championships in England before the 1957 Wimbledon championship. She was ready for her third Wimbledon attempt. Seeded first, her game fell into place, and she played Darlene Hard, another American, in the finals. Gibson won the singles title at Wimbledon, 6-3, 6-2. Thereafter, teamed with Darlene Hard, she continued winning by taking the doubles title at Wimbledon. The tough-minded kid

from Harlem succeeded at doing what no other black woman had accomplished before or since—winning the Wimbledon championship. Gibson's tennis accomplishments continued. She won the national clay court and Forest Hills singles titles in 1957, and in 1958 she returned to Wimbledon to win yet another singles and doubles championship.

Gibson retired from professional tennis in 1959. She played exhibition tennis on tour with the Harlem Globetrotters, appeared in the movie *The Horse Soldiers* (1959) with John Wayne and William Holden, and played professional golf from 1963 to 1967. In later years she served as program director for a racquet club and a parks commission in New Jersey. A few of her honors have included Associated Press Woman Athlete of the Year, 1957–58; Lawn Tennis Hall of Fame; and Black Athletes Hall of Fame. Althea Gibson remains the benchmark by which other black women measure their achievement in the sport of tennis.

JUDITH GEORGE

Glenn, Lula Mae Hymes (1917–)

One of Tuskegee Institute's leading track stars of the 1930s, Lula Mae Hymes Glenn was born in Newman, Georgia, on March 5, 1917. She belonged to the era of segregation when even the most outstanding black women athletes might go virtually unnoticed. With Glenn's participation, Tuskegee became the first black team to win the Amateur Athletic Union (AAU) championship in the first fourteen years of the competition. Years of effort to build up the women's athletic program at Tuskegee under coach Amelia C. Roberts led to the 1937 Tuskegee victory at the women's track and field championship sponsored by the AAU. The star of the Trenton, New Jersey, competition was Lula Hymes, who took first place in the long jump with a 17 foot, 8-inch jump. She also took second place in the 50-meter dash and second place in the 400-meter relay, along with three other participants.

In 1938, the Tuskegee women's team again won the AAU women's track and field championship, with Hymes as the high-point winner in the 100-meter dash and the broad jump. In the 1939 nationals, Glenn set a new American record with an 18 foot, 1-inch jump in the running broad jump competition. She married Miles Alfonso Glenn that same year.

Glenn was the first all-around star for the Tuskegee women's team and continued to be a leading figure until 1941. In the years since, Tuskegee Institute has continued to field a leading women's team in the track and field competition.

JOHN L. GODWIN

H

Harris-Stewart, Lusia (1955–)

High scorer Lusia Harris-Stewart led the American women's Olympic basketball team to a silver medal in the 1976 Montreal Olympics. This was the first time women's basketball appeared as an Olympic sport, and Harris-Stewart scored the first two points in Olympic women's basketball history. She also led her small, previously unknown, Delta State University (Cleveland, Mississippi) basketball team to three Association for Intercollegiate Athletics for Women (AIAW) National Collegiate Basketball Championships in 1975, 1976, and 1977. As a high scoring, six-foot three-inch-tall center she was the best of the new breed of star collegiate players. She broke hundreds of records and won numerous American and international honors. She was the dominant woman basketball player of her era.

Harris-Stewart was a pioneer woman player at Delta State University on an academic scholarship. Her ability was central to attracting large crowds to Delta State's basketball arena. As the only black player on her school's team, and one of the few black players on the collegiate basketball teams in the mid-1970s, she served as a lonely superstar role model for black girls and women. She was a member of the women's team that played at Madison Square Garden in New York in February 1976—the second women's team ever to do so. (The first played in 1975.) The fans came, in part, to watch Harris-Stewart, who at twenty-one years old was enjoying a three-year, fifty-game winning streak. She led Delta State to victory by scoring a dazzling forty-seven points, a high-score record that season for man or woman, college player or pro. Harris-Stewart, however, was not just a basketball player; she was an active leader at Delta State. She made a place

Lusia Harris-Stewart was one of the first two women players inducted into the Basketball Hall of Fame. (NAISMITH MEMORIAL BASKETBALL HALL OF FAME)

96

for herself in the white community, not only as a top basketball recruit but also as an acknowledged leader on campus and as the first black woman to be chosen homecoming queen.

Born in 1955, Lusia Harris grew up the seventh of nine children on a vegetable farm in Minter City, Mississippi, a town with a population of 200. Her love of sports and pursuit of excellence in school dominated her life. Her basketball career started in her backyard with her brothers and sisters. She played basketball at Tucker Young Junior High School and became a star player at Amanda Elzy High School. When she was about to enter Alcorn A & M, she was recruited away to Delta State and became a central player in building their basketball successes. Lusia graduated from Delta State with B.S. and M.S. degrees in physical education. While still a graduate student, she became an assistant basketball coach and admissions counselor at Delta State. For a brief time in 1980, Harris-Stewart played for the Houston Angels in a new Women's Pro League. Her husband, George E. Stewart, and their four sons live in Mississippi, where she teaches physical education and coaches women's basketball.

Lusia Harris-Stewart's achievements have merited many national honors and awards. As a college player, she was selected for the AIAW All-Tournament team; she was selected three times for the Kodak All-American team; and she was voted most valuable player at an AIAW National Championship. In 1976, she was Mississippi's first Amateur Athlete of the Year. The next year, she won the Broderick Award for the top basketball player in the AIAW, and she received the Broderick Cup for the outstanding female collegiate athlete. On the national and international level, Harris-Stewart was high scorer in the 1975 World University Games in Bogota, Colombia, in the Pan-American Games in Mexico City the same year, and in the 1976 Olympics. In May 1992, Harris-Stewart was one of the first two women basketball players inducted into the Springfield Basketball Hall of Fame. The other woman inducted was Nera White, an international player from the Amateur Athletic Union (AAU) of the United States.

Lusia Harris-Stewart remains a basketball legend and is an active role model for young people. She speaks to the importance of accomplishing through sacrifice, working to overcome obstacles, and pursuing goals.

JOAN HULT

Hudson, Martha B. (1939–)

Her nickname was "Pee Wee." At four feet, ten inches, she was the smallest athlete who had ever competed in the Olympics—at least six inches shorter than the runners she beat at the 1960 Rome Olympics. A talented sprinter who never let her size get in the way, Martha Hudson was a track star from the Tigerbelles, the extraordinary team from Tennessee State University.

Born in Eastman, Georgia on March 21, 1937, Hudson was the oldest of three children. Her father was a truck driver for a local factory, while her mother was a housewife. Hudson was a tomboy who liked to race the boys and, little as she was, she often won. At Twin City High School she not only excelled at basketball, she also became team captain.

While competing at the famed Tuskegee relay races, Hudson was spotted by Ed Temple, a coach who was building the women's track team at Tennessee State University. It was 1955, and Temple was just beginning the summer training programs for high school girls that was later to yield a crop of Olympic greats. Hudson attended that first summer high school program and went to two more in the following summers.

By 1955, while still in high school, Hudson was a national competitor. That year at the Amateur Athletic Union's (AAU) national meet at Ponca City, Oklahoma, she won the 75-yard run. She then helped the Tennessee State team to a victory in the relay race. The following year, in 1956, Hudson won the 50-meter run at the AAU's Track and Field Championships in Philadelphia.

In 1957, Hudson graduated as class salutatorian and received a work-aid scholarship to Tennessee State. She started the same year as fellow championship sprinter **Barbara Jones**, on a team that included such world-class competitors as **Mae Faggs** and **Margaret Matthews**. In 1959, she won the 100-yard run at the AAU indoor national meet and was on the AAU All-American women's track-and-field team.

The next year, Hudson made the team for the 1960 Rome Olympics along with many of her teammate Tigerbelles, including Jones and the famed **Wilma Rudolph**. In the discouraging early races, none of the racers did well except for Rudolph. The 400-meter relay team was all Tigerbelles, but only Rudolph had won any races. The rest of the team decided it was time to make a comeback. They did, and the Tigerbelles won a gold medal with their split-second timing in the relay race.

That evening the Tigerbelles were the toast of Rome. They were wined and dined at Bricktop's, a cabaret (run by the celebrated nightclub owner of the same name) that catered to millionaires and titled figures in Rome. In the States, Hudson came back to an awards ceremony hosted by the governor of Tennessee, with the mayor of Nashville awarding the gold-medal winners gold watches. Back in Georgia, Hudson's hometown declared a Martha Hudson Day.

After graduating from Tennessee State, Hudson returned to Georgia. She became a elementary school teacher in 1963, in the small town of Thomaston. Aside from her teaching duties, she coached elementary school girls in basketball.

Aside from winning a gold medal and becoming a celebrity in Rome, Hudson had one ambition—just once to beat her admired team captain, Mae Faggs. That was the one thing she never accomplished.

Hyman, Flora (1955–1986)

"The floor wasn't a good friend of mine," said Flora Hyman when describing the demanding sport of volleyball. She was born in Inglewood, California, in 1955 and began to play volleyball as a teenager.

Hyman studied math and physical education at the University of Houston for three years. She then decided to pursue volleyball instead, thinking that she could resume her academic career later in life. Hyman, a three-time all-American at the University of Houston and the outstanding collegiate player of the year 1976, reached her full potential only after years of work on the United States team. She was a member of the U.S. team in the 1978 and 1982 world championships and the world cup tournaments in 1977 and 1981. In 1983, she and the coach of the women's volleyball team, Dr. Arie Selinger, accepted the Team of the Year Award from the Women's Sports Foundation.

Hyman was a dedicated athlete who insisted on learning as much as possible about the game and practicing at every opportunity. She was described as "one of the world's strongest hitters at the net, who spikes the ball the way Julius Erving dunks a basketball." She was faced with limited prospects as a female athlete after the U.S. team won the silver medal in the 1984 Olympics, so she and several of her teammates traveled to Japan to join a semiprofessional team, "Daiei," sponsored by a Japanese supermarket chain.

It was in Japan, on January 24, 1986, that Hyman died of Marfan's syndrome, a hereditary disorder of the connective tissue. She was survived by her father and seven brothers and sisters. Hyman brought a vigor, vitality, and aggressiveness to women's athletics that helped pave the way for women in sports.

FLORA R. BRYANT

J

Jacket, Barbara J. (1935–)

When Barbara J. Jacket became head coach for the U.S. women's track-and-field team at the 1992 Olympic Games in Barcelona, Spain, she became the second African-American woman to hold that honor. The first was Jacket's coach and mentor, **Nell Jackson**. No stranger to pioneering roles in athletics, Jacket holds many honors and awards as athlete, coach, and manager. In 1990, she became the first and only female athletic director in the Southwestern Athletic Conference (SWAC) when Prairie View A & M University in Prairie View, Texas, named her to that position.

Barbara Jacket, daughter of Eva Getwood, was born in Port Arthur, Texas, on December 26, 1935. She was educated at Port Arthur's Lincoln High School and then went to Tuskegee University, where her track-and-field abilities led to her induction into the Tuskegee Athletic Hall of Fame (1987). However, Jacket is even better known for her work as a coach. She has been named National Association of Intercollegiate Athletics (NAIA) Coach of the Year in various categories on twenty-seven different occasions. She had Olympic assistant coaching responsibilities for U.S. teams in 1973 meets in Germany, Poland, and Russia; in 1975 in Russia; and in 1977 in Bulgaria. She was assistant coach in the Pan-American Games in 1979; and head coach in the World University Games (Japan 1975); the World Championships (Italy 1987); and the World University Games (England 1991). Her Prairie View women's track teams have won the following national championships: NAIA, 1974 and 1976; U.S. Track and Field Federation, 1975 and 1976; Track and Field Association-USA, 1979 and 1980; NAIA Indoor, 1984, 1987, and 1991; and NAIA Outdoor, 1982-90.

JEWEL LIMAR PRESTAGE

Jackson, Nell Cecilia (1929–1988)

Nell Cecilia Jackson, one of the pioneers in women's track and field, was born July 1, 1929, in Athens, Georgia, to Dr. Burnette and Wilhemina Jackson. The second of three children, she spent most of her early life and college days in Tuskegee, Alabama, where her father was a dentist and her mother worked at the Veterans Administration hospital. Nell loved sports, and by the time she was fourteen she was a member of the Tuskegee Institute Track and Field Club. The club was for talented girls at both the high school and college levels and was the avenue for their entry into national meets. From then on, Nell Jackson's life revolved around track as she became a competitor, educator, coach, and official.

As a competitor, she was an All-American sprinter who was a member of the 1948 U.S. Olympic team. She competed in the first Pan-American Games in 1951, placing second in the 200-meter relay and winning a gold medal as a member of the 400-meter relay team. In 1949, Jackson set an American record time of 24.2 for the 200-meter relay that lasted for six years.

Jackson received a bachelor's degree from Tuskegee Institute in 1951, a master's degree from Springfield College in 1953, and a Ph.D. from the University of Iowa in 1962. She taught physical education and coached track at the Tuskegee Institute, Illinois State University, the University of Illinois, and Michigan State University. She also was women's athletic director at Michigan State University and, at the time of her death in 1988, professor and director of athletics and physical education at the State University of New York at Binghamton. A renowned scholar, she wrote many track articles for periodicals and books, and she authored a definitive text, *Track and Field for Girls and Women* (1968).

In addition to her collegiate experience, she was coach of the U.S. women's track team at the 1956 Olympic Games in Melbourne, Australia, the first black head track coach of an Olympic team and, at twenty-seven, one of the youngest head coaches of any sport. Nell Jackson was also head women's track coach at the 1972 Olympic Games in Munich, Germany. In 1980, she was one of five Americans selected to attend the International Olympic Academy in Olympia, Greece. In 1987, she was manager of the U.S. women's track team that competed in the Pan-American Games. She also conducted innumerable track workshops and clinics all over the country.

As an official, Jackson served in many capacities. She was the first of two women to serve on the board of directors of the U.S. Olympic Committee, was a vice president of The Athletic Congress (TAC), and, at the time of her death, was secretary of TAC. She also served in varying committee assignments for the American Alliance for Health, Physical Education, Recreation, and Dance, the National Association for Girls and Women in Sports (NAGWS), and the National Collegiate Athletic Association.

Through the years Nell Jackson received many honors. She was inducted into the Black Athletes Hall of Fame, and she won the NAGWS Honor Award twice for her track contributions. Tuskegee Institute (now Tuskegee University) honored her three times, the last time with its Outstanding Alumni Award. The University of Iowa also recognized her with its Alumni Merit Award.

Nell Jackson epitomized loyalty, honesty, dedication, and excellence. Her untimely death from the flu occurred on April 1, 1988, in Binghamton, New York. She was survived by two brothers, Dr. Burnette L. Jackson, Jr., and Thomas P. Jackson, both of Philadelphia. Posthumously, on December 1, 1989, Nell Jackson was inducted into TAC's National Track and Field Hall of Fame and was awarded its highest honor, the Robert Giegengack Award, given for outstanding leadership and contributions in track and field.

JOANNA DAVENPORT

Jones, Barbara (1937–)

She was a high-strung sprinter and, at the age of fifteen, the youngest woman in Olympic history to win a track-and-field event. Ladylike and her mother's pet, she was not a rough-and-tumble competitor; but before she hung up her track shoes, Barbara Jones won fifty-six trophies and 335 medals, including two Olympic gold medals.

Born in Chicago on March 26, 1937, Jones was a well brought-up young lady. She lived on the sometimes rough South Side of

Barbara Jones is still the youngest woman in Olympic history to win a track-and-field event. At the age of fifteen she won a gold medal at the 1952 Helsinki games on the relay team led by Mae Faggs. (TENNESSEE STATE UNIVERSITY)

Chicago, but there was no question of young Jones getting into trouble. When she joined the Brownies, her mother was the den mother. When she became a Girl Scout, her mother was troop leader. Jones went to St. Elizabeth Catholic High School and, when she went out for track, her mother was there to cheer her on.

Jones showed her athletic talent quite young. Running for the Catholic Youth Organization (CYO), she tried out for the Olympics at only fifteen years old, earning a place on the team for the 1952 Helsinki games. She won a gold medal on the relay team led by **Mae Faggs**, even though Faggs had to coerce her into practicing by threatening not to set her hair.

Jones did equally well in competitions in the United States. From 1953 through 1955, her CYO relay team won the Amateur Athletic Union (AAU) races. In 1954 and 1955 she won the 100-yard run at the AAU indoor meets. Then, to her great disappointment, at the qualifying meet for the Olympic trials in 1956, Jones was beaten by members of the Tennessee Tigerbelles—the women's track team from Tennessee State University—again and again. She didn't get to go to the Melbourne Olympics.

Instead, she decided to train with the Tigerbelles. Jones already had a year at Marquette University, but she transferred to Tennessee State, where she was offered a work-aid scholarship. It took heart and humility to start over at Tennessee State: Jones was not a hero there, and her mother was not there to spoil her. **Margaret Matthews**, another sprinter, seemed to delight in upsetting Jones before a race, but Jones stuck it out. Her form improved, and Jones went back to winning races.

Jones won the 100-yard run in the AAU national championships in 1957, and won the 50-meter run in 1957 and 1958. The latter year, she set a world record that was matched in a dead heat with fellow Tigerbelle **Isabel Daniels**. They both ran the 50-yard run in a time of 5.7 seconds.

Jones seemed to thrive on large crowds and foreign competition. In 1958, in the 100-meter run, Jones was the first American female to win against Soviet racers. The next year she did the same in Philadelphia, besting the Russians again at 100 meters.

The next Olympics, held in Rome in 1960, Jones made the team. She did not do well in the individual races, but she and a team composed of fellow Tigerbelles set a new Olympic record in the semifinals in the 400-meter relay, with a time of 44.5 seconds. After problems with rain on the clay track, the same team took the gold medal in relay, losing only one tenth of a second off their previous time. The Tigerbelles celebrated that night at one of the finest nightclubs in Rome.

Jones graduated from Tennessee State in 1961. She married Marcellus Slater and moved to Chicago, where she became a physical education teacher.

ANDRA MEDEA

Jones, Leora "Sam" (19??–)

"I'm beginning to think I was put here to play handball," says Sam Jones. Certainly anyone who has played against her would think the same. For many years, she was the best team handball player in the United States.

The daughter of a domestic worker and a pickle factory foreman, Sam Jones grew up in Dudley, North Carolina, where she attended Southern Wayne Senior High School and was All-American in basketball. After graduating in 1978, she attended Louisburg Junior College in Louisburg, North Carolina, where she was All-American in basketball as well. In 1980, she moved to East Carolina State University, where she majored in special education and minored in criminology. She continued playing basketball and added volleyball. She was named Most Valuable Player on the basketball team for each of the three years she attended.

In 1983, the national team handball coaches came to East Carolina State on a recruiting mission and Jones tried out for the team. Two weeks later she was on the team and competing in France. The next year she was a member of the U.S. team at the Los Angeles Olympics. The U.S. team took fourth place. After the Olympics, Sam Jones moved to Europe and began playing for two European teams, Bayern Leverkusen in Germany and Hypo Bank Vienna in Austria. The two teams were national champions for the next three years.

Sam Jones played for the U.S. handball team in the next two Olympics—1988 in Seoul, South Korea, and 1992 in Barcelona, Spain. She participated in her fourth Olympic Games in 1996 as the assistant coach for the U.S. Team Handball Women's National and Olympic Teams.

HILARY MAC AUSTIN

Joyner, Florence Griffith (1959–)

Born in Los Angeles in 1959, Olympic medalist Florence Griffith Joyner, the seventh of eleven children, began running track at age seven, through a program at the Sugar Ray Robinson Youth Foundation. At fourteen and fifteen she won the Jesse Owens National Youth Games Awards and while at Los Angeles' Jordon High School set records in sprinting and long jumping.

In 1979, Joyner attended California State University in Northridge, but was forced to drop out because of lack of funds in 1981. Fortunately, University of California at Los Angeles Assistant Track Coach Bob Kersee recognized her athletic talents and engineered an athletic scholarship to UCLA for her in 1981. While attending classes on the Westwood campus, Joyner won the National Collegiate Athletic Association

200-meter championship in 1982 and the 400-meter championship in 1983.

After graduating with a psychology degree in 1983, she was not very successful when she competed in the U.S. nationals and the world championship games. Later to become well known for her flamboyant clothes, nails, and hair, Joyner first caused a stir when she ran the first two rounds of the 1984 World Championship games in Rome wearing a skin-tight leotard-like suit.

At the twenty-third Olympiad in Los Angeles in 1984, Joyner garnered a silver medal in the 200-meter race.

After the 1984 Olympic Games, Joyner worked at a bank during the day and styled hair and nails for clients in the evenings. From September 1986 to April 1987 she was retired from athletic competition.

Joyner resumed training by spending endless hours watching a tape of Ben Johnson's 100-meter world-record run in order to improve her start. Success came at the 1987 World Championship games, when she was a member of the winning relay team and won a second-place award for the 200-meter event.

It was at the 1988 Olympic trials in Indianapolis, however, that Joyner's flamboyant beauty and exciting taste in track attire combined with her athletic performance to capture the attention of the world press. Her outfits included a sparkling apple green "one-legger" bodysuit, a plum purple "one-legger" bodysuit, a fluorescent gold bodysuit, and a white lace bodysuit with see-through tights and midriff. She came in first in the 100- and 200-meter events and shattered the world record for the 100-meter race in the quarter finals.

Wearing the conventional American uniform at the twenty-fourth Olympiad in Seoul (1988), Joyner won the 200-meter event, setting new world records in both the semifinals and the final race. In addition, she established a new world record in the 100-meter heat and won the gold in the final event. The gold was again cinched in the 400-meter relay (4 x 100) and silver was garnered in the 1600-meter relay (4 x 400). Following her multiple victories in Seoul, Joyner received the Sullivan Award and the *Track and Field News* Athlete of the Year award.

She retired from competition shortly after the 1988 Olympics, and kept herself busy for a time acting, writing books, and designing her own line of sportswear. She and her husband, Al Joyner (the triple-jump gold medalist in the 1984 Olympics and brother of **Jackie Joyner-Kersee**, the Olympic heptathlon gold medalist) have one child, a daughter, Mary Ruth.

In 1993 Joyner was appointed by Bill Clinton to be cochairwoman of the President's Council on Physical Fitness and Sports. The *New York Times* caught up with her at the end of a frenetic stay in Washington, D.C., during which she jogged four miles with the President. (Her husband dropped out after three miles.) Joyner told the paper's reporter that "what I'd like to do on the President's council [is] make athletics available to every youth in America, not just one day a week like it was for me, but every day." She credits the Sugar Ray Robinson Foundation, which runs recreational programs for disadvantaged children in California, with giving her and other children in Watts a chance to swim, run and jump in grassy playgrounds where "swings weren't broken and you didn't get ringworm from playing in the sandbox." Given her goal-driven dedication in the past, you can be certain that she'll try to accomplish just that.

D. MARGARET COSTA/JANE D. ADAIR

Joyner-Kersee, Jackie (1962–)

As she ran a victory lap at the 1992 Summer Olympics, the tall Illinois native was approached by the former Olympic decathlon champion Bruce Jenner. "You're the greatest athlete in the world," he told her. "Man or woman, the greatest athlete in the world." Seven times in the history of the Olympic Games a woman has scored more than 7,000 points in the challenging and grueling heptathlon. Six of those times, the woman was Jackie Joyner-Kersee. More than a superb athlete, more than a repeated winner of Olympic gold medals, she is a legend.

Jacqueline Joyner was born on March 3, 1962, in East St. Louis, Illinois. Joyner's grandmother insisted that the child be named after First Lady Jacqueline Kennedy because "some day this girl will be the first lady of something." Her parents, Alfred and Mary Joyner, were in their teens when she was born. Mary Joyner worked as a nurse's assistant, and Alfred Joyner traveled to other cities to work in construction before he got a job as a railroad switch operator.

At the age of nine, Jacqueline Joyner ran in her first track competition. Soon she was bringing home first prizes every time, sometimes four or five of them. When she was fourteen, she won her first National Junior Pentathlon Championship. Then she won it three more times. At Lincoln High school, she set a state record for the long jump and played on a basketball team that defeated its opponents by an average of 52.8 points a game. All this time, she excelled in her academic work as well, graduating in the top ten percent of her class.

The University of California at Los Angeles recruited the remarkable young athlete, offering her scholarships in either basketball or track. She chose basketball and went off to UCLA as star forward. She qualified for the 1980 Moscow Olympics but was disappointed when the United States boycotted the games. However, a much greater sorrow overshadowed that loss. During Joyner's freshman year, her mother died of meningitis at the age of thirty-eight.

Joyner was concentrating on basketball and the long jump when she was spotted by assistant track coach Bob Kersee. He was stunned by her abilities but dismayed that they were not being encouraged to their fullest. After receiving special permission to coach her, he persuaded Joyner to begin heptathlon training; she went on to set collegiate records in 1982 and 1983. In 1983, she and her older brother, Al, were both chosen to compete in the world track-and-field championships in Helsinki. There, Joyner discovered that she was not invulnerable. She experienced her first serious injury, a pulled hamstring, and was unable to compete. However, a year later, she qualified for the 1984 Olympics in Los Angeles.

Joyner arrived at the Los Angeles stadium with another hamstring injury. In spite of that, and two fouls in her best event—the long jump—she went into the final event of the second day neck-and-neck with Glynnis Nunn of Australia. With her brother running beside her on the final leg of the 800-meter run, urging her on, she came within .06 seconds of winning the gold medal. Al, however, did win a gold, in the triple jump. It was the first time in Olympic history that a sister and brother had won medals on the same day and the first time an American woman had won any multievent medal. Joyner went home with the silver medal and the recognition by many of her peers that she was someone very special.

In 1986, Joyner and her coach, Bob Kersee, got married. That same year, she gave up basketball to concentrate on the heptathlon and changed her training to avoid hamstring pulls. Her performance immediately improved, peaking at the Goodwill Games in Moscow, where she shattered the 7,000-point mark—the heptathlon equivalent of running the four-minute mile. From that time on, she did it regularly. That same year she won the Sullivan Award for top amateur athlete. She also received the 1986 Jesse Owens Award.

For the next two years, Joyner-Kersee racked up wins and records. At the 1988 Summer Olympics in Seoul, South Korea, she won a gold medal in the heptathlon. Then, at the Olympics in Barcelona, Spain, in 1992, she did the unprecedented. At the age of thirty, after eleven years of competition, she won the gold for the second time. This time, she was ahead after every single event. Her closest competitor, Irinia Belova, finished 199 points behind her. No woman had ever before won back-to-back medals in the heptathlon.

At the 1996 Olympics in Atlanta, she was forced to drop out of the heptathlon because of a hamstring injury, but she recuperated enough to come back to win a bronze medal in the long jump competition. "Of all the medals I've won," she said, "this one is special because I really had to work for it."

D. MARGARET COSTA/JANE D. ADAIR

L

Love, Lynette (1957–)

At six feet two and a half inches and 178 pounds, Lynette Love is built to be a champion in tae kwon do karate. A gold medal winner at the 1988 Olympics, and a holder of national and world champion titles, Love is a third-degree black belt who has gone on to train a new generation of Olympic competitors.

Born in Chicago on September 21, 1957, Love was the daughter of Delores Preston-Cooper and Willie Love. She grew up in Detroit, Michigan, where she attended Cass Technical High School. Her size and athletic ability made her a basketball star in high school, but she realized there were few opportunities for women in basketball. After graduating from high school, she went on to study speech and theater at Wayne State University.

Love shifted her interest from basketball to dance in order to stay physically active. She became involved in tae kwon do almost by accident. As she said, "I was driving by a tae kwon do center and saw people doing jump kicks. I took one look and said to myself, 'That's something I want to try.'" She went in and talked to the head instructor, Hwa Chung, who seemed like someone special who cared about his students. Chung eventually became the manager of the U.S. Olympic team.

Love entered her first national competition also nearly by accident. It was 1979, and she was attending the meet but not intending to compete. But her karate uniform was in the car, and her instructor suggested that she compete for the fun of it. She did, and won the national title.

Since then, Love has won nine consecutive national championships in tae kwon do and become the world heavyweight champion in the sport. She is taller and leaner than most of her competitors, which lends speed and agility. But she attributes her success to her intense concentration, which is the key to mastery in the art.

Love graduated from Wayne State University in 1983 and moved to Brooklyn, where she studied dance with the famed Alvin Ailey's dance school. She also studied tae kwon do in Brooklyn. To make ends meet, she sewed theatrical costumes on the side.

Love moved to Maryland to study more intensively for the 1988 Olympics at Seoul, South Korea, where women's tae kwon do was introduced as a demonstration sport. She trained at **Howard University**, which has one of the finest tae kwon do training schools in the country. Since women's tae kwon do was not sponsored in the United States, Love worked full-time at a bank and fit in five hours of training daily. The work paid off with a gold medal in the Seoul Olympics.

In September of 1990, Love opened her own tae kwon do school, the National Institute of Tae Kwon Do and Fitness, in Bethel Hills, Maryland. She returned to the Olympics in 1992 as captain of the women's tae kwon do team and took a bronze medal in the heavyweight division. She retired from competition after those games and has since gone on to coach the women's teams for the 1995 Pan-American Games and the Olympic Sports Festival. She is now a full-time tae kwon do instructor at her new facility, Love's Tae Kwon Do Academy in Clinton, Maryland.

ANDREA MEDEA

M

Matthews, Margaret (1935–)

She was a tough young girl who became a tough young track star. Uneven in her training and performance, but with the sheer grit and determination to win, Margaret Matthews was a Tigerbelle who set national records in broad jump, as well as being a championship sprinter and relay team member.

Born in Griffin, Georgia, on August 5, 1935, Matthews grew up in a rough part of Atlanta. Her father worked occasionally as a construction laborer, and her mother supported the family on meager wages doing laundry. There were two other children in the family and hardly any money. Matthews grew up fighting and scrapping, but she knew she wanted to make something of herself.

Matthews' chance to make good started at David T. Howard High School, in the track program coached by Marian Armstrong-Perkins. Armstrong-Perkins had coached a series of young women who went on to the Olympics and she encouraged Matthews. While still in high school, Matthews was on the All-State basketball team and held state records in 50-, 57-, and 100-yard sprints, as well as long jump. Later Matthews said, "I found out you don't have to be pretty to be recognized, to be known, to be somebody." Matthews carried the picture of Armstrong-Perkins in her wallet for years.

Matthews graduated from Howard High School in 1953 and went to **Bethune-Cookman** College in Florida. That did not work out, so Matthews went on to Lewis College in Chicago, where she joined the Chicago Comets and competed within the Catholic Youth Organization (CYO). In Chicago she began competing against **Barbara Jones**, fellow Comet, a more ladylike sprinter whom Matthews dearly loved to beat.

Next Matthews went to Tennessee State, where she joined the famous Tigerbelles track team. Her roommate was team leader **Mae Faggs**, who was as warm as Matthews was rough. Between Faggs' warm heart and Matthews' tough contentiousness, the Tigerbelles were pushed to do their best.

Matthews was not an easy competitor. Her specialty was psychological warfare, goading her rivals into mistakes. Sometimes it worked and sometimes it didn't. Often, her tactics only made the other women angry enough to beat her. More than once she reduced Jones to tears, but Jones still won.

Matthews did not like to lose or even see her rivals win. In college, her main interest in broad jump seemed to come from trying to outdo her rival **Willye White**. The fierce competition between the two resulted in a series of American broad jump records.

Matthews won the 1956 Olympic trials in broad jump, with an American record of 19 feet, 9½ inches. She beat White, who still made the Olympic team. However, at the Melbourne Olympics, Matthews succumbed to the pressure, fouled repeatedly on her early jumps, and failed to jump far enough to make the finals. Instead, her rival White won a silver medal. Matthews did win a bronze medal as a member of the 400-meter relay team, but the setback still hurt.

Back in the United States, Matthews redeemed herself by winning the broad jump at the Amateur Athletic Union (AAU) outdoor meet in 1957. However, by this time, White had regained the American record with a jump a little under twenty feet. Matthews only jumped 19 feet 5½ inches, well under White's record. But at the outdoor AAU competition in 1958, Matthews broke White's record and became the first American woman to surpass twenty feet, with a jump of 20 feet, 1 inch.

At the same 1958 meet she bested Jones, her longstanding sprinting rival, in the 100-meter run. Then she, Jones, and the other Tigerbelles won the relay for a new track record.

These victories enabled Matthews to join the American team that competed in Europe that year. Once again, Matthews had trouble against foreign competition. In contrast, White, who nearly did not make the touring team, broke Matthews' record with a jump of 20 feet, 2½ inches in Warsaw, Poland. Foreign meet or not, Matthews was not about to stand for that. Just two days later, Matthews came back in Budapest, topping White's record with a jump of 20 feet, 3½ inches. Then she added another two gold medals for sprinting and relays.

Matthews dropped off her form for the rest of the tour, allowing White to beat her several times. But White was never able to break Matthews' last broad-jump record. In 1959, Matthews maintained her title in broad jump at the AAU All-American meet. Later that year she came in second to a Soviet jumper, although they both made remarkable jumps: Matthews jumped 20 feet, 3 inches against her rival's 20 feet, 2 inches.

In 1960, Matthews graduated from Tennessee State, and married Jesse Wilburn, another Tennessee State athlete. They settled in Memphis, where Matthews became an elementary school teacher. The rumor is that she mellowed.

ANDRA MEDEA

McDaniel, Mildred   (193?–)

Many black women athletes have achieved great things because somebody believed in them—or told them they couldn't do it. Mildred McDaniel was inspired by a little of both. A gold medal winner and Olympic record setter in the women's high jump, she excelled at track and field because her coaches had faith in her. And she set a new world record because a track official didn't think she could do it.

McDaniel grew up in a poor part of Atlanta, where her father was a checker in a department store. She had the good fortune to go to David T. Howard High School, where Marian Armstrong-Perkins coached girl's track and field. No fewer than five of Armstrong-Perkins' girls made it into the Olympics, and McDaniel was going to be one of them.

McDaniel began her athletic career not in track and field but in basketball. She started after the gym teacher offered a free pair of sneakers to any girl who shot ten consecutive foul shots. The next day McDaniel got her sneakers. She played on a high school team with **Margaret Matthews**, later an Olympic medalist, and Margaret McNabb, who also went to the Olympics. When McDaniel started out on the team, McNabb scored the most points. The next year McDaniel topped her.

McDaniel had a particularly effective way of dealing with hecklers. Kids cheering for the other side would yell, "Get Skinny," meaning her. McDaniel didn't appreciate this, so she would walk over to the stands and yell, "You call me 'Skinny' again and I am going to shoot another goal." Then she would do it. Pretty soon the crowd learned to call her by the number on her jersey.

McDaniel was happy with basketball and did not want to bother with track and field. Armstrong-Perkins, however, could see her potential and asked her to hang around the track and see what she liked. After a while, she noticed a girl who couldn't make a high jump. McDaniel could and so she went on to learn the high jump.

After graduating from Howard, McDaniel was recruited by what was then the foremost women's track team in the country, at Tuskegee Institute under Coach Cleveland Abbott. At the Amateur Athletic Union (AAU) national outdoor meet in 1953, McDaniel won the high jump. She lost to her teammate Janette Cantrell the next year but won again in 1955 and 1956, at both AAU indoor and outdoor competitions.

McDaniel won at the 1955 Pan-American Games, but that was the last time Coach Abbott saw her win. He died soon afterwards. **Nell Jackson**, who also coached for Tuskegee, led the American team for the 1956 Melbourne Olympics.

Even though McDaniel had won repeatedly in AAU meets, no one expected her to do particularly well at the Olympics. McDaniel had usually quit trying after she had beaten her competitors and so she had never jumped over 5 feet, 6½ inches. At Melbourne there were four other competitors who had already jumped 5 feet 8 inches.

Sportswriters had not even bothered to rate McDaniel's chances.

The jumper who held the current world record was Iolanda Balas from Romania. The Rumanian was eliminated early in the competition, but McDaniel kept jumping. McDaniel had already outdistanced the competition, she was just trying to better her score. It was cold, McDaniel was tired, and the officials were getting restless. Finally one of the officials muttered to another, "Well, we may as well pack up, she can't go any higher." That irritated McDaniel so much that she had them set the bar at 5 feet, 9¼ inches, a full inch over the world's record. McDaniel missed her first jump, but she got over the bar the second time.

McDaniel became the first American woman to set a world's record in the high jump. Her world mark went unsurpassed for two years and stayed the American record until 1967.

McDaniel graduated from Tuskegee after returning to the United States. She became a gym teacher in Pasadena, California.

McGuire, Edith Marie (1944–)

The year 1964 was the big one for track star Edith McGuire. She set six records in that year alone, at both national and international levels. She brought back three medals from the Tokyo Olympics. She was the first black woman to do so since **Wilma Rudolph** made three medals in one Olympics the goal to strive for.

Born in Atlanta, Georgia, on June 3, 1944, McGuire was an honors student at David T. Howard High School, as well as an athlete. She won awards in both track and basketball and was named best all-around student in her class.

Women's track at Howard had developed into an outstanding program under the guidance of Coach Marian Armstrong-Perkins. Track stars who had trained under Armstrong-Perkins competed on every U.S. Olympic team from 1952 through 1964, when McGuire won at Tokyo.

McGuire made her first international team when she was just out of high school at the age of seventeen. She joined the 1961 women's team that competed at the British Commonwealth Games in Jamaica, and went on to race against the best racers of the Communist bloc. She was not entirely pleased with the honor. She was so homesick she cried until she got to East Germany. She was in central Europe before it began to look like fun.

At the 1964 Tokyo Olympics Edith McGuire won a gold medal in the 200-meter race, setting a new Olympic record. (TENNESSEE STATE UNIVERSITY)

McGuire's teammates included established stars such as Wilma Rudolph, so no one paid much attention to McGuire. To everyone's surprise, she matched a 1958 sprinting record in Jamaica at the Commonwealth Games. In Kiev, USSR, after a history of painful defeats against Polish racers, **Wyomia Tyus** and McGuire shut out the Polish champions, coming in first and second in the 100-meters. At 200-meters McGuire came in first, and Tyus second, followed by their Polish rivals. In Warsaw, McGuire lost to the Polish racers, but won in West Germany at 200 meters. Then she raced with the team that won the 4 x 100-meter relay.

Back from Europe, McGuire went to college at Tennessee State, home of the famed Tigerbelles. This was the alma mater of many black track greats, such as **Mae Faggs** and Wilma Rudolph. While training with the Tigerbelles, McGuire proved herself a master of the longer sprints. In 1963, she won the gold at 100 meters at both the indoor and outdoor Amateur Athletic Union (AAU) nationals. At the Pan-American races in São Paulo in 1963, she set a Pan-American record for the 100-meters: 11.5 seconds.

But 1964 was McGuire's year to shine. She specialized in the longer sprints and was undefeated that season in races over 200 meters. She set six major records that year—a world record in the 100-yard run, an American record in the 100 meters, senior level California record in the 100 meters, both Olympic and Olympic tryout records in the 200 meters, and an American outdoor record in the 220-yard race.

That year was also the year of the Tokyo Olympics, and McGuire continued her successes there. She won a gold medal in the 200-meter race, setting a new Olympic record of 23.05 seconds. She took a silver medal in the 100-meter race and helped her teammates win an Olympic silver in the 400-meter relay.

After the Olympics, McGuire continued to excel at the national level. She won at 200 yards in the AAU indoor nationals in both 1965 and 1966. In 1966 she shared a victory with the 440-yard relay team at the national AAU outdoor meet. At the same meet she took second at 100 yards, and third at 220. But in 1966 she graduated from Tennessee State and the Tigerbelles, and there were few avenues for women athletes at the time. Her running career was over. McGuire went on to teach school and work with underprivileged children in Detroit.

ANDRA MEDEA

Miller, Cheryl de Ann (1964–)

She's been called the greatest female player in basketball. And that was by an opposing coach. Cheryl Ann Miller is credited with creating modern women's basketball, bringing new speed, agility and excitement to the game. The leader of two Olympic gold medal teams and holder of virtually every award available to a women's basketball player, Miller was a dazzling athlete who changed the sport and brought new high standards to the court. And if it hadn't been for Title IX sports legislation, she probably wouldn't even have played.

Born in Riverside, California on January 3, 1964, Miller is the daughter of Saul and Carrie Miller. Her father worked on computer systems, first in the Air Force and then in a Riverside hospital. Her mother was a nurse. Miller was the oldest of the family with three brothers, all of whom were talented in sports. Her parents were supportive of them equally. They agreed that at least

Cheryl Miller is the greatest woman basketball player of all time. (NAISMITH MEMORIAL BASKETBALL HALL OF FAME)

one parent should be at each game, even though this sometimes got hectic. As Miller's father said, "If there were four games, I'd go to two and their mom would go to two. If there were three games, I'd start at one, Carrie would start at another, and we'd meet at the third."

Miller often played one-on-one with her brother, Reggie, who later became a professional basketball player. In the fifth grade she played on the boys' basketball team. As she put it, "The boys on the other teams laughed at me in the beginning, but then they'd see the score at the end of the game and they weren't laughing any more."

Miller benefited from Title IX legislation that mandated that girls were entitled to the same team sports that boys had. Had she been born a decade earlier, her talent might have remained undiscovered because there were so few girls' teams, and those that existed received so little support. That began to change when the 1972 legislation took effect. By the time Miller was in high school and college, her talents had an avenue. At one point she told *Sports Illustrated*, "Without Title IX I wouldn't be here."

Miller attended Riverside Polytechnic High School, where she quickly became a basketball star. At 6´3´´, she had speed, skill, flamboyance and agility. During her stay at Riverside, her team compiled a startling record of 132 wins and four losses. During one game, she scored 105 points! She also set conference records for points scored in a season (1,156), and points scored during her high school career (3,405). She led her team to a California Interscholastic Federation championship during her senior year.

Miller was the first athlete, male or female, to be named to *Parade* magazine's high school All-American Team for four years running, from 1979 to 1982. She was chosen consensus All-American for the same four years. She was *Street and Smith's* top high school basketball player in both 1981 and 1982. While still in high school she was named *Sports Illustrated* Player of the Week in December, 1983. In 1982, she was the only prep school athlete asked to play on the American National basketball team to tour Europe.

When Miller graduated from Polytechnic in 1983 she received approximately 250 scholarship offers, making her probably the most recruited women's basketball player in history. She enrolled at the University of Southern California in 1983, where she continued her stellar success. As a freshman Lady Trojan, she led the team in scoring, steals, and blocking. She set a single-season scoring record with an average of 22.2 points per game. Her first year, she helped her team win the National Collegiate Athletic Association (NCAA) championship by scoring almost one half of her team's points. She was voted the tournament's most valuable player.

It only got better. In her first two seasons Miller accumulated a total of 1,399 points, 670 rebounds and 235 assists. As a sophomore, she led her team to a 24-4 season, with another NCAA championship. Again she was voted the tournament's most valuable player. Miller was named All-America player for four years while at USC, and NCAA Player of the Year three times.

In 1983, Miller won a gold medal playing basketball at the Pan-American Games. She followed this with another victory at the 1984 Olympics in Los Angeles, with the first American women's basketball team ever to win the gold at the Olympics. Miller was leading scorer in the women's division, with a total of 99 points.

In the 1984 season, Miller improved her performance yet again, averaging 26.8 points per game for USC. Her senior year, her average dropped slightly to a still remarkable 25.4 points per game. That year the Lady Trojans made it to the NCAA championship but lost to the University of Texas, 97 to 81.

While in college Miller won basketball awards too numerous to list. They included the Female College Athlete of the Year in 1984; the Broderick Award; college player of the year in 1984 and 1985; the Naismith Trophy in 1984, 1985, and 1986; and the Women's Basketball Coaches' Association Player of the Year in 1985 and 1986. After her last season at USC, the Trojans retired her number.

Miller graduated from USC in 1986, with a degree in communications. She went on to win a gold medal at the 1986 Goodwill Games in Moscow, and to play in the World Basketball Championships that August.

Miller's basketball career was cut short by a severe knee injury in early 1987. She was not able to play at the 1987 Pan-American Games or at the 1988 Olympics at Seoul. Instead, she used her communications degree to become a sports commentator for ABC, covering college basketball and football.

If Miller's career had not been ended by a knee injury, it might have been ended by economics. There was simply no place in the United States, for a women's basketball player of her caliber because there were no women's professional teams. When Miller was inducted into the Basketball Hall of Fame in 1995, many of the questions were about her younger brother, Reggie, who had become a highly successful professional player. Cheryl Miller was good-natured about answering the questions about a brother she is close to and proud of, but the irony was obvious.

In the late 1980s, Miller became an assistant coach for her old team at USC. By 1993 she had become head coach. In 1994 she had coached USC to a Pac-Ten title, and had brought the Lady Trojans to the NCAA championships in both 1994 and 1995. In 1995 Miller abruptly left USC, anticipating another stint as a television announcer.

Miller was inducted into the International Women's Sports Hall of Fame in 1991 and into the Basketball Hall of Fame in 1995. Acknowledged as perhaps the greatest woman basketball player, it is the least she deserves.

ANDRA MEDEA

Mims, Madeline Manning   (1948–)

She was the first American woman to win an Olympic gold medal in the 800-meter race, and she set an Olympic record doing it. Considered one of the greatest women distance runners America has ever produced, Madeline Manning Mims struck gold at the 1968 Mexico City Olympics. Her track-and-field career lasted nearly fifteen years. As a small child, she was not expected to live.

Born in 1948 in Cleveland, Ohio, the daughter of a domestic worker, Mims was raised in a housing project by her mother and stepfather. When only three, she was struck by spinal meningitis, a deadly disease. She survived but was expected to be mentally retarded and physically handicapped. Although anemic, sickly, and shy, Mims recovered and eventually began to run track in high school. There she came into her own.

After high school Mims went to Tennessee State University, where many of the greatest women stars of track and field had trained. Specializing in the 800-meter run, she won at the 1966 World University Games and at the 1967 Pan-American Games, where she set a new American record. In 1968, she won the Olympic trials at 800-meters, and followed this with a victory at the 1968 Mexico City Olympics. She was the first American woman to win in the Olympics at 800 meters. To cap her victory, she came in at 2:00.9, a new Olympic record.

During the late 1960s and early 1970s, Mims continued to win at national meets, with a total of seven Amateur Athletic Union (AAU) outdoor championships and five AAU indoor championships. Equally remarkable, Mims earned membership on four different Olympic teams—in 1968, 1972, 1976 and 1980. She did not make the 800-meter team in 1972, but that year she won a silver Olympic medal as part of the 400-meter relay team.

In 1976, Mims became the first American woman to break the two-minute mark in the 800-meters, with a time of 1:59.9. The same year at the Olympic trials, she broke her own record with 1:57.9. This record stood until 1983.

After the 1976 Olympics, Mims began to pursue what she considered her true calling, the ministry. While studying at Oral Roberts University, she came out of retirement and began to train once again for the 1980 Olympics. She was then thirty-two. In the 1980 Olympic trials she ran the second best time of her career but lost the chance to compete when President Carter ordered a boycott of the Moscow Olympics.

Since 1975 Mims has ministered in women's prisons. She has also become a highly regarded gospel singer. In 1982, after completing graduate school, she was or-

Madeline Mims set an Olympic record when she became the first American woman to win an Olympic championship in the 800-meter race in the 1968 games. She is shown here with three of her teammates that year. From left to right are Madeline Manning Mims, Martha Watson, Una Marsh, and Estelle Baskerville Diel. (TENNESSEE STATE UNIVERSITY)

dained in the Faith Christian Fellowship International. She then started her own ministry to women's prisons, Friends Fellowship, Inc.

Mims has been made a member of the National Track and Field Hall of Fame, the U.S. Track and Field Hall of Fame, the Olympic Track and Field Hall of Fame and the Ohio Track and Field Hall of Fame. She was also chosen as women's distance runner on the All-Time, All-Star Indoor Track and Field Team in 1983.

Mims continues to offer running clinics, and does public speaking along with her ministry. She lives in Tulsa, Oklahoma.

ANDRA MEDEA

Murray, Lenda (1962–)

She looks simply astonishing. The winner of the Miss Olympia Bodybuilding Contest for five years running, Lenda Murray is a chiseled mass of muscle and sinew, a moving human sculpture. She is also the result of years of hard work. She can do squats with a 315-pound barbell resting across her shoulders, and that's just part of her job. The rest involves jetting around the world for photo shoots and appearances, running the business of owning the most incredible body in the world.

Lenda Murray did not start out this way. The second-oldest of six girls, she ran track in high school and at Western Michigan University. She graduated from Western Michigan with a bachelor's degree in political science. She was then a cheerleader for the Michigan Panthers, which was part of the long-gone U.S. Football League. In 1982, she was ready to move up to cheerleading for the Dallas Cowboys, where she'd made the next-to-last cut, so she began to work

Lenda Murray's daily workout includes three hours of weight training, including wrist curls with twenty-two-pound barbells. It is this kind of dedication that has made her the winner of the Ms. Olympia contest every year since 1991. (LENDA MURRAY)

out to "improve" her body. She never made it onto the squad. Instead, she was destined to have other people cheering for her.

When Murray started working out, she was trying to develop a standard cheerleader body, which in her case meant smaller thighs. However, her thighs got larger and considerably more muscular. She discovered that she wasn't born to be a small cheerleader type. She was born to be a powerhouse.

Other people at the gym noticed her remarkable strength and musculature. The ability to develop into a competition bodybuilder is genetic, a matter of wide shoulders, long arm and leg muscles, and a low percentage of body fat, less than half that of a normal woman. Murray had that combination, and she decided to develop it.

There is only one major competition each year for women bodybuilders: the Ms. Olympia contest. Murray entered in 1990, when it was held in New York City. She won her first competition, displacing the six-time champion Cory Everson. In 1991, Murray followed up her victory with another win, proving that she wasn't a temporary phenomenon. And she went on winning title after title into 1995.

Bodybuilding is part sheer grit and part aesthetics. Since the body itself is the shape to be molded, the sport of bodybuilding is subject to the same shifts of fashion as the rest of society. What does the ultimate female body look like? Is it the strongest body, the most tapered, the most sharply defined? No one has been entirely sure.

In 1992, the International Federation of Bodybuilders issued femininity rules in women's bodybuilding that confused contestants and bodybuilders alike. What was feminine? Small? Lean? Most of the contestants were guessing, as was Murray. Most women showed up smaller, including Murray. Fortunately she and the judges were in sync, and she won again.

Murray's daily workout includes one to three hours of serious weight training, including wrist curls with twenty-two-pound barbells. Getting ready for a competition, she works considerably harder. As the established Ms. Olympia, she has a schedule that might include trips to Italy, Japan, and several cities around the United States, all in the space of a month.

Now living in a suburb of Detroit, Murray has appeared on an ESPN program on bodybuilders. In 1994, she came out with her first workout video, *The Shape of Things to Come*. Wherever she goes, she gives people new reasons to think about what female beauty really is.

ANDRA MEDEA

P

Patterson-Tyler, Audrey (Mickey)
(1926–1996)

Audrey "Mickey" Patterson had the distinction of being the first black woman to win an Olympic medal and the first American woman to compete in the 200-meter run. Born in New Orleans on September 27, 1926, she was in high school when, after hearing Jesse Owens speak, she decided to start running.

After graduation, in 1947, Patterson moved on to Tennessee State University, where she joined the prestigious track team. At the final trials during the 1948 Olympics in London, Patterson won the 200 meters and came in second in the 100 meters before going on to win her bronze medal. Unfortunately a shadow was cast over her win when, twenty-five years later, a reexamination of the finish line photograph suggested that the Australian runner Shirley Strickland had, in fact, crossed the finish line ahead of her.

Following her retirement from sprinting, Mickey Patterson enjoyed an active life as a mother, grandmother, and inspirational speaker.

For many years she coached her world-renowned track team Mickey's Missiles in San Diego, California, where she settled in 1964. She coached more than 5,000 youngsters, including two who later followed in her footsteps as Olympic sprinters. Of her years of competition, she told *Essence* magazine in 1984, "At the time I competed, you know, we were still sitting at the back of the bus and eating at separate lunch counters. Just imagine what it was like for me."

Fortunately, the world has changed somewhat. It is no longer an "event" for a black woman to win a medal at the Olympics and there are no longer laws that separate the races on buses and at restaurants. All of us are also lucky that women like Mickey Patterson helped to make those changes and can remind us of how far we've come.

Patterson-Tyler died in August 1996 at the age of 69.

HILARY MAC AUSTIN

Pickett, Tidye (19??–)

"Olympic Village, California: July 26—Lily-whiteism, a thing more pronounced than anything else around here on the eve of the Olympic Games," wrote the *Chicago Defender*, "threatened to oust Tidye Pickett and **Louise Stokes** from participation and put in their stead two girls who did not qualify." Tidye Pickett and Louise Stokes were the first black women ever to become members of a U.S. Olympic team, but they were not allowed to compete in the 1932 Olympic Games held in Los Angeles.

Both young women qualified, with Pickett running sixth in the 100-meters. They were told that they would run as part of the 400-meter relay team. The trouble started

119

before they even arrived in Los Angeles. During a stopover in Denver, Colorado, they were not allowed to eat with their teammates in the hotel dining room, but instead their food was sent to their rooms. Back on the train, future star athlete Mildred "Babe" Didrikson, in what might have otherwise been considered "youthful highjinks," threw a pitcher of ice water on Pickett and the two exchanged words. Some reports imply that those words were abusive.

Once in Los Angeles, Pickett and Stokes continued to prepare for their race and practice with their teammates. Then word came from Olympic officials that two other women had been given their positions on the relay team. The *Chicago Defender* reported that, "Tidye Pickett of Chicago and Louise Stokes of Boston are two girls who qualified at the final trials held in Evanston two weeks ago. . . . However, a meeting held Tuesday resulted in the officials deciding that two of the girls failing to qualify on the coast are much faster and should be placed ahead of the Race stars."

Neither woman gave up after this blow, however. Pickett continued to prove herself at meets all over the country. The indoor national meet, in 1933, gave her a second place medal in the 50-meter run. At the same meet, in 1936, she won the 50-meter hurdles. At the Olympic trials she qualified for the team by finishing second in the 80-meter hurdles. Tidye Pickett had secured her place in history. Despite the efforts to keep her from competing in 1932, she succeeded in becoming the first black woman to compete in the Olympics for the United States.

Unfortunately, Pickett's illustrious career did not end with a resounding victory. She was eliminated during the semifinals when she hit a hurdle. It would be wise to remember, however, that she had already leapt over many other, much higher hurdles to be able to participate in that race. She prepared the way for the many who followed.

HILARY MAC AUSTIN

Powell, Renee (1946–)

If you want to talk about Renee Powell, you have to begin with her father. Bill Powell loved golf. To get around the problem of segregated all-white golf courses, he built his own, the Clearview Golf Club in East Canton, Ohio. It is the only golf course in the United States totally designed and built by an African American. He introduced his daughter to the game he loved when she was only three. By the time Renee Powell entered Ohio State University, she had participated in over one hundred amateur golf tournaments. While at Ohio State she became captain of the ladies' golf team.

Then, in 1967, Renee Powell did what only two black women before had been able to do: she became a member of the Ladies Professional Golf Association (LPGA) tour. During her professional life she played in at least 250 tournaments all over the world. Retiring from the tour in 1980, Powell didn't stop playing or promoting golf. She became a sports commentator for ABC and CBS, taught golf clinics, played in exhibition tournaments in Africa, and became the first (and to date, only) woman in history to be named as a head golf professional (at the Silvermore Golf Club) in the United Kingdom.

Recently, Renee Powell returned to East Canton and her father's golf club. On taking over as head golf professional at

Clearview, she said: "It means a great sense of personal pride to be involved with my father's dream. He wanted to build a golf course that would benefit all people, regardless of race or creed." Both Renee and Bill Powell have a lot of reasons to be proud.

HILARY MAC AUSTIN

R

Rudolph, Wilma   (1940–1994)

At the 1960 Rome Olympics, Wilma Glodean Rudolph made her mark in track by becoming the first American woman ever to win three gold medals. That achievement established her as one of the world's outstanding female athletes.

The twentieth of twenty-two children, Wilma was born near Clarksville, Tennessee, on June 23, 1940, to Ed and Blanche Rudolph. Polio had left Wilma at four years old with little chance of ever walking, but with her family's help Wilma was able to discard her brace and corrective shoes by the age of twelve. By age sixteen, six-foot-tall "Skeeter," as she was nicknamed, had already been named an All-State player in basketball and won a bronze medal at the 1956 Olympics in the 4 x 100-meter relay. Just two years later, Rudolph believed her dreams of a college education and Olympic gold medal were over when she discovered she was pregnant.

With the support of coach Ed Temple, Rudolph attended Tennessee State University on a full track scholarship. In 1960, she returned to the Olympics and won gold medals in the 100-meter dash, 200-meter dash, and 4 x 100-meter relay. She held world records in all three events at the time she retired from amateur competition in 1962. After graduating from Tennessee State University in 1963, Wilma married her high school sweetheart, Robert Eldridge, with whom she had four children: Yolanda (1958), Djuanna (1964), Robert, Jr. (1965), and Xurry (1971). She subsequently worked as a teacher, coach, and director of youth foundations, finally settling in Indianapolis, Indiana.

Wilma Rudolph was one of the most celebrated female athletes of all time. During her competitive years she was voted the United Press Athlete of the Year (1960), the Associated Press Woman Athlete of the Year (1960, 1961), the James E. Sullivan Award (1961), and the Babe Didrickson Zaharias Award (1962). Rudolph's more recent honors include being inducted into the Black Sports Hall of Fame (1973), the Women's Sports Hall of Fame (1980), and the U.S. Olympic Hall of Fame (1983). In 1984, she was one of five sports stars selected by the Women's Sports Foundation as America's Greatest Women Athletes.

During a period of reemergence of the female athlete, Wilma Rudolph had a significant impact. She was one of the first major role models for both black and female athletes, and her success and popularity during the 1960 Olympics gave a tremendous boost to women's track in the United States. In addition, her celebrity caused gender barriers to be broken in previously all-male track-and-field events such as the Millrose Games and the Penn Relays.

Although remembered primarily for her Olympic achievements, Rudolph also has

A victim of polio at age four, Wilma Rudolph overcame many obstacles to become the first American woman ever to win three gold medals in the Olympics. Shown here at far left with her 400-meter relay teammates Lucinda Jones, Barbara Jones, and Martha Hudson in 1960, she has since received numerous honors and awards, including being named one of America's Greatest Women Athletes. (NATIONAL ARCHIVES)

made significant contributions through her work with youth. In 1977, her autobiography, *Wilma*, was published and adapted for a television movie. In 1981 she started the Wilma Rudolph Foundation, a nonprofit organization that nurtures young athletes.

She died of cancer in Nashville, Tennessee on November 12, 1994.

BRENDA MEESE

S

Stokes, Louise (19??–)

"The fastest thing in the schoolyard at Beebe Junior High School is a little colored girl named Louise" (quoted in *Black American Women in Olympic Track and Field*). Although that little girl was fast and went on to win meets, set American records, and win a place on the Olympic team, she never ran an Olympic race, because she was black.

The story of Louise Stokes begins in Malden, Massachusetts, where her father worked as a gardener and her mother as a domestic. In 1930, William H. Quaine, the local commissioner of public parks was starting a track team and discovered "the fastest thing in the schoolyard." Stokes joined his Onteora Club. By 1931, she had established herself as one of "the fastest things in America" when she won first place in the 100-meter run and second place in the 50 meters. She received the Curley Cup for outstanding track performance of the year. An all-around track-and-field athlete, she also placed third in the high jump and, at the first indoor track meet ever held in Boston, set an American record and tied the world record for the standing broad jump.

Then came the Olympics of 1932. At the trials, Louise tied with another Boston runner, Mary Carew, for fourth place in the 100-meter run. Tidye Pickett, a black athlete from Chicago placed sixth. Both of these young black women were told that they had made the Olympic team and were to compete for the U.S. in the 400-meter relay.

Problems started as soon as the team set out for Los Angeles, where the games were being held. During a stopover on the trip Stokes and Pickett weren't allowed to eat in the hotel dining room; instead, food was sent up to their room. Later, on the train, there was an altercation between Pickett and another member of the team, Mildred "Babe" Didrikson. Abuses were hurled. Finally, after arriving in Los Angeles, Stokes and Pickett learned that officials had decided that two other women were faster and should run in their stead.

Stokes described the situation saying, "a pretty fast stunt was pulled. The only thing that would have helped us was to have a man stand up for us as well as going to all the meetings. This is what happened when we didn't have anyone to support us."

Stokes didn't give up and, in 1935, she was the national outdoor 50-meter champion. In 1936, she again competed for a place on the Olympic team. This time the tables were turned. Stokes didn't qualify for a place on the team, but officials decided to give her one anyway. Oddly enough, they made this decision but were not able to guarantee her passage to Berlin. The Olympic committee was chronically short of funds. As the *Chicago Defender* described it, "it was almost sailing time before Miss Stokes was aware that she would go along. There is no happier athlete on the boat than she."

Unbelievably, what happened to Stokes in 1932 happened to her again in 1936. Thinking that she would run in the 400-meter relay, she was told that another would run instead. The first black woman to be chosen for an Olympic team never got to run in the Olympics and never got the chance to see if she could win a medal.

HILARY MAC AUSTIN

Stone, Lyle (Toni) (1931–)

The first black woman ever to play professional baseball, Toni Stone was considered an excellent fielder, an accurate thrower, and a creditable batter. She grew up in St. Paul, Minnesota, and began playing baseball when she joined the boys' team in high school. In 1953, when she was twenty-two, talent scouts for the Negro American League team, the Indianapolis Clowns, saw her playing on a local St. Paul team and signed her to a $12,000 single-year contract. She played second base for four to six innings in about fifty of the Clowns' 175 games. Some historical reports refer to Ms. Stone as a "novel attraction," like the clowns and midgets who were used in the Negro Leagues to increase attendance. Yet even these sources have to give her credit for being an above-average player, batting .243 in her lone season with the Clowns.

HILARY MAC AUSTIN

Stringer, C(harlene) Vivian (1948–)

C. Vivian Stringer, coach of Rutgers University's women's basketball team, is the most significant black basketball coach in the history of the women's game. For the last two decades she has been committed to breaking gender- and race-related barriers. Stringer's leadership and the respect she commands as an exceptionally talented coach enabled her

Now the women's basketball coach at Rutgers, C. Vivian Stringer first made her reputation by leading a small, unknown Cheyney State College basketball team to a second-place finish in the first NCAA Women's National Basketball Championship in 1982. (PUBLIC RELATIONS OFFICE, UNIVERSITY OF IOWA)

to become the first black woman head coach of a U.S. national women's basketball team. Her squad won a bronze medal in the 1991 Pan-American Games in Havana, Cuba. She successfully coached the 1989 U.S. World Championship zone qualification team. No stranger to the winner's circle in earlier years, Stringer also led a small, unknown black Cheyney State College (Pennsylvania) basketball team to a second-place finish in the first National Collegiate Athletic Association (NCAA) Women's National Basketball Championship in 1982.

Charlene Vivian Stoner was born to Charles and Thelma Stoner in Edenborn, Pennsylvania, March 16, 1948. Participation in a variety of sports and a desire for education were the two driving forces in Vivian's early life. She played softball, basketball, and field hockey during her high school years and competed in the latter two sports at Slippery Rock State College in Slippery Rock, Pennsylvania. She received the college's Most Valuable Player Award in basketball, made the Mid-East Field Hockey Team, and played on the nationally ranked (second place) Pittsburgh Orioles softball team. She holds B.S. and M.Ed. degrees in physical education from Slippery Rock State College. In 1972, she went to Cheyney State College as an assistant professor of physical education and coach for women's basketball and volleyball. In 1978–79, she held the unique position of assistant coach for the University of Chihuahua, Mexico, men's basketball team.

After coaching the Cheyney State College team to the second place title in the 1982 NCAA national games, she was actively recruited by many institutions. She selected the University of Iowa in 1983 and coached the women's team to four straight Big Ten conference titles (1987–90). Her record during her twelve seasons at the university is 269 games won, 84 lost.

In the summer of 1995 she became the women's basketball coach at Rutgers, at a salary of $150,000, more than Rutgers paid their men's basketball and their football coaches. Her career record at that time was 520–135 (.794), the fourth-highest among all women's coaches, and her winning percentage also ranked as the nation's fourth best.

Vivian and her husband, William D. Stringer, have three children, David, Janine, and Justin. To encourage girls in basketball, she has run her own summer basketball camp and conducted clinics throughout the country. In the summer of 1991, her basketball team toured Japan.

Stringer's contribution to the basketball world is phenomenal. She represented the NCAA on the 1992 Olympic Games committee for Barcelona. She is vice-president of U.S.A. Basketball's administrative committee and serves on NCAA, U.S.A. Basketball, and Women's Basketball Coaches Association committees.

Stringer's numerous accomplishments include coaching the 1985 World University Games, the 1982 U.S. Olympic Festival East Team, the 1982 Parade All-American South Team, and the 1981 Women's Touring Team trip to China. Among Stringer's Coach of the Year awards are the Philadelphia Sports Writers Award (1979), NCAA Award (1982 and 1988), and the prestigious Converse Award (1988). Other honors include the Distinguished Faculty Award from Cheyney State and the Smithsonian Institution Black Women in Sports Award.

Sports Illustrated invited Stringer, one of ten prominent sports figures, to share her thoughts about the opportunities available to black athletes, in the article "The Black Athlete Revisited" (August 5, 1991). She focused on three primary themes: setting priorities, combating racism, and providing direction for black youth. Stringer reminded readers that education is more important than athletics and that the reality for black youth is that they must overcome barriers to their educational and economic success. Black athletes and leaders must save "our own people" by providing direction and support for individual achievement. For Stringer, sports in general, and basketball in particular, offer rich opportunities for both personal and political advancement.

JOAN HULT

T

Thomas, Debi (1967–)

The first African American to win a national championship in figure skating, Debi Thomas was also the first woman of African descent to win a medal at a Winter Olympics. A powerful, graceful skater with crowd-winning charm, Thomas bested the greatest of the Soviet-bloc skaters in competition and was ranked among the world's best.

Born on March 25, 1967 in Poughkeepsie, New York, Thomas is the daughter of Janice Thomas, a computer analyst, and McKinley Thomas, a manager. Her parents were divorced when Thomas was young, and she grew up with her mother in San Jose, California.

Thomas discovered skating at the age of four, when her mother took her to see an Ice Follies performance. She began skating lessons at the age of five and quickly attracted the attention of the co-owner of the Redwood City Ice Lodge. The co-owner persuaded Thomas's mother that the girl had talent and should have serious training. Since coaching cost around $25,000 a year, and her mother's salary was only $35,000 per year, this was not easy. However, thanks to tight budgeting and the help of her grandparents, half brother and father, plus occasional grants and loans, they managed. The training also required that Thomas's mother drive her daughter back and forth to lessons in Redwood City—some 150 miles of driving each day.

Thomas took part in her first competition at the age of nine and won. She passed the U.S. Figure Skating Association's tests at age fourteen. In 1985, she took a gold medal at the National Sports Foundation. After graduating from San Mateo High School with a 3.5 grade point average, Thomas was accepted at Harvard, Princeton, and Stanford. She chose Stanford and kept practicing at Redwood City.

By her freshman year at Stanford in 1985, Thomas was competing at the national and international levels and winning at the National Sports Festival, Skate America 85, and the St. Ivel Competition. Then she won the U.S. Nationals. From 1986 to 1989, she skated in sixteen competitions, winning eight of them and placing second in three. She won in the women's competition at Skate Canada, first place at the Grand Prix International of France, and captured the Nelhorn Trophy in West Germany. After such a spectacular showing she was named Amateur Sportswoman of the Year by the Women's Sports Foundation in 1986 and McDonald's Amateur Sportswoman of the Year for the same year.

In spite of her skating successes, financial problems persisted. Stanford cost $16,000 a year, and Thomas still had her coaching costs. Thomas' only sponsor was her family. There were times when she had to take breaks in her training, simply for financial reasons. But in yet another victory in 1986, she upset Olympic champion Katrina Witt of East Germany at the World Championship in Geneva, Switzerland. Witt came back to beat her in another competition the same year, but the rivalry attracted attention. Her coach told reporters that it was sad that a skater such as Thomas had no sponsors, while her greatest rivals from East Germany and the Soviet Union were sponsored by their governments. Soon corporate sponsors stepped forward.

This took some of the financial pressure off, but the time pressure remained. Thomas was a pre-med major at Stanford, which was an extremely demanding program. People advised her to postpone college and concentrate solely on the 1988 Winter Olympics. Thomas maintained her exhausting schedule until 1987, when she took a leave from Stanford and moved to Boulder, Colorado, to devote herself to skating practice.

In previous competitions Thomas had shown herself to be highly athletic, with remarkable speed, power, and exuberance. However, she tended to lose points on artistic interpretation, which is a major factor in figure skating. In Boulder she took advice from famed ballet star Mikhail Baryshnikov and began working with George de la Pena, his assistant choreographer.

When it finally came time for the 1988 Winter Olympics in Calgary, Canada, Thomas was beset with difficulties. She had inflamed tendons in her ankles, and Olympic skating is an unforgiving sport. After problems on the ice, Thomas' confidence seemed to falter, and she was finally edged out for second place by a narrow margin. She did win the bronze. Thomas went on to compete at the World Championship at Budapest, where she also won a bronze medal.

Thomas had long insisted that her medical career was more important than her skating and that she did not wish to become a one-dimensional athlete. Now she decided to get on with her life. She officially retired from skating. She had previously declared that she might skate professionally to get money for college, and she now spent some time with professional companies such as the Ice Capades and Stars on Ice. She won first place in her first professional competition, the World Professional Figure Skating Championship. Her dream, however, remained becoming an orthopedic surgeon. She graduated from Stanford University in 1991 and entered medical school at Northwestern University.

ANDRA MEDEA

Thomas, Vanessa (19??–)

"Graceful . . . wild . . . sensuous . . . an amazing act . . ." These are descriptions of Vanessa Thomas' elephant acrobatic act, which she performs in the Big Apple Circus.

Vanessa Thomas was born in Philadelphia, Pennsylvania, and began dancing at the age of four. In 1981, on a whim, she auditioned for a dancing job with Ringling Brothers and Barnum and Bailey Circus. "They called on Saturday and asked if I could leave Sunday. In a split second, my life and career changed." She danced first with Ringling Brothers, then with Circus Vargas; then, in 1985, she found her home at the Big Apple Circus. With Big Apple she expanded her repertoire, performing as an aerialist, as a whipcracker, and in the knife-throwing routines. She belly danced, twirled the hula hoop, and entertained the audience with a double-dutch jump-roping display. But it is her "dancing with elephants" that has earned her special recognition and critical praise. Her performance is eight to nine minutes long, during which she does fourteen different acrobatic mounts with the elephants, interspersed with her own interpretive dances.

She has begun a master's degree in arts management at New York University, choosing the history of blacks in the circus as her thesis project. As for her circus career, she says, "I've developed skills I never thought I possessed. Every season, I get to do something new and different. . . . I'm having the time of my life." So is her audience.

HILARY MAC AUSTIN

Tyus, Wyomia (1945–)

She was a record-setting runner and the first athlete, male or female, to defend an Olympic sprinting title successfully. A quiet, low-key athlete, Tyus was sometimes overlooked around more famous competitors. But she had a gift for delivering under pressure that led her to three Olympic gold medals and one silver.

Tyus was born on August 29, 1945, in Griffin, Georgia. Her father, Willie Tyus, was a dairy worker. Her mother, Maria Tyus, was a laundress. The young Tyus was the only athlete in the family, which also included three boys. Her father encouraged her interest in competitive sports but he died when she was only fifteen.

Tyus's first attempt at track and field at Griffin High School was in the high jump, but she could barely clear four feet. Instead, she turned to running, which was the only varsity sport she could qualify for. She was a good high school sprinter, but not an outstanding one. In 1961, she was noticed by Ed Temple, the coach who trained the famed Tigerbelles of Tennessee State University. He saw her potential and invited Tyus to his summer intensive track-and-field training program. There she got in shape and polished her sprinting technique.

The following year, the conditioning paid off. At the 1962 American Athletic Union (AAU) Championships held in Los Angeles, Tyus won the 100-yard run at the age of 17, setting a new American record for her age. In the same meet she won the 50- and 75-yard runs. In 1963, she repeated her victory in the 100 yards and, within a month, raced in her first AAU senior women's competition. There she finished second to the established sprinter **Edith McGuire**.

In the fall of 1963, Tyus accepted a scholarship to Tennessee State. There, the other Tigerbelles were pushing their training to the limit with a view to the 1964 Olympics. Tyus, only a freshman, worked out with the others, but had more modest goals. "I had plenty to do," she says, "just getting in shape for regular meets." Nonetheless, in 1964 she defeated McGuire in the AAU 100-meter run and, immediately afterwards won a place on the Tokyo-bound Olympic team.

No one thought much of Tyus at the Olympic Games. Her personal best for the 100-meters was 11.5 seconds, well short of the time that won the 1960 Olympics. But in the qualifying heat, she came in first with 11.2 seconds, which tied a standing record. In the final race she won first place, beating McGuire by a full two yards. Next, Tyus won a silver medal with the American 400-meter relay team. Suddenly, she had become an athlete to take seriously.

Tyus' family failed to appreciate the victory. Her mother suggested that she give up track because it was "unladylike." But Tyus went back to her scholarship and the Tigerbelles.

In 1965 and 1966, Tyus won the AAU 100-meter runs. In 1965, she broke her standing world's record with a time of 11.1 for that event and matched the world's record with 10.3 seconds in the 100 yards. In 1965, she was timed racing at 23 miles an hour, a phenomenal speed for a human being. She also won the AAU championship at 220 meters. In 1967, she won the 200-meters at the Pan-American Games in Winnipeg, Canada.

The greatest challenge was the 1968 Olympics in Mexico City. It was the greatest

The 1968 Olympics drew the greatest field of women sprinters ever assembled. Wyomia Tyus bested them all in the 100-meter race in a new world record time of 11.0 seconds. (TENNESSEE STATE UNIVERSITY)

field of women sprinters ever assembled. There were five women on the planet who had matched the world's record time of 11.2 seconds in the 100-meter sprint, and all five of them would be present at Mexico City. Four of them made it to the final round. Tyus won with a new world's record time of 11.0 seconds, making her the first Olympic athlete ever to defend a sprinting title.

At this point Tyus announced her retirement, but she joined the American team to win the 400-meter relay. She and her teammates dedicated their gold medals to Tommy Smith and John Carlos, who had been thrown out of the Olympic village for raising the black power salute while on the winner's platform.

After receiving her degree from Tennessee State, Tyus began teaching in Los Angeles and raising a family. After not competing for five years, she was lured out of retirement in 1973 by the Professional International Track Association (PITA), a newly formed organization for professional athletes. There was only one women's event, the 60-yard run. Working hard to get back into shape, Tyus won it. She went on to win eight out of eighteen races that year and all twenty-two of her races the next year.

Apart from racing, Tyus was a goodwill ambassador to Africa and a founding member of the Women's Sports Foundation. She was a consultant to the Olympic Experience Group, was on the Post Fun and Fitness Council, and took part in the "Help Young America Campaign" sponsored by Colgate-Palmolive.

Tyus was elected to the National Track and Field Hall of Fame in 1980 and the International Women's Sports Hall of Fame in 1981. In 1983, she was chosen as women's sprinter when sports reporters and statisticians named the All-Time Team.

Tyus continues to be a successful coach and public speaker and is a public relations representative for a major soft drink company. One of the finest and most well-balanced of American athletes, Tyus remains a great representative of black women athletes.

ANDRA MEDEA

W

Washington, Ora (1898–1971)

"Courage and determination were the biggest assets I had." So says Ora Washington, who was "one of the greatest pioneering inspirations for black women athletes."

Urged into sports as a way to work through her grief following the death of her sister, Ora Washington quickly became the most prominent black woman athlete in the early years of this century, a time when organized sports for blacks were just beginning. When the first black woman's national tennis tournament, the African American Tennis Tournament, was held in Baltimore, Maryland, in 1924, Ora Washington won it. She held onto the championship for twelve years, undefeated among her peers in the American Tennis Association and the African American National Tennis Organization.

During this same period, Ora Washington was also playing basketball with the Germantown Hornets, scoring a majority of their points. In 1931, she helped to found the famed Philadelphia Tribune basketball team. She was their star player for eighteen years. The Tribune team traveled across the United States giving clinics and playing the best teams, both black and white. During the 1930s, the team only lost six games.

A champion who never had the chance to challenge the other great champions of her day, Ora Washington suffered from the prejudice of the times. The United States Lawn and Tennis Association was closed to blacks. Ora Washington wanted to play the white female tennis champion of the day, Helen Wills Moody, in a private match to determine the better player. Moody refused.

After a career in which she won 201 trophies, Ora Washington had to earn her living as a domestic. Toward the end of her life, she had saved enough to purchase an apartment house, and she threw herself into coaching the youth of Germantown, Pennsylvania, for free. "No one who ever saw her play could forget her, nor could anyone who ever met her. She was a quiet person, gracious, yet a fierce competitor." It's too bad that ignorance and stupidity denied her the wider audience she deserved and denied America her gifts.

HILARY MAC AUSTIN

White, Willye B. (1940–)

Willye B. White, a five-time Olympian (1956, 1960, 1964, 1968, and 1972) and silver medalist, is a modern sportswoman committed to being a black role model and leader for female track-and-field athletes. She won her first silver medal in the 1956 Melbourne, Australia, games at age sixteen in the long jump, and she won another in the 1964 Tokyo Olympics. White works with youth for the city of Chicago, assisting in the training of young Olympian track hopefuls and other track performers. She has competed for more years than any other female Olympian. She used her participation in her last two Olympics in particular to encourage young women to fulfill their talents, to provide good competition, and to be a goodwill ambassador in foreign countries. The longevity of her Olympic participation is a tribute to her commitment to the Olympic ideal. As a pioneering black female athlete who had to confront both racist and sexist stereotypes, she worked to ensure that all female athletes had the opportunity and inspiration to compete successfully and to develop and prepare for leadership roles.

Willye B. White was born on New Year's Day, 1940, in Money, Mississippi. She had one sister and two brothers. Throughout her childhood, she lived in Greenwood, Mississippi, with her grandparents. She later moved to Chicago's South Side. At age eight, she started chopping cotton, using a long hoe called "the ignorant stick" and earning $2.50 for a twelve-hour day. Her training in track started early in Greenwood. In fifth grade she played on the high school varsity basketball team, where her high-scoring feats called attention to her abilities. Subsequently, the track coach at Tennessee State University, Ed Temple, invited her to attend the university's summer clinic for potential Olympians. She spent four summers at Temple's clinics and competed in the 1956 Olympics with the coaching of Temple and in the colors of Tennessee State.

Returning to Chicago after the Olympics, White completed high school while participating in the band, choir, and basketball training every day. She won a track scholarship to Tennessee State University, but left after one year to study nursing. Perceiving that her athletic goals and her race presented barriers to earning a nursing degree, she became a practical nurse instead. She later returned to college, and in 1976 earned her bachelor's degree in public healthcare administration and a coaching certificate at Chicago State University. By this time she held a position with the Chicago Health Department. With relatively secure employment, White was able to continue her work as a volunteer coach for Mayor Richard Daley's youth foundation and other local track clubs. She aggressively demanded more programs for young black athletes and, despite minimal financial backing, succeeded in gaining a reputation for assisting young athletes. After more than twenty years with the health department, White became director of recreation service, Chicago Park District, empowering her to better serve youth in Chicago.

White counts two events as especially important to her. The first was Willye B. White Day on March 12, 1972, when she returned to her hometown from the Olympic Games. Her second was when she received the coveted Pierre de Coubertin International Fair Play Trophy in 1964 from France. During her competitive years, White was a member of thirty-nine international teams, including four Pan-American teams and five Olympic teams. She held the American long-jump record for sixteen years. In addition, she has coached The Athletic Congress (TAC) international teams, U.S. Olympic Committee (USOC) Sport Festival teams, and the Special Olympics.

Among her other achievements, White has been inducted into the National Track and Field Hall of Fame and the Black Athletes Hall of Fame. The Women Sports Foundation appointed her as a board of trustees member and an officer. She served on the President's Commission on Olympic Sports, and has been a member of and consultant to the President's Council on Physical Fitness and Sport. The Amateur

Athletic Union (AAU) recognized, in the 1970s and 1980s, her contributions to track by selecting her for committee membership, and the Illinois AAU elected her president of the state organization from 1980 to 1986. White has also been a member of TAC's Athlete's Advisory Council and a representative to the USOC House of Delegates. Recently she was a candidate for membership on the powerful executive committee of the USOC.

Willye White is divorced and has one grown son. She is praised for her skill, tenacity, longevity, and her commitment to athletes and athletics. She is frequently honored, recognized with awards, and asked to speak to youth, women, and athletic organizations. She was an athlete par excellence, and she is an inspirational role model, coach, lecturer, and charismatic leader.

JOAN HULT

Williams, Lucinda (1937–)

They called her "Lady Dancer"—graceful, well-groomed, and a terrific competitor. One of the famed Tennessee Tigerbelle track team and a gold medal winner in the 1960 Rome Olympics, Lucinda Williams was one of the black woman sprinters who dominated American track in the 1950s and 1960s.

Born on August 10, 1937 in Savannah, Georgia, Williams grew up in Bloomingdale, Georgia. She began attending the Tennessee State University summer track program while still in high school. By the time she graduated she held the state championship track record. She was also named senior outstanding athlete at her high school.

In 1954, Williams became a freshman at Tennessee State at Nashville. Champion sprinter **Mae Faggs** was already at the school, helping to teach and encourage other women in track. Tennessee State soon became the premier training ground for women runners in the country, and the women's track team, the Tigerbelles, became the foremost track force in the country. Under the coaching of Ed Temple, the Tigerbelles brought back the lion's share of Olympic gold time and time again.

The new training and hard work first paid off for Williams in 1955 at the Ponca City, Oklahoma meet of the Amateur Athletic Union's (AAU) outdoor nationals. Williams was on the Tennessee State team that won the 440-yard relay in 49.1 seconds, setting a new American record for the event.

Along with other Tigerbelles, Williams made the 1956 Olympic team for Melbourne. The weather was bad and results were discouraging. Williams was eliminated in her second heat, and other Tigerbelles failed even to place in their races. When it came to the relays, little was expected of the American team. But after fierce practicing, an all-Tigerbelle relay team unexpectedly came in third, winning the Olympic bronze medal.

Williams continued to excel at the AAU national meets, winning the outdoor title at 220 yards in 1958. In 1957 and 1959, she won the AAU indoor competition. She was also on the AAU women's All-America track-and-field team, which enabled her to compete against the best runners of other nations in 1958 and 1959.

Williams did particularly well in the cold war contests held between America and Communist-bloc countries in the late 1950s. American women runners were often considered hopelessly inferior to their communist counterparts, but Williams helped prove that wrong. At a 1958 meet in Moscow she won in the 200 meters, and then again against the Russians in the 1959 games in Philadelphia.

In 1959, at the Pan-American Games, Williams won both the 100- and 200-meter runs. Then she followed up her victory by running anchor for the winning American team in the 400-meter relay.

In the 1960 Rome Olympics, Tigerbelles were responsible for all six gold medals for the American women's track and field. Although Williams did not make the finals in her individual race, the 200 meter, she ran the second leg on an all-Tigerbelle team for the 400-meter relay race. Williams set a terrific pace, and the Tigerbelles won in 44.75 seconds.

Williams ran on eight championship relay teams for the Tigerbelles, more than any other graduate of Tennessee State. She graduated with a master's degree in physical education in 1961 and ended her career in competitive track. She later taught high school gym in Dayton, Ohio.

ANDRA MEDEA

Named in the mid-1980s as the most outstanding one-on-one basketball player in the world, Harlem Globetrotter Lynette Woodard was brought up in the game by her Globetrotter cousin Hubert "Geese" Ausbie. (HARLEM GLOBETROTTERS)

Woodard, Lynette (1959–)

Reared in the game of basketball by her cousin, Hubert "Geese" Ausbie of the Harlem Globetrotters, Lynette Woodard dreamed of one day stepping into his shoes. She was born on August 12, 1959, in Wichita, Kansas, and achieved fame in 1975 and 1977 when she led her high school team in Wichita to 5A state championships for both years. A member of the Kansas Grand State Team in 1975, she was cited for All-State honors in 1975 and 1977, and made All-American her senior year. As a college freshman at the University of Kansas, Woodard led the nation in rebounds, averaging fifteen per game, and she was national leader in steals for the next three seasons. Considered at the time perhaps the most outstanding woman player in America, she single-handedly propelled the University of Kansas program into nationally recognized competition. By the time of her graduation she had amassed a total of 3,649 points, more than any other player in the history of division one women's basketball. Four-time All-American, and two-time Academic All-American, Woodard was a 1981 Wade Trophy winner. She was captain of the gold-medal-winning team representing the

United States at the Pan-American Games in 1983 and captain of the gold-medal-winning U.S. team at the 1984 Olympics at Los Angeles.

After a brief stint as an assistant coach at the University of Kansas, Woodard won a competition against twenty-six other women athletes to become, with her co-competitor Jackie White, one of the first two women players to be hired by the Harlem Globetrotters. Woodard made her debut with the Globetrotters in Brisbane, Australia, in 1986. Woodard acknowledged that her cousin Ausbie, who played professionally for twenty-four years with the Globetrotters, prompted her to dream as a child of one day playing for the Harlem showteam. Named in the mid-1980s as the most outstanding one-on-one player in the world, the six-foot forward had been coached by her cousin at an early age and preferred the Globetrotters to an unlikely start in the all-male National Basketball Association. By this time she was considered the most visible professional woman player in the game.

In 1993 Woodard retired from the Globetrotters and returned to her home state to became the athletic director for the Kansas City (Kansas) school district.

JOHN L. GODWIN

Chronology

1895
Black colleges hold the first tennis matches and tournaments open to African Americans in the United States. Both men and women participate.

1896
Stanford University and the University of California at Berkeley hold the first women's intercollegiate basketball game ever.

1900
The second Olympic Games allow two women's events—golf and lawn tennis.

1904
The third Olympic Games allow women one event—archery.

1906
In Chicago, Mrs. C. O. "Mother" Seames begins teaching tennis on dirt and clay courts to African Americans in the community.

The Interim Olympic Games are held, and women are allowed to compete in singles and mixed doubles tennis.

1908
At the fourth official Olympics, there are thirty-six women and 1,999 men. The women compete in tennis, archery, and figure skating. None of these women are Americans.

1910
In New York City, the Public School Athletic League (PSAL) holds the first major indoor track meet organized by African Americans.

The first black tennis tournaments are held in suburban Washington, D.C.

1911
In Washington D.C., the first official swim meet for African Americans is started by the Interscholastic Athletic Association (IAA).

1912
Mrs. C. O. "Mother" Seames becomes a charter member of the Chicago Prairie Tennis Club, a group that is still active today.

At the Olympic Games in Stockholm, Sweden, women are allowed to compete in swimming events for the first time.

1916
Excluded by white sporting organizations, black tennis players form their own governing group, the American Tennis Association (ATA).

1917
Black women are allowed as co-participants in ATA competitions. **Lucy Diggs Slowe** becomes the first black woman to win an athletic title of any kind when she wins women's singles at the ATA championships held in Baltimore, Maryland.

1920
Mrs. C. O. "Mother" Seames builds four courts on the south side of Chicago that become the first private black tennis club.

1923
The Amateur Athletic Union (AAU) holds the first major outdoor track-and-field meet for women.

1924
The first African-American men go to the Olympics. DeHart Hubbard and Edward Gourdin win gold and silver medals in the long jump.

1926
While attending the University of North Dakota, **Era Bell Thompson** sets five different records in women's track-and-field.

In Washington, D.C., African Americans form the United Golfers Association.

1927
Major Cleveland Abbott starts the Tuskegee Relays, which include two track events for women—the 100-yard dash and a 440-yard relay. Tuskegee is also the only college in the United States to create varsity-level sports for women.

1929
Anita Gant wins the national ATA mixed-doubles championship. She will win the same championship again in 1930.

At Temple University, athlete Inez Patterson, qualifies for six all-collegiate teams: hockey, tennis, basketball, track, volleyball, and dancing.

1931
Founded by **Ora Washington**, the *Philadelphia Tribune* women's basketball squad begins touring the country, playing both black and white teams. The team dominates women's basketball until it is disbanded in 1940.

1932
Louise Stokes and **Tidye Pickett** are the first black women to make the U.S. Olympic Team, are not allowed to compete. U.S. Olympic officials replace them with white runners.

1936
Tidye Pickett is the first black woman to compete in any Olympic Games when she runs in the 80-meter hurdle race at the Berlin Olympics.

The Tuskegee track-and-field team enters the American Athletic Association (AAU) Nationals for the first time and comes in second.

1937
The Tuskegee track-and-field team wins the AAU Nationals, with **Lula Mae Hymes [Glenn]** as its star. The Tuskegee team will win the championships every year, except 1943, until 1948.

The first largely black intercollegiate golf tournament is held at the Tuskegee Institute.

1944

Jesse Abbott (Cleveland Abbott's daughter) founds the nation's second black women's track team—the famed Tigerbelles—at Tennessee A&I, (later Tennessee State University.)

1947

Althea Gibson wins her first ATA women's national championship. She will win the championship for the next nine years as well.

1948

At the Olympic Games held in London, nine of the eleven women on the U.S. track-and-field team are black. **Audrey Patterson-Tyler** wins a bronze for the 200-meter run and **Alice Coachman** a gold in the high jump, setting an Olympic record in the process. They are the first black women to win Olympic medals of any kind.

The Ladies Professional Golf Association is founded. Blacks are effectively barred from the organization, though this is not spelled out in the organization's constitution.

The Women's International Bowling Congress and the American Bowling Congress allow black membership.

1949

Althea Gibson breaks tennis' color barrier when she plays in the United States Lawn Tennis Association's (USLTA) Eastern and National Indoor Championships, but she is still barred from the National Championships (the U.S. Open) at Forest Hills.

1950

Althea Gibson wins the USLTA Eastern Indoor Championship and is allowed to compete in the U.S. National Tennis Championship, becoming the first African American to play in the U.S. Open.

1951

Althea Gibson plays at Wimbledon and reaches the quarterfinals.

The Amateur Fencer's League accepts its first black woman member, Sophronia Pierce Stent.

1952

At the Olympic Games in Helsinki, Finland, fifteen-year-old **Barbara Jones** becomes the youngest person ever to win a gold medal in track-and-field, as a member of the 400-meter relay team. The team, which also includes **Mae Faggs**, Catherine Hardy and Janet Moreau, sets a new world record of 45.9 seconds.

1953

"Big Mo" Aldredge becomes the first black woman to make the national AAU women's basketball team.

Toni Stone is possibly the first woman to play in baseball's Negro American League when she joins the league champion Indianapolis Clowns.

1955

The Women's AAU Track and Field Championship is won by Tennessee State University's track team, the Tigerbelles.

1956

At the Olympic Games in Melbourne, Australia, **Nell Jackson** becomes the first

African American to coach any Olympic team when she is chosen to be head coach for women's track-and-field. Team member **Mildred McDaniel** is the first black woman to set an Olympic record and a world record when she wins the gold medal in the high jump.

Earlene Brown wins the South Pacific AAU shot-put title.

Ann Gregory is the first African American to play in an integrated women's amateur golf championship.

Althea Gibson is ranked the second-best woman tennis player in the USLTA.

1957

Althea Gibson wins both the singles and doubles (with Darlene Hard) titles at Wimbledon. She also wins the U.S. National Championship at Forest Hills and becomes the first black woman to appear on the cover of *Sports Illustrated* magazine.

1958

Althea Gibson successfully defends both her Wimbledon and U.S. National Tennis Championship titles.

1960

At the Olympic Games in Rome, Italy, **Wilma Rudolph** becomes the first American woman ever to win three gold medals. She also sets world records in the 100 and 200-meter dashes and, with **Martha Hudson, Lucinda Williams,** and Barbara Jones, in the 400-meter relay.

Winning the bronze medal, Earlene Brown becomes the only American woman to win a medal in the shot put in the history of the Olympic Games.

1961

Wilma Rudolph beats her own world record in the 100-meter dash, lowering it from 11.3 to 11.2.

1964

At the Olympic Games in Tokyo, Japan, **Wyomia Tyus** begins her fantastic Olympic career when she takes home a gold medal (and a world record) in the 100-meter dash and a silver in the 400-meter relay.

Edith McGuire becomes the second woman (after Wilma Rudolph) to win three medals in one Olympiad, bringing home a gold in the 200-meter dash and silvers in the 100-meter dash and the 400-meter relay.

1967

Renee Powell becomes the first black woman to join the LPGA.

The Olympic Project for Human Rights is formed to protest the treatment of African Americans in the Olympics and in America. The group attempts to arrange a boycott of the 1968 Olympics but is not successful.

1968

At the Olympic Games in Mexico City, Mexico, Wyomia Tyus becomes the first athlete to win two consecutive 100-meter golds, setting another world record in the process.

Madeline Manning is the first black woman to win the gold medal for the 800-meter run.

1969

Nell C. Jackson joins the U.S. Olympic Committee board of directors. She is the first African American to sit on the board.

Tina Sloane-Green joins the U.S. National

Lacrosse team. She is the first African American on the team.

Ruth White wins the national fencing championship. Already holding four national titles, she is the youngest woman and first black woman to win the championship.

1972

Congress passes the education amendments to the Civil Rights Act. These amendments include Title IX, which assures equal opportunity for women in athletics at any school that receives federal funding.

The first women's intercollegiate basketball championships are inaugurated by the Association for Intercollegiate Athletics for Women (AIAW).

1973

The Professional International Track Association (PITA) is formed.

1974

Gloria Jean Byard joins the U.S. National field hockey team. She is the first black woman on the team.

Wilma Rudolph is inducted into the National Track and Field Hall of Fame.

1975

Alice Coachman is inducted into the National Track and Field Hall of Fame.

1976

Anita DeFrantz wins an Olympic bronze medal for rowing.

Evie Dennis is the first black woman to become an officer of the United States Olympic Committee.

Linda Jefferson leads the Toledo Troopers to the National Women's Football league championships.

Mae Faggs is inducted into the National Track and Field Hall of Fame.

1977

The Women's Basketball league is founded.

Lusia Harris is the first black woman to be drafted by the NBA but declines offers from the New Orleans Jazz and the Milwaukee Bucks.

Donna Lynn Mosley, thirteen years old, breaks the color barrier in gymnastics by becoming the first African American to compete in the U.S. Gymnastics Federation Junior Olympic National meets.

Nell C. Jackson is inducted into the Black Athletes Hall of Fame.

1979

Edith McGuire is inducted into the National Track and Field Hall of Fame.

1980

Wyomia Tyus is inducted into the National Track and Field Hall of Fame.

1981

Zina Garrison is the first black player to win the junior singles tennis championship at Wimbledon.

The Women's Basketball League folds.

Willye B. White is inducted into the National Track and Field Hall of Fame.

1983

Mildred McDaniel is inducted into the National Track and Field Hall of Fame.

1984

At the Olympic Games held in Los Angeles, California, **Evelyn Ashford** wins first place in the 100-meter run and sets a new Olympic record of 10.97 seconds. Eighteen days after the Olympics end, she sets a new world record of 10.76, beating her own time of 10.79 set the previous year. She also wins a contract to endorse the American Express card.

Lynette Woodard is named captain of the U.S. Olympic women's basketball team. The team wins the gold medal, and team member **Cheryl Miller** is considered the best woman in the history of the sport.

Diane Durham becomes the first black gymnast to be internationally ranked. She is injured before the Olympics, however, and cannot attend.

Madeline Manning is inducted into the National Track and Field Hall of Fame.

1985

Coach **Vivian Stringer** of the University of Iowa leads her team against Ohio State University. The largest crowd ever to attend a women's basketball game is watching.

Lynette Woodard becomes the first woman member of the Harlem Globetrotters. She plays with the team for two years.

1986

Debi Thomas becomes the first black woman to win the World Figure Skating Championship.

1988

At the Olympic Games in Seoul, South Korea, **Jackie Joyner-Kersee** wins the gold medal for the heptathlon along with another for the long jump.

Evelyn Ashford, thirty-one years old and a mother, wins a silver in the 100-meter run and shares a gold in the 400-meter relay.

Florence Griffith Joyner wins four medals, three gold (in the 100- and 200-meter dashes and the 400-meter relay) and a silver in the 1600-meter relay. She also sets world records in the 100- and 200-meter dashes.

Zina Garrison wins an Olympic gold medal in tennis.

Lynette Love brings home a gold medal in tae kwon do when it is inaugurated as a demonstration sport at the Olympic Games.

At the Olympic Games in Calgary, Canada, Debi Thomas becomes the first African American to win a medal at a winter Olympics when she wins the bronze medal for figure skating.

Anita DeFrantz joins the International Olympic Committee. She is the first African American to serve on the ninety-nine member Committee.

Barbara Ferrell is inducted into the National Track and Field Hall of Fame.

Nell C. Jackson is inducted into the National Track and Field Hall of Fame.

1990

Zina Garrison is the first black woman to play on Wimbledon's center court since Althea Gibson.

The Boston Red Sox baseball team hires Elaine Weddington to be their assistant general manager.

Bernadette Locke becomes the assistant coach of the University of Kentucky men's basketball team. She is the first woman to hold an on-court coaching position on a college men's team.

1991

Cheryl Miller is inducted into the International Women's Sports Hall of Fame.

The NCAA awards Althea Gibson the Theodore Roosevelt Award, its highest honor. She is the first woman ever to receive the award.

1992

At the Olympic Games in Barcelona, Spain, Jackie Joyner-Kersee becomes the first woman to win a second gold medal in the heptathlon.

Dominique Dawes joins the U.S. Olympic Gymnastics team. She is the first black woman on the team.

Barbara J. Jacket is named head coach of the U.S. Olympic track-and-field team. She is the second black woman to hold this position.

Lynette Love becomes captain of the U.S. Olympic tae kwon do team and wins a bronze medal.

Vivian L. Fuller is the first black woman to be named athletic director of a Division I (the NCAA top competitive level) university when she is asked to lead the department at Northeastern Illinois University.

Lusia Harris is inducted into the Basketball Hall of Fame.

1993

Cheryl Miller becomes head coach of the Lady Trojans, the women's basketball team at the University of Southern California.

1994

Cheryl Miller coaches the Lady Trojans to a Pac-Ten title.

Dominique Dawes, at the National Gymnastics Championships in Nashville, takes gold medals in all four events—the vault, uneven bars, balance beam, and floor exercise. It is the first time that feat has been accomplished in almost three decades, since 1969.

1995

Cheryl Miller is inducted into the Basketball Hall of Fame.

Mae Faggs is inducted into the New York Track and Field Hall of Fame.

Vivian Stringer is hired as the coach of women's basketball at Rutgers University at a salary higher than that of both the men's basketball coach and the football coach.

VISUAL ARTS

Introduction

THE ARTISANS

The impact of black women on art in America did not begin in an art school or a gallery. It began at a crudely crafted kiln in a New England village, at a loom in a "cloth house" on a Southern cotton plantation, in the sewing room of the home of a middle-class white family. In all these places, black women brought their creativity and love of beauty to bear on their tasks and helped to shape the look and feel of America.

Africans were brought to the shores of America to work. Most were agricultural workers, either on small farms in the North or on large plantations in the South. However, there was a significant minority of slaves who worked as artisans, crafting the tools, clothing, dishes, and other implements of both their own households and those of their white masters. Many of these items were made strictly to order, following the designs of the slaveowner's own culture. Many others, however, allowed the creativity of the artisan, as well as his or her African heritage, some expression. In these practical crafts we can first see the traces of African-American artists.

Black women were among these first slave artisans. They were involved in the making of pottery, for example, for their own use and for the master's household. In South Carolina, where workers on the rice plantations used the skills they had brought with them from Africa, women were involved in the crafting of rice storage baskets, rice fanners, winnowers, and other forms of basketry. They fashioned these implements according to African patterns, bringing that influence into American practical arts.

Perhaps the most significant area of participation for black women artisans was in textiles. On the cotton plantations of the South, at least a portion of the raw cotton was usually spun and woven into cloth. It was the women who did the spinning and weaving, in buildings called cloth houses. They also, in both the North and the South, did much of the sewing of clothes and linens for white households.

Black women in slavery also made personal items for their own households. They made dolls, beads, bone carvings, pots, and baskets for their families. Some of the most fascinating and loveliest of these items were, again, textiles—the patchwork quilts in which black women expressed their African heritage within the limits of a very American art form.

The skills black women developed in making and working with cloth sometimes provided them with a path to freedom or a way of making a living in freedom. During slavery, there were four types of artisans. First, there were those who worked directly for a master. Then, there were slaves who were apprenticed to other white business owners or craftsmen. Third, there were those who were hired out by their masters

147

What work of art could more appropriately open an introductory essay on black women artists than Faith Ringgold's The Sunflower Quilting Bee at Arles *(1991). Depicted in the artwork are (from left to right) Madam C. J. Walker, Sojourner Truth, Ida B. Wells, Fannie Lou Hamer, Harriet Tubman, Rosa Parks, Mary McLeod Bethune, and Ella Baker. Vincent van Gogh is on the far right.* (FAITH RINGGOLD; COLLECTION OF OPRAH WINFREY)

to others. And finally, there were slave entrepreneurs. This last group conducted their own businesses and paid over to their owners the largest portion of their profit.

Slave entrepreneurs were sometimes able to purchase their freedom with the money they made at their businesses. Among black women, this most often happened with those who provided health and laundry services, and with cooks and dressmakers.

Elizabeth Keckley learned her dressmaking skills as a slave from her mother. She supported her owner's entire family through the business she built up in St. Louis in the

1840s and 1850s. Then, through loans from her customers, she bought her freedom and that of her son. She paid off her loans with the profit from her dressmaking, moved first to Baltimore and then to Washington, D.C., where she began to design clothes for the white elite of that city, including the wife of Senator Jefferson Davis. Her reputation grew and she came to the attention of Mary Todd Lincoln, the wife of President Abraham Lincoln. Soon, she was designing all of Mrs. Lincoln's clothes, including her inaugural ball gown, which is now on display in the Smithsonian Institution.

Elleanor Eldridge, a black woman born in about 1784, learned all about the spinning and weaving of cloth as a teenager, while she was working as a servant in a white household. When she was in her late twenties, she opened a business with her sister in Warwick, Rhode Island, weaving cloth. The business was quite successful, and Eldridge soon bought a vacant lot, built a house on it, and rented it out. In the next few years, she bought more real estate and developed a respectable fortune.

As the population of free African Americans grew, many black men made their livings as artisans, working as ironworkers, stonemasons, carpenters, and woodcarvers. Black women found these occupations closed to them, just as white women did. However, they were able to use the skills they and their mothers had developed as slaves and servants. By 1860, 15 percent of free black women were dressmakers.

But dressmaking did not lead easily into any of the fine arts, as did some of the occupations of black men. Among the very first black artists to gain any recognition were Joshua Johnston, who was, as far as we know, the former slave and apprentice of a portrait painter; Robert M. Douglass, Jr., who was a sign painter and portraitist; David Bustill Bowser, who supported himself by painting emblems and banners; and Patrick Henry Reason, who was an engraver and lithographer. All of these men worked professionally at their crafts while they developed as artists. They gained their training through apprenticeship and through work with other male artisans. That path was closed to women.

At the same time, the handful of white women who emerged as artists at this time usually gained their training in schools or from artists who taught private lessons. That path was closed to African Americans. Gender barred black women on one hand, and race barred them on the other.

Still, by the beginning of the 1800s, there were black women who were painting and drawing. They came from the ranks not of sign painters, but of teachers.

FIRST NAMES

The earliest documented paintings and drawings by an African-American woman anywhere in the United States are various pieces by **Sarah Mapps Douglass**, a schoolteacher in Philadelphia. Mapps started her own school in the mid-1820s, teaching the children of many successful African-American citizens in that city.

At that time, teaching was virtually the only occupation open to a respectable woman, black or white. Educated daughters of middle-class families could teach until they were married or instead of getting married. Otherwise, they stayed home. This was as true among the free black elite as it was among the white middle and upper classes.

However, teaching had another meaning among African Americans and therefore a great significance for young black women. Education was seen as the surest avenue of escape from oppression, the salvation of the race. As a result, teaching was more than a respectable profession: It was almost a holy calling. Young black women committed themselves to educating their people with a fervor that grew out of their love of freedom. This fervor also grew out of their belief that no black American could be truly respected until all were raised up to a level of some prosperity and dignity.

Because teaching had this tremendous importance in the black community, young women with leanings toward literature, music, journalism, or the visual arts all tended to become teachers. Their interest in the arts and other professions became incidental to their work in the classroom. But it also enriched that work. Evidence of this exists in the scrapbooks and notebooks that were used by women educators as instructional aids in educating female students.

Steven Loring Jones, a Philadelphia-based scholar, explains this phenomenon in nineteenth-century America, saying, "Notebooks were started by female teachers for adolescent female pupils who, for a decade or more, would have important people in their lives contribute a treasured poem, personal thought or visual paean, sometimes borrowed but occasionally original. These albums appear to be both pedagogical and inspirational in nature, providing the pupils with brief examples of themes and thoughts with which an 'educated' person ought to be familiar, as well as tangible examples of African American success within a larger world of conflict and struggle."

It is in these albums that the first work by African-American women in the traditional European style is found. In about 1836, Sarah Douglass contributed a stunning, signed painting of a rose-dominated bouquet and a prose dedication to an album belonging to Elizabeth Smith. Under her painting Sarah Douglass wrote, "Lady, while you are young and beautiful/Forget not the slave, so shall Heart's Ease ever attend you." This is the first painting by an African-American woman that we know about.

Of course, it is unlikely that this painting was actually the first ever created by an African-American woman. Sarah Mapps Douglass came from a prominent family. Two of her brothers were artists. Her mother was a leader in the Philadelphia anti-slavery movement. We know much more about the Douglasses than we do about the average black family of that time. There is no way of knowing how many paintings and drawings decorated the walls of black family homes or were slipped into letters from one young woman to another. Another example of Douglass' work was found in just such a correspondence. In a March 1, 1833, letter, she sketched a kneeling female slave, the most important abolitionist symbol of the time, at the head of her communication. Douglass continued her artistic work throughout her life. An 1874 letter discussed some drawings of quilt patches that she was doing for the son of a good friend. Other works include a watercolor bouquet of forget-me-nots with a poem, circa 1843, and an 1846 watercolor, *Fuchsia*, accompanied by a full-page essay on the flower in a scrapbook. It is also known that she advertised at her brother Robert's studio the silk scarves she painted.

These are sparse evidences of creative work among black women of the time, but two things must be remembered. First, in the history of African-American artists and in the history of women artists—and therefore especially in the history of black women artists—each scrap of preserved work represents hundreds of pieces that have been lost. Art that is not valued by the mainstream culture is not saved. Art that is not recognized by the art establishment is not safeguarded.

And second, while Douglass and others in the middle class were beginning to draw and paint, other black women continued to work as artisans. They did not stop making pottery, clothing, and dolls because some black women were now making pictures. They did not stop fashioning quilts because others were doing watercolors. The rich tradition of black craftswomen continued.

Although some of their works remain, the names of most of these craftswomen have been lost. One, however, we know. That one is the name of **Harriet Powers**, one of America's most famous quiltmakers.

Powers was born into slavery in Georgia in 1837, about a year after Sarah Mapps Douglass painted her rose bouquet in Elizabeth Smith's album. After the Civil War, she and her husband and their two children lived on their own farm and were fairly prosperous. In 1886, Powers exhibited one of her quilts at the Athens (Georgia) Cotton Fair. It was seen by Jennie Smith, a white artist from Athens. Smith was immediately struck by the power and originality of the quilt and proceeded to track down its maker. Eventually, Smith bought the quilt and wrote down Powers' explanation of its narrative and symbolism.

Both the Smith quilt and another, commissioned by a group of faculty wives for the president of Union Theological Seminary, are preserved in American museums, the Smithsonian Institution and the Boston Museum of Fine Arts, respectively. They are stunning pieces of work. They combine imagery from the Judeo-Christian Bible with African symbolism and were made using the appliqué technique which flourished between 1775 and 1875 in the South.

Although narrative quilts are a distinctly American art form, the appliqué technique used by Powers and many other Southern black women is traceable to historic Eastern and Middle-Eastern civilizations, with roots in African culture. Gladys-Marie Fry, who has chronicled the life of Powers and other quilters, writes that

> Powers' quilts form a link to the tapestries traditionally made by the Fon people of Abomey, the ancient capital of Dahomey in West Africa. These people brought to the South this knowledge of appliqué, which in Dahomey was executed by men but in America was perpetuated by slave women. In Dahomean tapestries and in Harriet Powers' quilts, stories from oral tradition and oral history are illustrated with appliquéd figures. Many of the Dahomean tapestries contain animals as symbols of kings or as the central figures of proverbs. The Powers quilts include some of the same animals . . . as proverbial characters, and made in a similar style.

To those who have seen and studied the Powers quilts, it is clear that Harriet Powers was an artist. But she was also a craftswoman. This brings up a question that takes on great importance in any discussion of the art of black women. Quite simply, what qualifies as art?

People have been making art for thousands of years. They've made masks and murals, tapestries and teapots. They've woven carpets never intended to touch a floor and sewn thousands of beads and feathers in intricate patterns on ceremonial robes. They've made statues that tower several stories into the sky and pyramids that dominate desert landscapes. And they have also made carved ivory figures of exquisite detail that are no larger than a walnut.

There is even a town in Africa where, well into the second half of the twentieth century, the townspeople created new patterns in the sand of their streets and painted new patterns on the walls of their buildings every single day. The main activity of the town was art.

However, in the last couple of hundred years, in the Western world, the term "art" has been narrowed to refer primarily to portable paintings and sculpture. From whole towns to a piece of painted canvas—what a fall! How could this strange imprisonment of the notion of art within the confines of a picture frame have happened? "Why portable paintings have acquired such prestige," writes Germaine Greer in *The Obstacle Race*, "is not immediately obvious, especially because we have all grown up taking their prestigiousness for granted and calling other art forms, including the massive ones of architecture and gardening, *minor* arts."

Greer goes on to explain how the art market may have influenced this definition. "In financial terms, portable paintings are, like rare stamps, small repositories of enormous value. This value is not primarily or even secondarily related to aesthetic values.

The same painting may be worth a hundred times as much when attributed to one painter as it is when attributed to another. Authenticity is the highest index of value, rarity the second."

In other words, paintings on canvas are the highest form of art because they are best suited to buying and selling. And this definition is remarkably widely accepted. In 1976, an important book entitled *Women Artists: 1550–1950* was put together by two women art historians. It was based on an exhibition of art by women. Every single work in the book, as in the exhibition, was a painting, drawing, or print. There were not even any sculptures included. There certainly were no quilts, weavings, masks or pots.

It is not accidental that there were, in that book, no black women represented. The narrowness of the definition of art had excluded them. During the four centuries the book covered, black women made just about every kind of art imaginable, from quilts to monumental sculptures. But most of them did not choose to paint with oil on canvases. And there are very good reasons for that.

BREAKING INTO THE INSTITUTIONS

For women, art schools and studios have long been hostile territory. For African Americans, male and female, they were, until late in the nineteenth century, forbidden territory.

There were at least fifty fairly important American artists—all white men—before the middle of the nineteenth century. John

Singleton Copley, Gilbert Stuart, George Catlin, and dozens of others had begun to enter the ranks of recognized, important American artists. At that point, no American art school had yet admitted either a woman or an African American. That gave white men a pretty good head start in the history of American art.

Then, in the 1850s, some schools began to admit white women. But the men were not exactly giving up the inside track. Women were kept from participating equally in the activities of the schools in many ways. A clear example of the restrictions laid upon them is life drawing.

One of the most important aspects of training in the European tradition of painting is drawing the human figure from nude models. You simply have to see the human body in order to draw or paint it. But, as late as the 1890s, the stated policy in art institutions dictated that only men could draw nudes of either sex. Women who were permitted in anatomy classes used casts from antiquity. In other words, men drew people and women drew statues.

By the 1880s, another dozen or so white men had been added to the list of important American artists, including Frederic Remington, James McNeill Whistler, John Singer Sargent, and Winslow Homer. The first African Americans were finally being admitted to the schools. And women were still drawing statues.

The policy of denying women access to nude models was rigorously enforced. Thomas Eakins, one of America's finest painters, reorganized the antiquated curriculum at the Pennsylvania Academy of the Fine Arts around the study of the nude and anatomy. His students did extensive life drawing and even dissections. His reputa-

tion as one of the finest teachers in the world was established. Among his students was the first African-American painter recognized by the American art establishment, Henry O. Tanner. Then, in 1885, Eakins displayed a completely nude male model in a class with women in it. He was fired.

So, at a time when artistic achievement was judged by the artist's ability to respond to classical attitudes and sensibilities, women artists were expected to master academic drawing and muscular anatomy without access to the nude. When they couldn't master this skill, many women instead cultivated the "minor" fields of still life, genre painting, landscape painting, or portraiture only, fields that did not require life drawing.

One victim of this policy of exclusion was Annie E. Anderson Walker (1855–1929). Born in Flatbush, at that time a suburb of Brooklyn, New York, Anderson entered the teaching profession at an early age. She had brief assignments in Jacksonville, Florida, and Orrville and Selma, Alabama, where she married an attorney named Thomas Walker in 1875. The couple moved to Washington, D.C., and in 1890 Annie Walker began private lessons in drawing and painting. After a year's study, she showed a marked improvement in her abilities as a draftsman and applied to the Corcoran Gallery of Art.

After approval by the admissions committee, Walker was admitted to the elementary class for drawing and given a date to begin classes. However, when Walker appeared at the Corcoran, she was told by the admitting instructor that "the trustees have directed me not to admit colored people. If we had known that you were colored, the committee would not have examined your work."

Humiliated and insulted, Walker went for help to the highly respected political leader Frederick Douglass. Douglass wrote a powerful appeal on her behalf to the committee of the Corcoran, requesting them to "reconsider this exclusion and admit Mrs. Walker to the Corcoran Gallery of Art, and thus remove a hardship and redress a grievous wrong imposed upon a person guilty of no crime and one in every way qualified to compete with others in the refining and ennobling study of art." The committee refused to change its mind.

Walker was eventually able to continue her studies because of her husband's financial resources. In order to get her training, she had to travel to New York City to attend the Cooper Union for the Advancement of Science and Art. She graduated in the class of 1895 and then continued her studies in Europe. But her position as the wife of a successful professional man was a two-edged sword. After she returned from the Continent, in December 1896, she was expected to take up her responsibilities as a socially active wife. By 1898, because of the strain of her work and the other pressures of her life, Annie Walker suffered a nervous breakdown. She remained an invalid in her home until her death in 1929.

It's impossible to conceive of a young man of the nineteenth century, or any other, being confronted with Annie Walker's dilemma. Having pursued her studies with determination and some success (her drawing, *La Parisienne* was exhibited in the Paris Salon of 1896), she had to split her time and her emotional energies between her need to be an artist and her duties as a society wife . . . or become a social pariah. This was not a time when a woman artist from a respectable family could move out of her parents' or husband's house, find a gallery, and sell her paintings. Or get a part-time job to pay her rent while she worked away on her art in a garret.

In 1896, the year Annie Walker returned to Washington, D.C., women could not vote. In most states, they could not own property. They would not be awarded custody of their children in case of a divorce. The only available jobs were live-in domestic work, mind-numbing factory work, or, for women who were educated and unmarried, teaching.

Whether Annie Walker would have made a name for herself as an artist under other circumstances is impossible to know. She had only three productive years, and that is far too little to judge by. But her life illustrates what a young black woman had to overcome in trying to be an artist. If she had the money and connections to overcome racism and get training, she was hemmed in by the extreme limitations put on women of that time.

The art establishment's method of exclusion, working hand in hand with social pressures on women, was remarkably successful. Gradually, because they gained access to the inner sanctum, a few African-American men began to produce work that was taken seriously in some artistic circles. And one or two women with unusual resources gained some grudging acknowledgment. The vast majority of women, however, both black and white, remained on the outside, as did most black men.

And when black women finally entered the artistic scene, they attacked on an outer flank.

THE SCULPTORS

These are the first recognized black women artists in America: **Edmonia Lewis**, sculptor (born 1843); **Meta Vaux Warrick Fuller**, sculptor (born 1877); **May Howard Jackson**, sculptor (born 1877); **Laura Wheeler Waring**, painter (born 1887); Nancy Elizabeth Prophet, sculptor, (born 1890); Augusta Savage, sculptor (born 1892); **Selma Burke**, sculptor (born 1900). To any student of American art, the fact stands out like a bronze casting in a room full of watercolors; most African-American women artists of significance have been sculptors. Trying to understand why this is true is very revealing of the experience of black women artists in general.

There are, first, some very practical considerations. Sculpting is cheaper than painting, unless you're working in Carrara marble. Clay and plaster are less expensive than fine pigments and canvas or watercolor paper. And since most black women had limited financial resources, that was almost certainly involved.

Also, black women began to come into their own in the United States during the "Gilded Age." There was a great demand for monuments and portrait busts, for sculpture of all kinds. There was employment for skilled sculptors.

But these two factors, while important, do not tell the whole story. The tradition of art in West Africa, where most African Americans came from, emphasizes sculpture, rather than painting. Of course, you would then expect that black American artists of both sexes would be sculptors, but this isn't true. Most African-American men were painters. There were only a few sculptors,

primarily men who made their living as stonecarvers.

The men, of course, had earlier access to training in European methods. Is it possible that, because they were denied that training, black women remained more closely connected to their African artistic heritage?

Here's another possibility. Reality, the world around us, exists in three dimensions. One of the primary focuses of Western painting is to translate that reality to two dimensions. That's where the rules of perspective and a great many other techniques taught in art schools and studios come in. In order to paint in a way that is acceptable to the Western tradition, you have to know and master all those techniques.

Sculpting, however, does not involve that translation. It interprets three-dimensional reality in three dimensions. As a result, when an artist with natural talent sculpts, that talent can show itself with far less formal training. Black women, as we know, had the least access to art education of any group. Perhaps the only black women who could gain recognition for their art were those who did not require extensive training in order for their natural gifts to shine through.

Then, too, any African-American woman who was able to overcome the obstacles set between her and success as an artist had to be a very strong woman. Perhaps these early artists, with their tremendous strength of character, were drawn to sculpture because of the strength of vision and of body that it requires. This was certainly true of the first black woman artist to gain recognition in this country, Edmonia Lewis.

Mary Edmonia "Wildfire" Lewis was born to a Chippewa mother and an African-American father. The circumstances of her life were unusual. When she was very young, her parents died, and she went to live with her mother's family. She was raised as a Chippewa, swimming and fishing and wearing moccasins. Her tribal name was Wildfire, and she never used any other until she went away to school.

Lewis was able to go to **Oberlin College**'s preparatory school because her brother was making a substantial living in the California gold mines. He paid for his sister's education and, later, set her up in a studio in Boston, in the same building as noted African-American painter Edward Bannister. After a brief period of study with Boston sculptor Edmond Brackett, to whom she was introduced by an abolitionist who took an interest in her career, Lewis began sculpting medallion portraits of abolitionist leaders and Civil War heroes.

Edmonia Lewis' situation was perfect for a young woman artist in the nineteenth century. She was an orphan and, sad as that might be personally, she had no protective middle-class parents to restrict her actions. However, she had a brother who was devoted to her and willing to give her financial support. And because she was raised by the Chippewas, outside mainstream American life, she had not absorbed American notions of the proper life for a woman. She was described by her contemporaries as tomboyish and was certainly charismatic, determined, and unconventional.

She also came into her own during a time when history was being made and momentous issues were being decided all around her. As Cedric Dover put it in *American Negro Art*, "Above all she was alight with the surety of success and the certainty that what she wrought belonged to the great struggle for freedom and beauty surrounding her."

In 1864, Lewis created a piece of work that would launch her as a sculptor. It was a bust of Colonel Robert Gould Shaw, a young Boston man who had been killed leading an all-black Union Army battalion against Confederate forces in the Civil War. Lewis exhibited it at the Boston Fair for the Soldiers' Fund, where it was seen by Shaw's wealthy and prominent mother. Mrs. Shaw bought the bust, and several hundred other copies were sold as well. Within a year, Lewis had moved to Rome. She remained there, although she made several visits back to the United States, and enjoyed a successful career executing commissions for portrait busts and for doing monumental marble pieces.

Clearly, Lewis had advantages that few black women of the time could even imagine. But it would be a mistake to think of her as free from the constraints of racial and sexual discrimination. Throughout her career, she struggled desperately to be taken seriously as an artist, apart from both her gender and her race. For example, contrary to the practice of the day of hiring Italian carvers, Edmonia Lewis did her own carving for years, fearing accusations that others created her work. This seriously limited her output and her ability to make a living. She also remained isolated from other artists so that she could not be accused of being overly influenced by them. This limited her artistic growth.

The problems Edmonia Lewis faced have continued to trouble women artists, especially black women. Remarkably, however, African-American women have expressed their visions in art worthy of respect and attention throughout the twentieth century.

PROPHETS OF A NEW AGE

Edmonia Lewis spent virtually her entire career in a studio in Rome. She was following in a tradition accepted by most American artists until the beginning of the twentieth century, embracing European culture and its values. Little merit was seen in the native culture of the United States in art, music, theater, or any other field. And African-American artists were as likely as any others to try to adopt this foreign heritage. Indeed, they were even more likely, according to Samella Lewis in *African American Art and Artists*.

"Most African American artists of the nineteenth century," she writes, "attempted to escape their country's prejudice and provincialism through study—and, in some cases, permanent residence—abroad. They usually found their way to one of the major European capitals, where, removed from American life and from the scenes of their early personal experiences, they sought to become internationally known. For some of these artists the flight from racial prejudice also included a complete avoidance of racial subject matter in their work."

Lewis goes on to say that this avoidance prevented the African-American artists of the second half of the nineteenth century from making any significant contribution to the development of an American, much less an African-American, style of art. Henry Ossawa Tanner, for example, was the most prominent black American artist of his time. At the beginning of his career, he painted several beautiful portrayals of African-American life. However, after moving to Europe in the 1890s, he moved away from this subject matter and began producing religious paintings. Virtually his entire artistic output from then on concerned life in the Old and New Testaments, rather than in Georgia.

Interestingly, black women were exceptions to this rule of ignoring—and in some cases denying—African-American themes and issues. Or perhaps it would be more accurate to say that they were among the first to turn their attention away from Europe and focus it on their own people.

By the turn of the century, women were accepted for training at the National Academy of Design, the Pennsylvania Academy of the Fine Arts, the Art Institute of Chicago, the Cincinnati Art Academy, and the Art Students League in New York City. Yet, the ultimate art education was still to be obtained in Europe. Paris attracted many women artists, who studied at the Ecole des Beaux-Arts and at the academies of Julien and Colarossi during the closing years of the nineteenth century. Although biases and discrimination continued to plague black women artists, some gained access to these institutions and, as assistants, to the studios of French masters. One such artist was Meta Vaux Warrick Fuller.

Born in 1877 into a middle-class Philadelphia family, Fuller studied at the Pennsylvania Museum and School for Industrial Art (now the Philadelphia College of Art) and, between 1899 and 1902, at the Ecole des Beaux-Arts and sculpture at the Colarossi Academy. In the summer of 1901, at twenty-four years of age, she had an appointment with Auguste Rodin, the most famous and respected sculptor of the time.

Rodin had agreed to review a portfolio of photographs of Fuller's work and a small clay model. Fuller hoped that he would accept her as his student. After leafing through the photographs, Rodin returned them without any comments. Disheartened, Fuller prepared to leave, but realized that she had not shown him the clay model of *Man Eating His Heart* (also called *The Secret Sorrow*). As he turned the sculpture, viewing it from every angle, running his hand over it, he proclaimed, *"Mon enfant, vous êtes un sculpteur, vous avez le sens de la forme!"* "My child, you are a sculptor, you have the sense of form!" was an extraordinary critique for this young artist. Rodin said regretfully that he could take no additional students, but he promised to visit her studio often.

Rodin seems to have helped Fuller expand her exploration of the psychology of human emotions. However, where Rodin's primary artistic interests were with love, Fuller looked to the suffering of her people. Because of her treatment of such powerful subject matter, her early work was sometimes termed macabre and gruesome. But she remained committed to these themes.

After her return to Philadelphia in 1902, Fuller became involved with the social and intellectual life of the black community. African-American themes continued to share a place with European influences in her sculpture. Several of her works were exhibited in the Paris Salon of 1903.

In 1909, she married Solomon C. Fuller, a Liberian who was a director of the pathology lab at Westborough State Hospital and a neurologist at Massachusetts Hospital. In 1910, a fire in a Philadelphia warehouse destroyed sixteen years of work she had done at home and abroad. She also gave birth to three sons between 1910 and 1916. However, she remained an active member of the cultural community.

During this period, one of Fuller's most important works resulted from the invita-tion of W. E. B. DuBois to reproduce *Man Eating His Heart*, lost in the fire, for the Emancipation Proclamation's fiftieth anniversary in New York in 1913. Instead of replicating this piece, she created *Spirit of Emancipation*, a three-figured group standing eight feet tall. According to scholar Judith Kerr, it was "unlike any other of its genre. There were no discarded whips or chains, no grateful freedmen kneeling before a paternalistic Lincoln. Fuller had also not chosen to favor the female figure with Caucasian features, indicating her heightened race consciousness."

In the years that followed, Fuller created many political works, including a medallion for Framingham's Equal Suffrage League (1915) and a figure based on the infamous Mary Turner case (1919), and other works addressing the atrocities of war and violence against blacks. She explored African-American themes many years before James Weldon Johnson, DuBois, and others ushered in the Harlem Renaissance, with its emphasis on cultural expression among black Americans and a greater awareness of their African heritage. When that tremendous movement took hold, she became one of its leading figures. Her sculpture *Ethiopia Awakening* powerfully expressed its principles. It depicts a beautiful African woman who is emerging out of the wrappings of a mummy. Fuller wrote that she used the Egyptian motif to symbolize the black American who "was awakening, gradually unwinding the bandages of his past and looking out on life again, expectant, but unafraid."

Fuller's career continued into the 1960s and was rewarded by recognition from the black community and, to a limited degree, the American art establishment. Less success came to another black woman who also turned away from the influence of Europe, identified strongly with her black heritage, and foreshadowed the Harlem Renaissance. Her name was May Howard Jackson.

Like Fuller, Jackson was born in Philadelphia in 1877 and attended J. Liberty Tadd's art school. However, the lives of these two women offer sharp contrasts. Unlike Fuller, Jackson remained in America, studying at the Pennsylvania Academy of the Fine Arts. Her exploration of the African-American world was different as well. Most of her work, throughout her career, consisted of portrayals of African Americans, both famous and anonymous. While other black artists were still avoiding racial subjects and trying to fit into the white artistic establishment, Jackson was frankly and thoroughly preoccupied with the faces of black and mixed-race people.

Art historian Leslie King-Hammond calls Jackson "the founder of the first movement toward an Afrocentric aesthetic," but Jackson did not receive that kind of recognition during her own time. She did portrait busts of such prominent African Americans as Paul Laurence Dunbar, W. E. B. DuBois, and Jean Toomer, as well as such unnamed figures as *Mulatto Mother and Her Child* and *Shell-Baby in Bronze*. But her realist portrayals of black subjects were not welcomed by the art establishment. They were too far from the stereotyped sentimental or comic figures of African Americans that had been popular up to that time.

Jackson became increasingly bitter, but she continued to produce. She had some successful exhibitions and taught for several years at **Howard University**. But she paid a high price, emotionally and in terms of her career, for her contribution to the development of a genuinely African-American art tradition.

Both Fuller and Jackson were ahead of their time. In the years that followed, many male artists would answer the call to racial awareness issued by DuBois, Johnson, Alain Locke, and Marcus Garvey. Painters such as Aaron Douglas, Hale Woodruff, Palmer Hayden, and Archibald Motley would be hailed as the leaders of a new age of African-American art, and rightly so. It does no disservice to them, however, to remember these two sculpting women who showed them the way.

THE HARLEM RENAISSANCE

The twentieth century saw a host of technological and scientific discoveries. As the old order changed with philosophical and scientific advancements, so did the art world. A myriad of "isms" replaced or overlapped each other in rapid succession—Fauvism, Expressionism, Cubism, Dadaism, and Surrealism—radical styles that reflected the freedom of the artists. Many compositions, breaking free of the traditional representation of a subject, were now based instead on abstract arrangements of color and form. Women painters and sculptors were involved in these radical approaches. And although societal pressures for women to lead home-centered lives still had an impact, more women were able to overcome these obstacles and establish careers as professional artists.

Paris remained a source of inspiration for many American artists, especially those of African descent. But Harlem, in New York City, also became a center of African-American culture. There has been endless speculation about what caused the blooming of black art and culture that occurred in the 1920s and 1930s. Most say the large numbers of black Southerners who moved north, bringing with them their folklore and music, had something to do with it. The emphasis put on culture by such leaders as W. E. B. DuBois and Marcus Garvey was certainly part of the explanation. Coincidence may have brought together some of the remarkably talented people who lived within the borders of New York's Harlem. But whatever the reasons, black literature, art, music, and theater became startlingly alive.

Part of the excitement of the time came from the sheer number of gifted writers and artists creating lasting works. Then there were the night life and the music, the parties where the best and brightest came together to talk about life and art. Writing about it later, poet Arna Bontemps said, "In some places the autumn of 1924 may have been an unremarkable season. In Harlem, it was like a foretaste of paradise."

Musical comedy star **Florence Mills** was a sensation on Broadway in *Shuffle Along*. **Ethel Waters** would soon be the highest-paid woman, black or white, on the Broadway stage. The **Lafayette Players**, in Harlem, were producing serious drama starring black actors. **Ma Rainey** and **Bessie Smith** ruled the world of blues. But the most exciting aspect of the Harlem Renaissance was the redefining of black culture in America.

In 1925, Alain Locke, the first black Rhodes scholar and later a philosopher and professor at Howard University, edited a book called *The New Negro*. In it he commented that though some African-American artists had been "notably successful," they had developed no school of Negro art. He

said that African-American artists should do two things. First, they should look toward Africa to explore their "ancestral arts" more seriously. Second, they should develop the "Negro physiognomy," or physical features, in their work.

Of course, Meta Fuller had begun doing the first of these things two decades before, and May Howard Jackson had been doing the second for almost that long. As is often the case, an impulse in art had begun with artists, been interpreted by a critic, and then gone on to inspire other artists.

Although women artists played a crucial role in bringing about the rebirth of African-American art, they did not benefit as greatly as men did from its popularity. Meta Fuller continued to produce and to hold a respected position among black artists. And May Howard Jackson did some of her best work during this time. But few other women were carried forward on the wave that took a number of black men into the galleries and private collections of the time. And even black men did not have the impact in the visual arts that they did in literature.

Still, the artists of that period did influence American art in a significant way. Today they are being reevaluated, and history's final judgment has not been delivered. But it is clear that images of black people changed radically in that short time. Before then, African-American life had been seen in art almost exclusively through the eyes of white artists. Afterward, the black experience became the province of the black artist. As Mary Schmidt Campbell says of the Harlem Renaissance artists in her introduction to *Harlem Renaissance: Art in Black America*, "Their work has the look of something new, something raw and deliberate, a tradition freshly crafted and conceived. If they contributed anything, they contributed the sense that for the first time the Black artists could take control of Black America."

A controversial feature of the Renaissance was the Harmon Foundation. It was begun by white philanthropist and real estate baron William E. Harmon in 1922 to encourage self-help. In about 1926, Alain Locke and George Edmund Haynes, black head of the department of race relations of the Federal Council of Churches, persuaded Harmon to shift the emphasis of his organization from aid to the blind and student loans to support of African-American writers, artists, and professionals.

In the visual arts, the Harmon Foundation became very influential in the black art community through its establishment of an annual exhibition of the work of black artists, as well as monetary prizes. The foundation also helped its exhibiting artists sell their work to museums, colleges, universities, and private collections.

Even at the time, there were those who criticized the Harmon Foundation. Painter Romare Bearden attacked it in the pages of the magazine *Opportunity*, declaring that its attitude "from the beginning has been of a coddling and patronizing nature." On the other hand, Hale Woodruff, another important black painter, said that the foundation was "doing a wonderful piece of work toward furthering the interests and the achievements of the American Negro."

From the vantage of 1989, scholar Gary Reynolds called the foundation "conservative in nature and paternalistic in practice. At the core of its activities was a belief in a well-defined class system ('social order') that enabled wealthy white men such as Harmon to give assistance to those deemed worthy. The standards against which African Ameri-

cans were measured were clearly those of whites." Whatever the case, the Harmon Foundation continued its exhibitions until 1935. And many of the exhibitors, including several women, became important figures in African-American art.

The sculptural tradition established by Lewis, Fuller, and Jackson was continued by Nancy Elizabeth Prophet, Augusta Savage, **Beulah Ecton Woodard**, and Selma Burke. The painters who came to prominence were Laura Wheeler Waring and **Lois Mailou Jones**. The lives of these women reflect the situation of black women artists of the time in a number of ways.

Nancy Elizabeth Prophet, for example, was in lifelong conflict about her racial identity, made more intense by frustrated ambition. Born to a mother who described herself as a "mixed negro" and a Narragansett Indian father, she was the only black student at the Rhode Island School of Design (RISD) when she graduated in 1918. While still a student, Prophet married Francis Ford, one of the few African Americans to attend Brown University at that time.

According to Blossom Kirschenbaum, an adjunct professor at the RISD, "Prophet and her husband aspired to privileges more typically enjoyed by persons born to higher status than theirs, and they did so without much support." After graduation, Prophet shunned teaching positions, designing textiles, or any employment outside of the discipline. Instead she sought sponsors to help her financially. She was successful in receiving the support of at least three socially prominent women who provided funds and purchased her work.

Prophet studied at the Ecole des Beaux Arts in Paris and remained in France for ten years, where she participated in several salons and received exceptional reviews. Her friend Countee Cullen described her as "at peace with herself" and "content with the direction of her life and her art." However, when Prophet returned to the United States, one of the first pieces she exhibited was a polychromed wood head titled *Discontent*; she said it was "the result of a long emotional experience, of restlessness, of gnawing hunger for the way to attainment."

Even then, after her successes in Paris, Prophet felt that her life and her art were not what she should be able to achieve. At the urging of W. E. B. DuBois, she became an instructor at Atlanta University in 1933. The following year she joined the art department at **Spelman College**, introducing sculpture into the curriculum. There she remained through 1944.

It is unclear why Prophet left Atlanta, but Kirschenbaum suggests that "apparently she had suffered some sort of breakdown. For a while she was hospitalized in Rhode Island." Yet, she was able to mount a 1945 solo exhibition at the Providence Public Library.

Prophet never achieved the fame that she had hoped for, and her financial status was always unsure. Unable to find a teaching position in Providence, she became a live-in maid in 1958, receiving only room and board, with no salary. This arrangement lasted about six months. Living in isolation, poor, unable to secure employment, and unable to continue her creativity, Elizabeth Prophet died in obscurity in 1960.

Near the end of her embittered life, Prophet said that she "had no use for the colored." Proclaiming her Native American heritage exclusively, she refused to be included in Cedric Dover's 1960 publication of *American Negro Art*, stating that she

"was not a negro" and rejecting the limitations that identity imposed.

Being successful "for a black woman" fundamentally wrecked Elizabeth Prophet's life. She was remarkably talented, and there is little doubt that, had she been born white and a man, she would have enjoyed a considerably larger measure of success. And she knew it. She felt the injustice of her own situation intensely. But she did not react to this injustice by feeling kinship with others who experienced it. Instead, she rejected the part of her own identity that she held responsible for her humiliation.

Racial identity had a very different significance in the life of Augusta Christine Savage. Born in 1892, in Green Cove Springs, Florida, she was the seventh of fourteen children. Her father—a carpenter, farmer, house painter, and Methodist minister—discouraged her from creating clay objects. In a 1935 interview, she recalled that her father referred to her figures as graven images, and that he "licked me five or six times a week and almost whipped all the art out of me."

Married at fifteen, Savage gave birth to a daughter, her only child, in 1908. She was widowed a few years later. By 1915, Savage's father had moved the family to West Palm Beach, where there was no local clay, and for several years she did not sculpt. Then she met a potter and persuaded him to give her twenty-five pounds of clay. She sculpted several works that impressed the principal of the school she attended, and he hired her to teach a clay modeling class at the high school for six months, earning a wage of one dollar a day.

At the Palm Beach County Fair, Savage ran a booth where she sold clay ducks and chickens to wealthy tourists. She received a special prize of twenty-five dollars, an honor ribbon, and encouragement to pursue her interests in New York. The fair superintendent gave her a letter of recommendation to sculptor Solon Borglum, founder of the School of American Sculpture, and advised her to seek admittance there.

Arriving in New York in 1921 at the age of twenty-nine with $4.60, she announced her plans to become a successful artist in six months. But because of high tuition costs, Borglum referred her to Cooper Union, a tuition-free art school, for instruction. Within a month, she had been advanced to the third-year class, but money problems almost forced her to leave school while she was in the fourth-year class. The principal, recognizing her talent, found her temporary employment and persuaded the advisory committee to award additional funds for her living expenses. Friends of the Schomburg Library, also hearing of her difficulties, commissioned a bust of W. E. B. DuBois. As he sat for this portrait, Savage came under the influence of the philosophy and personality of this leader.

Receiving a scholarship from the French government in 1923 to attend a summer school in Fontainebleau, she was prepared to excel in her profession. However, she soon encountered racism of major proportions. When two recipients from Alabama were informed that an African American would be sailing to France on the same ship, the girls complained that they could not be expected to travel or room with a "colored girl," and Savage's scholarship was withdrawn.

The resulting publicity elicited an invitation from Hermon MacNeil, president of the National Sculpture Society, to study privately with him at his Long Island studio. Two years later, Savage received a working scholarship to the Royal Academy of Fine Arts in Rome but did not have enough money for travel and living expenses. Finally, her work was brought to the attention of the president of the Julius Rosenwald Fund, and she received her first Rosenwald Fellowship to study in France.

After a highly successful stay in Paris and another Rosenwald Fellowship, Savage returned to New York. She didn't, however, seek out white patrons, as Elizabeth Prophet had done. Instead, she established the Savage Studio of Arts and Crafts at 163 West 143rd Street. Some of the brightest young artists around, including Ernest Crichlow, Gwendolyn Knight, Jacob Lawrence, Morgan and Marvin Jones, William Artis, and Norman Lewis, became her students.

For the rest of her life, Augusta Savage combined creating her own sculpture with teaching young black artists. She also became an advocate, fighting for rights and recognition for all black artists. Being a black women had brought her difficulties and hardships, but embracing her identity had made her strong.

Both Elizabeth Prophet and Augusta Savage were teachers. So, too, were most of the other black women artists who came out of the Harlem Renaissance. To a large degree, they chose teaching because there was not a great enough demand for their work to provide for their support and that of their families. At the same time, they were usually committed, effective teachers. Like the thousands of black women before them who had taken the education of their people into their hands, they believed in the great significance of what they were doing. And the next development in American history found them once again in this familiar role.

THE WPA

The decade of the 1930s was a time of hardship such as the United States had never seen before. Unsound financial practices during the 1920s had caused the stock market to collapse, and with it much of American business. Drought had swept large areas of the country, leaving farmland and lives virtually destroyed. People were starving. The unemployment lines stretched for blocks. It seemed that this country's great bubble of prosperity had burst once and for all.

In the midst of this devastation, the country turned to a man who promised a New Deal—Franklin Delano Roosevelt. President Roosevelt entered the White House in 1933 with the hopes of the country on his shoulders. Very soon, he revealed one of his solutions to the problems of the Great Depression—the Works Progress Administration, later the Work Projects Administration (WPA). This was a series of government programs that provided jobs for the unemployed. People were put to work building roads, buildings, parks, playgrounds, and sewage systems. And, in the WPA's Federal Art Project (FAP), thousands of artists—black and white, men and women—were put to work painting, sculpting, and teaching art.

However, jobs were not passed out with an even hand. More men ended up painting murals, and more women ended up teaching children how to draw and paint. There were exceptions to this rule. Georgette Seabrook Powell, for example, painted murals in Harlem Hospital and Queens General Hospital. But most of the black women funded by the FAP worked in the community art centers. These women did not see their art on the walls of post offices, but they saw the talents of young people emerge in community cen-

ters around the country. And they had a profound effect on the generations of artists who followed them.

Augusta Savage was a major force in bringing black artists into the WPA. She fought for the right of African Americans to be included. She badgered politicians, conducted press conferences, and organized black artists to make their voices heard. Working with the Harmon Foundation files, she found material to support the WPA applications of many black artists. Her efforts resulted in commissions for muralists and sculptors who would otherwise have been passed over. Jacob Lawrence owed his first WPA assignment to Savage and never forgot it. He credited her with playing a major part in his highly successful career.

Savage also was able to establish, through the FAP, the Harlem Community Art Center, a national showcase where more than 1,500 residents took classes. Eleanor Roosevelt attended the ceremonies that marked the opening of the center, and Savage became the first director.

The center, located at Lenox Avenue and 125th Street in Manhattan, offered courses in drawing, painting, sculpture, lithography, etching, and photography. Savage's philosophy of teaching was, as she put it, to "teach [students] the essentials without making them bound down with academic tradition which will spoil the freshness of their work." Her approach was quite successful. Many of her students went on to have important careers.

In 1938, Savage took a leave of absence from the center when she was commissioned to do a work representing the African American's contribution to American music for the New York World's Fair of 1939. She created *The Harp*, inspired by the lyrics of J. Rosamond and James Weldon Johnson's

"Lift Every Voice and Sing," sometimes called the black national anthem.

Savage was the only black artist, except for the composer William Grant Still, represented in the fair. The sixteen-foot-tall plaster sculpture received wide publicity and became known in black communities throughout the country. However, funds from the New York Commission of the World's Fair were not available to cast the large plaster sculpture into bronze, and the money to do so was not found among private donors. *The Harp*, along with several other works, was bulldozed at the end of the fair. Only photographs and a few small souvenirs cast in iron from the original maquette remain.

Savage went back to work with her students in Harlem. And, while her most famous work was destroyed, another remains. Savage herself said, "If I can inspire one of these youngsters to develop the talent I know they possess, then my monument will be in their work. No one could ask more than that."

Working with Savage at the Harlem Community Art Center was another sculptor, Selma Burke. She, too, was the daughter of a Methodist minister and had begun sculpting with clay dug out of the earth near her home. She was early exposed to the beauty of African art because she had two uncles who were missionaries to that continent and who brought back with them to America many masks and religious figures.

At her mother's insistence, Burke trained as a nurse as well as an artist and, several times during her career, she supported herself with her nursing skills. Burke had a long and successful career, but she is probably best known for her 1944 profile portrait of Franklin Roosevelt. It later became the basis of the image on the Franklin dime.

Burke joined Savage at the Harlem Community Art Center teaching sculpture workshops, and she conducted art clinics under the auspices of the Friends Council on Education. She shared Savage's dedication to youth and strongly believed that young minds should not be discouraged for lack of training or an outlet to express their artistry.

Artist and writer **Gwendolyn Bennett** also taught at the Center, running it while Savage was on leave to create *The Harp*. So too did Riva Helfond and Louise Jefferson.

The Harlem Community Art Center was the most famous of the FAP community art centers, but there were others around the country, in Cleveland, Ohio; Chicago, Illinois; Atlanta, Georgia; Richmond, Virginia; Oklahoma City, Oklahoma; Memphis, Tennessee; and Jacksonville, Florida. These centers and others functioned not only as schools but as workshops. Black artists taught, learned, and worked in them. **Margaret Burroughs** was active in Chicago.

Painter and art historian James Porter, writing in 1943, stated, "The opportunities afforded . . . so far through the WPA's Federal Art Project raise the hope that equal opportunities will soon appear through private and commercial patronage and that the prejudice and mistrust that have restricted the Negro artist and warped his milieu will be abolished."

While overly optimistic, this statement makes clear the significance the FAP had for black artists of the 1930s and 1940s. For the first time in American history, black artists had a patron—the federal government. For the first time, they had places to work together, stimulating each other and exchanging ideas. And for the first time, black children by the thousands were being given the skills to express themselves artistically. Out of the FAP centers, often staffed and sometimes administered by black women, came a new generation of black artists.

MOVEMENT TOWARD FREEDOM

Freedom, for an artist, is a complex word. In the most basic sense, it means freedom to create whatever and whenever one wants. If the world were as it should be, that's all that would be important. In the world we actually live in, of course, it isn't.

For black Americans, whatever their role in life, freedom has always had other meanings. Freedom from slavery. Freedom from oppression. Freedom from discrimination, want, and fear. And so, for black artists, artistic freedom has never existed in a vacuum. It has always been connected to, and often limited by, the question of racial identity.

During the 1920s and 1930s, black artists were told by writers, philosophers, and political leaders—including Alain Locke, W. E. B. DuBois, and Marcus Garvey—that it was their duty to look to their African and African-American heritage. But this was not the only view heard.

James A. Porter, a major art historian and critic of the time, rejected the theory of "racial heritage." He criticized the Harmon Foundation for encouraging black artists to explore race-related themes. It was his belief that each black artist should feel himself or herself free to explore a unique, personal vision.

These two points of view, along with dozens of variations on them, have continued to be expressed in the decades since. The result is that black artists can be attacked for exploring racial themes one day and attacked for *not* exploring them the next.

During the late 1940s and into the 1950s, this question of racial identity in art became complicated by the dominance of abstract expressionism. Painting that is abstract, of course, has no obvious content. The patterns of color, light, and shape do not usually depict specific objects or people. When there are elements of representation in abstract painting, they are seldom recognizable enough to be identifiable by race.

Abstract painting swept across the American art scene with great force. Was it wrong for a black artist to be drawn in by its intensity, by the new possibilities it offered . . . by the freedom it represented?

Alma W. Thomas would have said no. She was born in 1892 and began studying art in the 1920s. She was the first graduate of the Howard University art department, but she spent most of her life teaching. All the while, she was doing representational painting and sculpture. "But I wasn't happy with that, ever," she told Eleanor Munro in an interview for *Originals: American Women Artists.* "I watched other people painting abstractly, and I just kept thinking about it, turning it over and over in my mind."

When Thomas finally turned to abstract painting in the early 1960s, she felt as if she had found her way. And her career took off. Within a decade, she was exhibiting at the Whitney Museum and being highly praised by New York critics. Her stunning colors put her, at the age of seventy, into the forefront of a new movement in art, color-field painting.

Representing the other point of view was sculptor and printmaker **Elizabeth Catlett,** who called her first solo show, in 1947–48, "The Negro Woman." Freida High Tesfagiorgis, professor of African and Afro-American art at the University of Wisconsin, said of Catlett's work, "This series . . . was indeed a landmark in the pictorial representation of Black women for it liberated them from their objectified status in the backgrounds and shadows of white subjects in the works of white artists, and from the roles of mother, wife, sister, [and] other in the works of Black male artists."

From the beginning, Catlett's art has reflected her deep beliefs about race, gender, and class. "Art should come from the people," she says, "and be for the people." Choosing subjects that embrace socio-political issues concerning women, African Americans, and Mexicans, her compositions evoke strength of form and polished craftsmanship. They employ the human figure, are Afrocentric, and always seem familiar. Like those of Prophet and Savage, her works evoke a reverence for the black image.

Like Catlett, Margaret Taylor Burroughs received training and experience through the FAP and began exhibiting in the late 1940s. Also like Catlett, she has carried through her career a belief in the importance of race and racial themes in art. Productive as a writer of children's books and poetry, and as a visual artist, her range of media includes painting, sculpture, and graphics.

Burroughs says, "The whole motivation of my work, be it a portrait, a vase of flowers, or people on a picket line or in a demonstration, is in the final essence, for the liberation of my people in particular and for the end of imperialist oppression of all the underprivileged people of the earth of all races, creeds and colors." In 1961, she and her husband opened the Ebony Museum of Negro History, later to become the DuSable Museum of African-American History, in Chicago.

These women, and almost all of their colleagues, supported their art by teaching. The woman who was the most prominent African-American woman artist of the period taught at Howard University for forty-seven years. In that time she touched the lives and influenced the aesthetic foundations of artists such as Delilah Pierce, Elizabeth Catlett, David Driskell, **Malkia Roberts,** Earl Hooks, Mildred Thompson, Mary Lovelace O'Neal, Lou Stovall, **Sylvia Snowden,** and legions of others.

Lois Mailou Jones, who has been called the grande dame of African-American art, began as a textile designer. Then, in the late 1930s, she traveled to Paris to study. She returned with a group of beautiful paintings in which she skillfully used the techniques of Impressionism and Post-Impressionism. She was hailed by a reviewer for the *Boston Globe* as having "the right to be called [the] leading Negro artist."

Her work was included in a number of exhibitions over the next few years. Because of racial bias, however, it was not always certain that her paintings would be accepted for consideration in major exhibitions. To avoid rejection and humiliation, Jones often shipped her work to museums and galleries instead of taking them in person.

Knowing that the Corcoran Gallery of Art had a policy that forbade participation by African-American artists, Jones had a friend submit *Indian Shops, Gay Head, Massachusetts* for the 1941 exhibition. A scene from Martha's Vineyard, it won the prestigious Robert Woods Bliss Prize for

Landscape of the Society of Washington Artists. With this award, Jones broke the color barrier. As her work began to receive first-rate critical opinion, her reputation grew, and she continued to exhibit throughout the United States during the 1940s.

In 1953, Jones married a Haitian graphic artist and traveled to that country. It was the beginning of a new way of seeing for Jones. Although the essence of Europe was still very much apparent at the beginning of her visits, the palette and the formal organization of her paintings gradually evolved into a brilliantly spirited style, fresh, energetically fluid, and highly individual. Such works as *Les Vendeuses de Tissus* and *Bazar*

du Quai, Haiti, both 1961, signaled clearly that European tradition and technique did not yield for Jones what she needed to express the vigor found in this African-based culture.

She and a number of other black artists were coming to this point in their art at the same time. Jones' experience came out of her exposure to Haiti, but for most artists the change came with the growing civil rights movement and the focus it put on black culture. For the second time in the century, black artists were looking toward Africa to find a way of portraying their world.

This time, however, the transformation of African-American art would go deeper than

Lois Mailou Jones has been called the grande dame of African-American art. Many of the greatest names passed through her classes at Howard University, either as students or as teachers. Meta Warrick Fuller is show here in 1943 giving a demonstration at one of Jones' sculpture workshops. (LOIS MAILOU JONES)

the faithful depiction of African physical features or the introduction of some African images. It would be a fundamental challenge to European standards in art.

For Jones, this meant challenging the distinction between fine arts and decorative arts. She used a colorful, hard-edged style that fused abstraction with decorative patterns and naturalism. To many who had admired her earlier, Post-Impressionist work, these paintings were shocking, with their graphic, poster-like quality. To others, they signaled exciting new possibilities.

These characteristics asserted themselves more powerfully in the 1970s and 1980s after Jones made a trip to Africa, where she conducted research on contemporary African artists. The impact of her trip was seen immediately in works such as *Magic of Nigeria* (1971) and *Ubi Girl from the Tai Region* (1972), and later in *Damballah* (1980), *Symboles d'Afrique I* (1982), and *Mére du Sénégal* (1985).

While not everyone would go as far as Jones, distinctly non-European elements began to appear in the work of a number of artists. At the same time, the subject matter changed. For most of the 1960s, the art of black women reflected the social and political turmoil of the country. And the decades that followed brought to the surface a profound need for expressing and defining what it meant to be a black woman.

OUT OF THE FRAME

In recent years, African-American women artists have broken out of the frame, both literally and metaphorically. They have burst out of the confines of what has been accepted as art in the Western tradition. And they have shattered the frame American society has tried to put around them as black women, the frame that defined who and what they should be.

American women in general have attacked the distinction between art and crafts in the last several decades. It is, on the face of it, a difficult distinction to defend. Reduced to its simplest terms, the Western tradition demands that, in order to be considered fine art, an object must have no function. Why uselessness should increase aesthetic value was never entirely clear. Moreover, techniques such as weaving or embroidery that were customarily used to create or decorate functional objects were considered to be contaminated. Even when employed to create pictures that hung on walls—otherwise acceptable as art—the use of such techniques disqualified these pictures from serious consideration.

Looking at this distinction with the feminist eyes of the early 1970s, women realized how often a particular medium would be classified as a craft simply because it was a medium women frequently worked in. And they began to reject the division, demanding that art be defined in other terms.

Black women brought to this movement an even more powerful motive. Many of the media that had been, and were still being, neglected and undervalued by the Western art world were ones that were highly respected in African cultures. To reject mask-making, weaving and sewing, jewelry, and leatherwork was to reject the African heritage.

Today, a work of art created by a black woman may be a quilt or a doll. It may be crafted from clay or plastic milk bottles or bones. It may have elements of sculpture, painting, weaving, sewing, and photography. It may fill a room or hang from an earlobe. The frame of "fine art" has splintered.

No one has wielded the hatchet more effectively than **Faith Ringgold**. In the early 1960s, when she began her quest as an artist, she realized that she could not and would not fit into the European tradition. "I appreciated the beauty of European art," she said in an interview with Eleanor Munro for *Originals: American Women Artists*. "The Rembrandts at the Uffizi anyone can appreciate. But I understood that that wasn't my heritage, the way you can enjoy a Chinese dinner and still not want to cook Chinese all the time."

She went on to say that this was not simply an individual dilemma: "Most black people who are artists have the same problem. Even if you want to adopt a culture that isn't yours, you can't. The only way you can make works of art in another person's style is to copy, but then you have to keep on copying and going back for reference to things someone did in the past. It hampers your own development. It's making art from art instead of from life."

So Ringgold set out to find her own style, one that came from the traditions of Africa and African America. One of her first important works was a twelve-foot-wide mural titled *Die*, which depicted a street riot. In it, she used techniques she had taken from African art. "By its decorative, flat appearance, it [African art] helps project the real look of black people. If you have a dark form, and you modulate it with shadows, you have nothing. But if you flatten it out and indicate the shadows in flat, contrasting colors, you have a strong pattern."

Throughout the 1960s, Ringgold explored in paint a new style and expressed a new consciousness. Her paintings were filled with the racial conflict of the time, as well as the growing racial pride of black Americans.

Then, in the 1970s, a new element entered Ringgold's work. She became a feminist and began to break out of painting and into forms influenced by sewing and textiles. There followed her *Family of Woman* masks and *Slave Rape* painting series, as well as her soft sculpture creations. Today, her quilts tell stories, using the traditional feminine craft to make statements about the lives of women, coming full circle from Harriet Powers and her symbolic quilts of the nineteenth century.

The cloth, fabric, and fiber employed by Powers and Ringgold have also been used by such artists as Senga Nengudi, Viola Burley Leak, Januwa Moja, **Joyce Scott**, Xenobia Bailey, and Julee Dickerson-Thompson, among others, as they draw upon the craftsmanship of the past to respond to the socio-political issues of today.

All of these women force new definitions and reassessments, as do the Saars, mother and daughter. **Betye** and **Alison Saar** both create art the way poets create poems. As a poet chooses words for their meaning, sound, and associations, the Saars choose objects from the world around them. Then, in the way they put these objects together, they create new meanings.

Betye Saar began her process of raiding the world for material early in life, but she began to put the material together as art in the 1960s after seeing artist Joseph Cornell's boxes filled with occult and astrological images. Saar began to use boxes to order the objects and images of her art. Many of the pieces she created contain African and Caribbean religious symbols. Saar moved then into collage and also into more sculptural

Perhaps never before in the history of American art has there been such a talented mother and daughter pair of artists as Betye and Alison Saar. (ANTHONY BARBOZA; COURTESY OF MIDMARCH ARTS PRESS)

forms. In all of the forms she uses, she reclaims and recycles, not just objects, but the cultural and spiritual life of the people who made, owned and used them.

Alison Saar has followed in her mother's footsteps, although her art has a very different feeling. The two go out collecting together, to flea markets and junk shops, but they are seldom interested in the same materials. Alison Saar's works are less abstract than her mother's and are more often char-acterized by bright colors, humor, and social comment than by ritualism.

Other artists have moved so far out of the frame that they can barely be contained by whole rooms. **Martha Jackson-Jarvis**, for example, creates "installations." In this art form, the artist uses a variety of media and objects to form an environment that the "viewer" can enter. In *The Gathering*, Jackson-Jarvis uses shards, or broken pieces of pottery, in huge concentric circles on the floor, surrounded by walls decorated with spears and tiles. The installation evokes the feeling that, as Belena Chapp writes in *Gumbo Ya Ya*, "the shard—the singular piece—makes sense only when it can be seen in context, reflected in the pool of its origins. By itself it remains unconnected, apart from, not a part of, its history."

Jackson-Jarvis herself says, "For me, art is the documentation of the human spirit. . . . It's very difficult to see ourselves in relation to time. We usually get caught up in the logistics of day-to-day living. But we have to get to the point where we know we have to matter. We have to be larger than the moment. We have to be larger than ourselves."

This sense of history and of community is present in much of the art made by black women today. And this is just one more way that these artists are breaking out of the frame. Art is, and must be, an intensely personal act. However, it can be an act of reaching out, of connecting to others. At certain times in history, it may be most powerful when it clarifies and strengthens the attachments that have been denied in the past.

Historically, the dominant culture of the United States, being white, has tried to deny that African Americans have a history of any significance. From the days of slavery, it has seen communication between and unity among black people to be dangerous, and has attempted to stifle it. That same culture, being controlled largely by men, has tried to divide women, to isolate them and deny them the comfort and strength that can be gained from fellowship.

And so, black women today are portraying each other. They are denying past images of themselves by creating new ones. They are showing their love and respect for each other. They are also demanding that their beauty be recognized. **Elizabeth Catlett**, who has long made black women her primary subjects, has said, "I make a lot of prints that have to do with women because I feel that art with women generally has to do with what I call the exploitation of women. Art by men has to do with nude women. It has to do with portraits of rich women. It has to do with what's considered a beautiful woman, which is a white standard of beauty and a middle-class standard of beauty."

Catlett has championed the beauty of Africa and African-American women instead of this standard. So, in different ways, have Gwendolyn Knight, **Valerie Maynard,** Phoebe Beasley, Varnette Honeywood, photographer **Jeanne Moutoussamy-Ashe,** and many others.

The last several decades, for black women, have been filled with activities and acts that challenge, confront, and, to a large degree, destroy the limitations placed on their work because of race, gender, and European preconceptions about art. The results of that struggle are mixed. Many fine artists are still unable to gain recognition from the art establishment. Many encounter condescension or even scorn from more orthodox artists. But, having proved that art is a larger and more generous concept than the white male establishment has seen it to be, black women now seem free to create as they see fit. They can even, if they choose to do so, paint in oil on canvas, inside the frame.

And there is a certain collective self-esteem that seems to be very sustaining. Valerie Maynard, in an interview with painter Mildred Thompson, said, "From what I see, we have been hoodwinked into thinking that this is a business, that this is a way of making a living. But we are a cultural voice of the people and we have to know that, acknowledge that. No matter what they are saying you are and what you should be doing, prior knowledge tells me that I could never use art that way."

More and more, this independence of spirit graces the community of black women who make art, each in her own way, and all together as a powerful contributing force in American culture.

by Tritobia Hayes Benjamin

B

Beasley, Phoebe (1943–)

She lives in two worlds. A successful advertising executive by day, and a successful painter and artist in the evening, Phoebe Beasley has risen to the top in two highly competitive careers. As a painter and collage artist who derives inspiration from the black community, she has become a respected and collected artist among celebrities such as television personality Oprah Winfrey, writer Maya Angelou, and executive Eunice Johnson.

Born in Cleveland on June 3, 1943, Phoebe Arlene Audrey Beasley is the daughter of George Beasley. Her mother died when she was seven. Her father remarried an artist, Mildred Gaines, who took her stepdaughter to art museums, exposed her to artists, and encouraged her talent.

Beasley attended public schools in Cleveland, where she excelled in art classes. After graduating from high school, she went to Ohio State University, where she received her bachelor of fine arts degree in 1965. Upon graduation she became an art teacher at Glenville High School in Cleveland, where she remained until 1969. Meanwhile, she took graduate classes at Kent State University from 1967 to 1969.

In 1969, Beasley stopped teaching, moved to Los Angeles, and took a job selling advertising time on KFI/KOST radio. She has stayed at that job ever since, rising to the position of senior account executive. She now handles large-volume local and national accounts.

But despite her busy advertising career, Beasley has never given up her art career. She continued art classes when she moved to Los Angeles, first at the Art Center of Design in Los Angeles, and then at Otis Art Institute. Meanwhile, she made the rounds of gallery owners to get them interested in her work. It wasn't easy. Whites in the art world told her things like, "We don't carry black art," or "Why do you always paint black subjects?" Since Beasley receives her joy and inspiration from the black community, these seemed to her to be bizarre questions. But they were all too typical of the art world.

However, Beasley reached success as an artist as her works caught on with black art collectors. Her first one-person show was in Seattle, hosted by one of her collectors, basketball star Bill Russell. From there she had more than a dozen one-person shows around the country, in such cities as Chicago, Atlanta, Cleveland, Savannah, Los Angeles, and Beverly Hills. Television talk show host Oprah Winfrey, another collector, hosted the gallery opening in Chicago. With patrons such as these, the rest of the art world began to take notice.

Beasley received international attention as well. In 1989, she had a showing at the Holler Museum in Bonn, Germany. She has also shown at the Museum of African-

American Art in 1985, and at **Howard University** in 1984, as well as at Arizona State University and the Savannah College of Arts and Design. Beasley is part of many major corporate collections, including those of Johnson Publishing Company, Hanes Hosiery, and the Denver Broncos.

Beasley has also won major commissions in the art world. Oprah Winfrey had her do a series based on "The Women of Brewster Place," centering on the different characters in the television series. She also did the official poster for the 1989 inauguration of President Bush. Beasley was named the official artist for the Los Angeles Marathon in 1987 and designed a trophy and medal for the 1984 Los Angeles summer Olympics.

Now an established artist, Beasley is a member of the executive board of the Arts Task Force and a grants panelist on the California Arts Council. She no longer has to convince anyone of the value of black art. Phoebe Beasley is now one of the judges who help define artists of the future.

ANDRA MEDEA

Blount, Mildred E. (1907–1974?)

Mildred E. Blount is considered one of the greatest milliners of all time. She was well known in the fashion world from the 1930s through the 1950s, designing headwear for Hollywood stars and other noted personalities.

Mildred Blount was born in October 1907, in Edenton, North Carolina, the youngest of seven children. Her parents died when she was two years old. Blount was raised by various relatives in Philadelphia and other northern cities. Working as an errand girl at Madame Clair's Dress and Hat Shop in New York City, she developed an interest in millinery. Blount and her sister, Clara, a dressmaker, soon opened a shop of their own, designing dresses and hats for wealthy New Yorkers.

In the 1930s Blount was hired by John Frederics' Millinery of New York, where her career escalated. While at Frederics', she created a series of hats based on previous designs from 1690 through 1900; this collection was exhibited at the 1939 New York World's Fair. As a result of this exhibition, she was commissioned to design hats for the classic film *Gone with the Wind*. Although Blount rarely received film credit for her designs, she lent her talents to numerous major films including *Back Street*, *Blood and Sand*, *Easter Parade*, and *The Lady Is Willing*. Among her clients were Rosalind Russell, Joan Crawford, Gloria Vanderbilt, Marian Anderson, and many wealthy black women.

The August 1942 cover of *Ladies' Home Journal* featured one of Blount's hats and, in 1943, she became the first black American to have her work exhibited at the famous Medcalf's Restaurant in Los Angeles. That same year she was awarded a Rosenwald Fellowship to conduct research on period hats in America. During the late 1940s, she opened her own shop in Beverly Hills. Very little is known about Blount's later years. It has been reported that she died in Los Angeles in 1974.

KATHY A. PERKINS

Brandon, Barbara (1958–)

Cartoonist Barbara Brandon was born in 1958 in the Bushwick section of Brooklyn, the youngest of three children of Brumsic Brandon, Jr. Her father was the creator of the comic strip "Luther," which first appeared in the late 1960s. The strip, which was about an inner-city black child, ran for seventeen years.

Brandon was brought up in New Cassel, Long Island, and attended Syracuse University, where she studied illustration. After graduation, she applied for a job at *Elan*, a magazine for black women. The editor wanted a comic strip to run regularly in the magazine, and Brandon created "Where I'm Coming From." When the magazine went out of business before the strip was published, Brandon moved to *Essence*. That magazine said no to the strip but yes to

Brandon, hiring her as a beauty and fashion writer.

In 1988, the *Detroit Free Press* asked Brandon's father if he knew of any black cartoonists. Brandon got out her strip, and it began appearing in the *Free Press* in 1989 and was acquired by Universal Press Syndicate in 1991. Brandon thus became the first black female cartoonist to be syndicated in the mainstream white press. (Jackie Ormes had been syndicated in black-owned newspapers beginning in the 1930s.) Not thrilled to be the "first black woman" anything in the last decade of the twentieth century, Brandon was nevertheless happy to get a

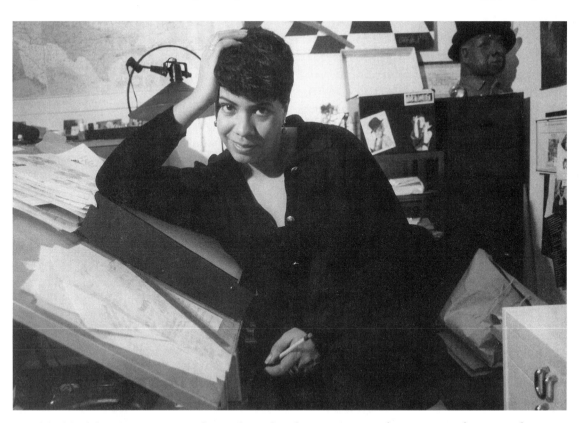

The first black female cartoonist to be syndicated in the mainstream white press, Barbara Brandon is carrying on a family tradition. Her father, Brumsic Brandon, Jr., created the comic strip "Luther." (EDWARD KEATING/NYT PICTURES)

Barbara Brandon's cartoon strip "Where I'm Coming From" features nine "girls" with diverse lives and points of view, talking about life from a black perspective. ("WHERE I'M COMING FROM" COPYRIGHT 1991 BARBARA BRANDON. DISTRIBUTED BY UNIVERSAL PRESS SYNDICATE. REPRINTED WITH PERMISSION. ALL RIGHTS RESERVED.)

larger audience for her increasingly political cartoons. "Where I'm Coming From" features nine black "girls" with diverse lives and perspectives.

KATHLEEN THOMPSON

Burke, Selma (1900–1995)

> I shaped my destiny early with the clay of North Carolina rivers. I loved to make the whitewash for my mother, and I was excited at the imprints of the clay and the malleability of the material.
>
> —Selma Burke, 1983

One of the chores assigned to the Burke children every Saturday was whitewashing the fireplaces with a wash made of local clay. Selma Hortense Burke discovered early that this clay could be molded into shapes that delighted her. Her varied career as a teacher, arts administrator, model, and nurse has been one of distinction and achievement, but it is her work as a sculptor that is the most memorable achievement. Working with a variety of woods, marbles, and stones, Burke infuses her figures with expressiveness, heroism, and power. She has consistently focused on the human figure, from the earliest clay figurines she created as a young artist to a statue she completed in the late 1970s of Martin Luther King, Jr.

Born December 31, 1900, in Mooresville, North Carolina, one of ten children of Neal Burke and Mary Jackson Burke, her introduction to and appreciation for the arts came early in her life. Her artistic interest was fostered by her father, a Methodist minister, who traveled throughout the world as a chef on several ocean liners. Neal Burke's globe-trotting landed him in South America,

Sculptor Selma Burke gained fame in 1945 when she created a plaque honoring Franklin Delano Roosevelt for the Recorder of Deeds Building. Her portrait profile of FDR probably served as the model for the Roosevelt dime. She is shown here with Eleanor Roosevelt at the dedication ceremony for the plaque. (MOORLAND-SPINGARN)

the Caribbean, Africa, and Europe, and he collected artifacts and fine art objects made in these various regions. Moreover, two paternal uncles who had graduated from Hood Theological Seminary traveled to Africa as missionaries during the late nineteenth century. As part of their mandate to teach Christianity to the Africans, they took the carved religious figures and masks and placed them in trunks rather than disposing of them. Upon their deaths, these artifacts

and other personal belongings were returned to the Mooresville home. African sculpture, therefore, became one of Burke's first references to art and the first objects that she duplicated. "I have known African art all of my life," she has explained. "At a time when this sculpture was misunderstood and laughed at, my family had the attitude that these were beautiful objects."

Mooresville had only an elementary school for black children, and Burke was sent to the **Nannie Burroughs** School for Girls in Washington, D.C. Her attendance at the school was brief, however, because "at Burroughs there was no encouragement for the arts. If you wore your silk-ribbed stockings, patent leather Mary Janes, and gloves, you were a lady. I wanted to be a lady and an artist."

When Burke was fourteen, William Arial, a white educator and superintendent of schools, took her into his home for tutoring. Arial, constantly battling some of the towns-people over his befriending a black child, became the first of Burke's patrons. The young aspiring artist had to travel to Winston-Salem (nearly fifty miles away) to obtain a high school education. She attended the Slater Normal and Industrial School (now Winston-Salem State University) where she studied with Frances and Jack Atkins and Lester Granger. Although her mother, an educator and homemaker (who lived to be 103) did not discourage her from pursuing the arts (her maternal grand-mother was a painter), she insisted that Selma get a practical education. So Burke pursued a nursing career at the St. Agnes School of Nursing (under the auspices of St. Augustine College in Raleigh, North Carolina), becoming a registered nurse in 1924.

In 1925, Burke moved to Philadelphia, where some of her relatives resided. To earn a living, the young artist practiced nursing in the area for two years. In 1927, Pennsylvania passed a law prohibiting nurses from giving anesthesia to patients. This curtailment of the range of services she could perform prompted Burke the following year to enroll in the Woman's Medical College, where a family friend was the president. There she specialized in operating room techniques to expand her nursing training.

While at the college, Burke rekindled a relationship with Durant Woodward, a lifelong friend from childhood. They were married in 1928. Tragically, however, Woodward, a mortician by profession, died of blood poisoning after only eleven months of marriage. A woman of great determination and purpose, Burke completed her extended course work at the medical college. Upon the recommendation of the president of the college, Burke in 1929 became the private nurse to

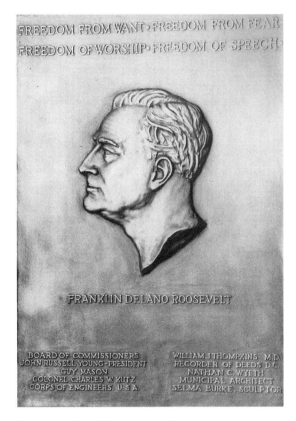

President Franklin Roosevelt agreed to sit for Selma Burke's plaque honoring him. She later remarked that she was "so imbued with the greatness of the man that my first seven studies of him were so idealized they were not good." (TRITOBIA BENJAMIN)

an heiress to the Otis Elevator business. She remained in this service for four years.

After the stock market crashed in 1929, the 1930s presented problems of epidemic proportions for most Americans. Burke was employed throughout these turbulent years, however, and was thus relatively unscathed by the Great Depression. Tom Sieg, writing in the Winston-Salem *Sentinel* (September 24, 1983), characterized those years as follows:

> [Selma Burke] ended up working for a charmingly crazy white woman, a Cooper, of the family for which Cooperstown, New York, was named. The woman turned out to be affectionate, generous, and very rich. By the time her employer died four years later, Miss Burke had a fantastic wardrobe, had become a regular at the Metropolitan Opera and Carnegie Hall, and had an acquaintance with royalty—and a nest egg.

Selma Burke's bust of Mary McLeod Bethune is one of several she made of black leaders. (NATIONAL ARCHIVES)

Selma Burke was able to remain afloat during the Depression years while many of her colleagues succumbed to economic deprivation. Nursing sustained her financially, but it was not the profession she desired to follow for life.

Seeking professional direction and study in sculpture, Burke went to New York City in 1935. To earn money when she first arrived, the artist took a job modeling at Sarah Lawrence College, while continuing her work in sculpture. Burke soon met Claude McKay (1890–1948), writer, author, a major figure in the Harlem Renaissance, and coeditor of the nation's outstanding avant-garde literary and political publication, the *Liberator*. Burke respected his accomplishments and his knowledge of European and African arts. Their relationship, though stormy, widened her circle of friends to include such luminaries as Eugene O'Neill, Langston Hughes, Max Eastman, Sinclair Lewis, James Weldon Johnson, Rosamund Johnson, and Ethel Waters, among others.

Burke immersed herself in work. She won a scholarship to Columbia University and a $1,500 Julius Rosenwald Award for a paper on sculpting materials. Further recognition came in 1936 with a Boehler Foundation Award.

In 1938, Burke went to Europe and spent nearly a year in France, Germany, and Austria gathering fresh material and experiences while improving her craftsmanship. In Vienna, Austria, she studied ceramics with Povolney, and in Paris, the cultural capital of Europe, she studied the human figure with Aristide Maillol, a major influence in early twentieth-century sculpture.

Feeling confident of her abilities, Burke resolved to obtain a professional degree in sculpture. She returned to Columbia University to work as an assistant to Oronzio Maldarelli, a well-known sculptor, and her quasi-classical leanings gave way to experimentation. Realizing that a creative insight could alter a composition in progress, she often used inexpensive materials. "It is very inspiring to release a figure from a piece of stone or wood," Burke declared. "Very often I look at a piece of stone or wood for a year or longer. Sometimes I will have completed the piece mentally before attacking the material."

The years at Columbia nurtured many meaningful relationships. Margo Einstein, daughter of Albert Einstein, was one of her classmates and a lifelong friend. Her visits to their home throughout the years, and the Einsteins' quiet support, encouraged Burke's aspirations as a sculptor. She graduated with an M.F.A. in 1941. In November of that year Burke exhibited at the McMillen Galleries in New York City with classic compositions.

When World War II broke out, Burke joined the navy and drove a truck at the Brooklyn Navy Yard, because, as she said, "I felt that during the war artists should get out of their studios." Then she injured her back and was hospitalized. It was during her hospitalization that she heard of the national competition sponsored by the Fine Arts Commission in Washington, D.C., to create a profile portrait of President Franklin Delano Roosevelt. Burke entered the competition and was awarded the commission in 1943.

Expected to create the profile from photographs, Burke researched newspapers and library records for such an image. Finding no photographs in profile (all were in full or three-quarter view), she wrote to the president requesting a sitting to make sketches of

him. He gave her an initial appointment for February 22, 1944.

Burke produced several sketches of the president on a roll of brown paper. Recalling the first two meetings with President Roosevelt, Burke remarked that she had been "so imbued with the greatness of the man that my first seven studies of him were so idealized they were not good." She explained that the president had been very gracious in his conversation with her concerning her work, and that she told him, on her second visit, that she wanted this work "to be the best piece of sculpture I had ever done."

The 3´6˝ by 2´6˝ bronze plaque depicting Roosevelt in profile listed the four freedoms that the president had vowed to uphold: freedom from want, freedom from fear, freedom of worship, and freedom of speech. The freedoms were placed at the top of the plaque. It was installed at the then-new Recorder of Deeds Building in Washington, D.C. Prior to its installation, however, approval was sought from First Lady Eleanor Roosevelt and members of the Fine Arts Commission.

On March 10, 1945, the president's wife visited Burke's studio to view the final draft. As she studied the plaque, Eleanor Roosevelt commented on the youthfulness of her husband and the height of his head. Burke later explained, "I have not done it for today but for tomorrow and tomorrow. Five hundred years from now America and all the world will want to look on our president, not as he was for the few months before he died, but as we saw him for most of the time he was with us—strong, so full of life, and with that wonderful look of going forward." Asked if she would like to visit with the president again, Burke accepted an appointment on

April 20; however, the president died, at Warm Springs, Georgia, on April 12, 1945. No further changes were made before the plaque's installation.

President Harry S. Truman spoke at the ceremonies on September 24, 1945. The plaque was unveiled by Frederick Weaver, great-grandson of Frederick Douglass, statesman, orator, and first black American to be recorder of deeds. After a celebratory whirlwind around Washington, D.C., Burke and members of her family returned to their homes the following day. As Burke recalled, "My mother was very proud of my achievements—she felt that I had delivered the Burkes from the cotton patch to the White House."

Much controversy has surfaced in recent years as to whether Burke's profile of Roosevelt on the plaque was used directly by the Bureau of the Mint of the U.S. Treasury for the Roosevelt dime. Few artists had had the opportunity of a private sitting with President Roosevelt during his lifetime, and Burke's profile had been evaluated as a good likeness of him. It is quite possible that John R. Sinnock, chief engraver at the Mint in 1945, credited with the design of the Roosevelt dime, consulted the Burke profile in his research, as it was the most recent rendering created from life. Burke's head of Roosevelt expresses a kind of hauteur that suggests, as she stated, "the going forward-ness that we needed at that time. I wanted to inject the feeling of pride and a positive direction." Sinnock, possibly seeking approval from Eleanor Roosevelt, who felt that in Burke's profile the president's head was too high, lowered Roosevelt's head for the design on the dime. The "J. S." initials that appear on the truncation of the neck, however, confirm the artist and the designer

of the coin. Artistically, the dime portrait is (with a few detail changes in the arrangement of FDR's hair) a mirror image of the plaque. Moreover, according to the National Archives and Records Administration of the Franklin D. Roosevelt Library in Hyde Park, New York, the source of the Roosevelt image on the coin was the "sculpture of FDR done by Selma Burke."

Determined that young minds would not be discouraged because of lack of training or an outlet to express their artistry, Burke taught in numerous school systems, workshops, and studios. Her work at the Harlem Art Center in New York City touched the lives of many now famous and nationally recognized African-American artists (Robert Blackburn, Jacob Lawrence, Ernest Crichlow). Under the supervision of sculptor **Augusta Savage** (1892–1962), Burke taught classes in sculpture. Located at Lenox Avenue and 125th Street in Harlem as a unit of the federally sponsored Works Progress Administration (WPA) program, courses were offered in drawing, painting, sculpture, lithography, etching, and photography. Burke also conducted sculpture workshops and art clinics under the auspices of the Friends Council on Education. She taught or lectured at numerous other institutions throughout her long career. Chief among them are the St. George's School in New York City; Old Solebury School in Bucks County, Pennsylvania; Friends Charter School in Pennsylvania; Swarthmore College; and the Pittsburgh School District.

Selma Burke married Herman Kobbe in October 1949. Marriage to the famous architect, author of *Housing and Regional Planning*, and a former candidate for lieutenant governor of New York (1934) meant a more public life for the artist. The couple moved in the 1950s to New Hope, Pennsylvania, long recognized as an artists' colony, home to writers, musicians, and visual artists. Burke became an intricate part of the Bucks County community. She was an active member of the local chamber of commerce, chairperson of the sculpture committee (Doylestown, Pennsylvania), and a member of the Bucks County Arts Council. Her success with this organization led to many years of hard work and dedication to the Pennsylvania Council on the Arts. As a member of this august body, Burke served three years under Governor William W. Scranton, four years under Governor Raymond P. Schaefer, and five years under Governor Milton Schapp. Selma Burke Day was proclaimed in Pittsburgh on June 20, 1975, by Governor Schapp in recognition of her statewide contributions to the arts.

With a strong sense of purpose and a desire to return something to the community, Burke opened the Selma Burke Art Center in Pittsburgh (1968–81). Located at 6118 Penn Circle South, the center was developed to answer the community's growing artistic needs. Offering studio classes both day and night in drawing, painting, ceramics, sculpture, visual communication, television production, and puppetry, it became an integral part of the Pittsburgh community. A full range of services included exhibitions by professional artists (group and one-person), concerts, lectures, demonstrations, and films. The theme of the center, "a place to grow and a place to show," was implemented and sustained through a variety of educational programs.

During her years as an arts administrator, Burke also served as a consultant to the A. W. Mellon Foundation in Pittsburgh. Throughout the decades of the 1950s,

1960s, and 1970s, Burke continued to exhibit in groups and one-woman shows and to teach at a variety of schools and art studios.

Her awards and honors are numerous and include an honorary doctorate in fine arts from the Moore College of Art, Philadelphia, Pennsylvania, 1979; an honorary doctorate of humane letters, Winston-Salem State University, North Carolina, 1979; a citation as Ambassador of Bucks County from the Central Bucks County Chamber of Commerce, 1979; an Award for Outstanding Achievement in the Visual Arts, Women's Caucus for Art, presented by President Jimmy Carter, Washington, D.C., 1979; a Bucks County Council on the Arts Citation, 1979; an honorary doctorate of fine arts from the University of North Carolina, Chapel Hill, 1977; an honorary doctorate from Livingston College, Salisbury, North Carolina, 1955; and a Yaddo Foundation, fellowship in 1955.

Burke's works are represented in many private and public collections, including Atlanta University; **Bethune-Cookman College**, Daytona Beach, Florida; Dry Dock Savings Bank, New York City; Gulf Oil Company, Pittsburgh; Hill Center House, Pittsburgh; Holy Rosary Church, Pittsburgh; **Howard University** Gallery of Art, Washington, D.C.; Jamaica High School, Long Island, New York; John Brown Association, Lake Placid, New York; Johnson C. Smith University, Charlotte, North Carolina; Livingston College Library, Salisbury, North Carolina; Mooresville Public Library, Mooresville, North Carolina; Museum of Modern Art, Miami, Florida; National Archives, Washington, D.C.; Scattergood School, West Branch, Iowa; United States Armory, New York City; and Winston-

Salem State University, Winston-Salem, North Carolina.

In the early 1980s, Burke retired from an active life as a sculptor, consultant, and arts administrator and returned to her New Hope, Pennsylvania, home. She died there on August 29, 1995.

TRITOBIA HAYES BENJAMIN

C

Catlett, Elizabeth (1919–)

I don't have anything against men but, since I am a woman, I know more about women and I know how they feel. Many artists are always doing men. I think that somebody ought to do women. Artists do work with women, with the beauty of their bodies and the refinement of middle-class women, but I think there is a need to express something about the working-class Black woman and that's what I do.

Sculptor and printmaker Elizabeth Catlett is an important figure in U.S. and Mexican art. Catlett's careful balance of dynamic form and content in both two- and three-dimensional works, and the acclaim that she has earned over a fifty-year period, firmly establish her contribution to the history of modern art. As a figurative artist, Catlett assimilates influences of modernist, social realist, expressionist, African, and pre-Hispanic styles into visual forms that imaginatively depict the human experience in subject matter ranging from heroic to ordinary characters and events. Though her stylistic influences have varied over the years, increasingly moving from realism toward abstraction, the work itself consistently adheres to perceptual reality. Preeminent in that reality is the theme of human dignity, a quality that Catlett interprets with penetrating emotional depth in both plastic and graphic form.

Catlett was born in 1919 in Washington, D.C., where she grew up during a period of overt segregation and oppression. She was the youngest of three children who were raised by their widowed mother, Mary Carson Catlett. John Catlett, Elizabeth's father, died shortly before she was born. He had been a math professor at Tuskegee Institute and a teacher in the public school system in Washington, D.C. Mary Carson Catlett and the children lived in a middle-class neighborhood in their own home, built by her father-in-law. Elizabeth Catlett recalls that they were "the poor cousins" within an extended family that included a famous surgeon; yet even so, they maintained a middle-class social standing because of their kinship ties. Catlett's mother supported her children with her job as a truant officer. As a young child, Elizabeth was inspired by both of her parents. Her mother encouraged Catlett to draw and paint and provided her with "materials, a place to work, and time apart." Her late father inspired Catlett through his history, including his artistic accomplishments in playing violin, mandolin, and piano, and in writing music and carving wood.

Catlett's formal education began at Lucretia Mott Elementary School in Washington, D.C., and continued at Dunbar High School, where she received encouragement in art. Upon graduating from Dunbar, in 1933, with academic honors, she participated in entrance examinations for one week at Carnegie Institute of Technology in Pittsburgh, but she was rejected in spite of her competitive art works. She overheard one of the teachers at the school say to another, "It's too bad she's a Negro, isn't it?"

Catlett began her formal study of art in 1933 at **Howard University**, where she studied with monumental figures in the history of African-American art. At Howard, Catlett studied drawing and painting with painter and art historian James Porter, author of *Modern Negro Art* (1943). She studied printmaking and crafts with leading printmaker James L. Wells, and design with leading painter **Lois Mailou Jones**. Catlett was exposed to the preeminent philosopher Alain Locke, author of *The New Negro* (1925), who encouraged black artists to turn to the ancestral arts of Africa for inspiration. Locke was a collector of African art, the influence of which is evident in Catlett's work. Catlett also was exposed to African art and classes in Western art in the art gallery of Howard University.

Catlett's education at Howard provided her with mentors and lifelong friends. She remembers, for example, how Porter "allowed her to spend time in his library and talked to her at length about life and art." Porter also encouraged Catlett to become involved with the Federal Art Project of the Works Progress Administration (WPA), a government program structured during the Great Depression by the Roosevelt administration to provide jobs by employing artists to produce art for public buildings. Catlett followed Porter's advice. In fact, it was through her involvement with the federal project that Catlett realized she lacked the necessary technique to paint a mural as she had planned. Research for the mural project introduced Catlett to the Mexican muralists who influenced her later work. Through

Howard, Catlett had acquired a foundation in drawing, painting, design, and woodcuts, and an appreciation of African, African-American, Mexican, and European art. She earned a B.S. in art, graduating cum laude in 1937.

For the next year Catlett taught art at the high school level and supervised art programs at eight elementary schools in Durham, North Carolina. During this time, she protested salary inequities—salaries of black teachers were equivalent to about half that of European-American teachers—and made plans to attend graduate school at the University of Iowa. There she studied with leading regionalist painter Grant Wood.

Catlett enrolled in the art department at the University of Iowa in 1938. Working under Wood's tutelage, Catlett expanded her styles and media while deepening her thoughts about art and its purpose. (Wood is also known for his work in interior design, stained glass, and carpentry.) Wood encouraged his students to paint what they knew. Reflecting on Wood's influence, Catlett noted, "That is probably why I do more work on black women than on any other single subject." Catlett completed her M.F.A. in 1940, the first student at the University to do so. Catlett's thesis piece was a mother and child figure that was carved in limestone; the work won the first place award in sculpture in the American Negro Exposition in Chicago the following year.

In summer 1940, Catlett got a summer teaching job at Prairie View College in Texas. From fall 1940 to 1942, she headed the art department at Dillard University in New Orleans. During the summer of 1941, Catlett studied ceramics at the Art Institute in Chicago and worked at the South Side Community Art Center, an active cultural center established during the WPA. Catlett interacted with Charles White, a painter and printmaker who worked in the realist tradition and became a major figure in African-American art. They married the same year and went to New Orleans, where Catlett taught another year at Dillard. The couple then went to Hampton Institute in Virginia for six months; Catlett taught and White painted a mural. They finally settled in New York City in 1942.

Catlett studied privately with French sculptor Ossip Zadkine, beginning in 1943. During that year she also studied lithography at the Art Students League. As Catlett expanded her techniques, she directed an alternative community school, the George Washington Carver School, where she taught for two years, from 1944 to 1946. Catlett was awarded a Julius Rosenwald Fellowship for 1945–46, an event that marked a turning point in the artist's life. The award was renewed in 1946–47, and in 1946 Catlett and White visited Mexico together and worked with Taller de Gráfica Popular (TGP), a collective of socially involved printmakers, an experience that had an important influence on the lives and works of both artists. Their marriage, however, failed and they soon returned to the United States to get a divorce.

Catlett subsequently returned to Mexico and became immersed in professional and social activities as she continued her work with TGP. She also studied pre-Hispanic ceramic techniques with Mexican artist Francisco Zuñiga at Esmeralda, Escuela de Pintura y Escultura. Between 1946 and 1947, she completed her graphic series on the "Negro Woman" for which she had received the fellowship. This significant body of work consisted of fifteen linocuts that were characterized by black linear rhythms that dramatically configured monumental real-type (as opposed to stereotype) images of black women. Her selection of and approach to her subjects uniquely inscribed convincing personalities, a quality that was rarely evident in American prints or painting depicting black women up to that time. Later identified as Afrofemcentrist (or Afro-female-centered), the series was exhibited at the Barnett-Aden Gallery in Washington, D.C., in 1947–48 and introduced Catlett to the public as an emerging professional artist. Its subjects and style evoked thoughts and emotions that suggested Catlett's empathy for humanity, her womanist/feminist proclivities, and her public voice for black women. It was a voice that challenged the oppression of all people of color, especially women. Subsequently, her position challenged the oppression of all women, though emphasizing women of color.

In 1947, Catlett married Mexican painter Francisco Mora, with whom she had three sons—Francisco, Juan, and David. Catlett and Mora continued to work with TGP until 1966. However, in 1956, Catlett returned in part to sculpture, studying woodcarving with José L. Ruiz at Esmeralda, Escuela de Pintura y Escultura. In 1958, she became a professor of sculpture in the National School of Fine Arts at the Universidad Nacional Autónoma de México, and in 1959, she became head of the sculpture department, remaining in that position until her retirement in 1976.

While expanding both her personal and professional responsibilities, Catlett remained politically active in Mexico. "Red-baiting" had marked her as an undesirable in the United States, a development that influenced her to become a Mexican citizen. With the change in citizenship, however, Catlett was prohibited from traveling in the United States. Her inability to enter the country attracted the attention of younger black American artists, politicians, museum directors, religious leaders, and others who wrote letters in her support to the U.S. State Department. Her status as an "undesirable" was finally changed in 1974.

Catlett's command of a variety of materials reveals her unusual versatility. She produces three-dimensional forms in marble, limestone, bronze, terra-cotta, and various types of wood, and two-dimensional works in linocut and lithography printmaking processes. Whether a geometricized sculptural representation of a black woman subject or an expressionist print on the theme of oppression, each work reveals a delicate balance of clarity, inventiveness, and philosophical conviction. The human figure remains prominent in this regard. In sculptural form (portrait bust, singular figure, or group figure), the representaton of the human subject calls attention to the beauty, character, and circumstance of specific or symbolic individuals. In graphic form, it expressively stimulates thought about social, cultural, historical, and/or political conditions.

Choosing to sculpt or print black and Mexican subjects, particularly women, Catlett depicts maternity, love, elderly wisdom, youthful beauty, feminine beauty, character, male and female leadership, work, female bonding, and identity, among other concerns. Her styles range from realism to semi-abstraction, and she sees form and meaning as inextricably bound.

Catlett's commissioned works are located in public spaces in the United States and Mexico; they include *Olmec Bather,* a ten-foot

bronze at the National Politechnical Institute in Mexico City (1966); *Phillis Wheatley,* a life-size bronze at Jackson State College in Mississippi (1973); *Louis Armstrong,* a ten-foot bronze in New Orleans (1975-76, presented at the U.S. bicentennial celebration); *Students Aspire,* a twenty-four-foot bronze relief on the Chemical Engineering Building at Howard University (1978); *Torres Bodet* and *Vasconcelor,* two life-size bronzes for the secretary of education in Mexico (1981); a thirty-six-foot-by-ten-foot bronze bas relief entitled *The People of Atlanta* for the new city hall in Atlanta (1989-91); and *Mother and Child,* a nineteen-inch black marble carving commissioned by Colgate-Palmolive (1992).

Catlett's prints are in important collections as well. Both her prints and sculpture are represented in major collections in the following institutions: Atlanta University in Georgia; the Cleveland Museum of Art in Ohio; Fisk University in Tennessee; Hampton University in Virginia; High Museum in Atlanta; the Library of Congress in Washington, D.C.; the Metropolitan Museum of Art in New York; the Museo de Arte Moderno in Mexico City; the Národniko Museum in Prague, Czech Republic; the National Museum of American Art in Washington, D.C.; the New Orleans Museum of Art; the Schomburg Center for Research in Black Culture in New York City; the University of Iowa, and the Studio Museum in Harlem, among others.

The commissions and collections in African-American, European-American, and Mexican institutions indicate Catlett's general historical importance. However, she is particularly important in the history of African-American art because of her representation in pioneering African-American exhibitions, including "Evolution of Afro-American Artists, 1800–1950" (New

York, 1967); "Two Centuries of Black American Art" (Los Angeles County Museum of Art, 1976-77); "Forever Free: Art by African American Women, 1862–1980" (Normal, Illinois, 1980); and "National Black Arts Festival" (Atlanta, 1988), among others. Given the few existing texts on African-American art, those exhibitions and their catalogue texts serve as important documents of the history of African-American art.

As her subjects and commissions might imply, Catlett has consistently made her works available to various communities in different domains of life. Her works are shown in major museums throughout the world. They are found on black college campuses and in the offices of community organizations. From Catlett's perspective, exhibiting in a community church or social club is as important as exhibiting in a museum or gallery, and this is the message that she has passed on to younger black artists. Her historic lecture, "The Negro People and American Art at Mid-Century," delivered at the National Conference on Negro Artists (NCA) on April 1, 1961, contained this message of social commitment. Catlett pre-

sented ideas that synthesized the populist ideology of TGP, cultural nationalist ideology, and activist positions of the civil rights movement. She encouraged an art of communication and emphasized the necessity of black artists to exhibit in black community spaces. Catlett said: "Let us take our painting and prints and sculpture not only to Atlanta University, to the art galleries, and to patrons of the arts who have money to buy them; let us exhibit where Negro people meet—in the churches, in the schools and universities, in the associations and clubs and trade unions. Then let us seek inspiration in the Negro people—a principal and never-ending source." These words were consistent with the thought that she conveyed to art historian and artist (and Catlett's former student) Samella Lewis in the late 1970s as she noted, "Art must be realistic for me, whether sculpture or printmaking, I have always wanted my art to service my people—to reflect us, to relate to us, to stimulate us, to make us aware of our potential. . . . We have to create an art for liberation and for life."

FREIDA HIGH W. TESFAGIORGIS

F

Fuller, Meta (1877–1968)

Meta Vaux Warrick Fuller was one of America's first studio sculptors of African-American ancestry. Called "elegantly Victorian" and "deeply spiritual," Fuller was, according to contemporary W. E. B.

In this formal photographic portrait of Meta Fuller, one can see why she was called both "elegantly Victorian" and "deeply spiritual."

DuBois, one of those persons of ability and genius whom "accidents of education and opportunity had raised on a tidal wave of chance."

Meta Vaux Warrick was born in Philadelphia on June 9, 1877, the daughter of William H. Warrick, Jr., a master barber, and Emma (Jones) Warrick, a wigmaker and hairdresser. Ten years younger than her brother William and sister Blanche, Meta was one of three surviving children of the Warricks. A sister, Virginia, died before Meta was born.

As a child, Warrick had been intrigued with the activities of her sister, Blanche, an art student. Outings with her father to the Philadelphia Academy of Fine Arts sharpened this interest.

In primary school, her own facility in art emerged. In high school she was one of those selected to attend J. Liberty Tadd's art school once a week for special training. Little is known of Warrick's record at Tadd's; however, a small woodcarving of hers was among the school's exhibits at the World's Columbian Exposition in Chicago in 1893.

After graduating from high school, Warrick applied for and received a three-year scholarship to the Pennsylvania Museum School for the Industrial Arts, where she studied from 1894 to 1897. One of the conditions of that scholarship was to produce a work of art for the school. Thus, in 1897, she executed *Procession of the Arts and Crafts*, a bas-relief composed of thirty-

190

seven medieval figures. The relief won a prize as one of the year's best works.

In 1897, the Pennsylvania Museum School granted her a postgraduate scholarship to continue her studies in sculpture. Sculpture proved to be her strength and vivid imagination her gift. Like many artists, she was inspired by theater, music, and mythology, but the subjects she chose to interpret tended to be sensational: *Medusa*, with "hanging jaw, beads of gore, and eyes staring from their sockets"; *Gestar*, portrayed in the dead of winter in order to show that romanticism could not exist in a cold and sterile environment, just as intellect proved insubstantial without spiritual content; and *Siegfried Slaying the Dragon* and the *Three Daughters of the Rhine*, inspired by Wagner's *Ring of the Nibelungs*. The latter diploma piece won a prize for modeling at her graduation exhibit in 1898. However, it was *Crucifixion of Christ in Anguish* that evoked the most comment. Some observers objected to so tormented a Christ. Warrick's reply combined the intellectual with the spiritual: "If the Savior did not suffer, wherein lay the sacrifice?" Generally, those evaluating her work viewed it positively; though perhaps too much toward the sensational in art, its handling was "masculine." Her boldness convinced many that she should continue her studies in Paris.

In September 1899, Warrick sailed for Europe. She arrived in England and spent a month with a friend of her mother, Harriet Loudin, whose husband, Frederick, was director of the touring Fisk Jubilee Singers. She then went to Paris, where a friend of her uncle, painter Henry Ossawa Tanner, had agreed to act as her guardian.

When she arrived at the Paris railway station on October 26, Tanner was not there to meet her. Consequently, she went alone to the American Girls Club, a hostel for young women studying in Paris. Warrick was horrified to discover that she could not stay there because of her race. However, with the help of Henry Tanner and the club's director, she found a room in a small hotel. The club's director also introduced Warrick to American sculptor Augustus Saint-Gaudens. During one of her many visits to his studio, he recommended that she not begin sculpting immediately but take drawing lessons instead. He also suggested teachers, thus aiding Warrick's search, which had been made more difficult by inadequate finances. During her first year in Paris she studied drawing, visited museums, and attended lectures at the Académie des Beaux-Arts; but by the summer of 1900, she was sculpting from live models.

The Paris Universal Exposition was held in 1900 and attracted a number of black Americans, some who had come specifically to participate in the event. Among those with whom Warrick toured the fair were exposition commissioner Thomas J. Calloway; agent Andrew F. Hilyer, an employee of the U.S. Department of the Interior, and his wife, Mamie, an accomplished pianist; Alonzo Herndon; Adrian McNeal Herndon, who taught at Atlanta University and was recognized as a talented actress; and Professor W. E. B. DuBois of Atlanta University. Before leaving Paris, DuBois suggested that Warrick specialize in African-American subjects. For her part, Warrick was unwilling to limit herself in this way. In the fall, she enrolled at the Académie Colarossi, where she continued to be guided by French sculptors.

In the summer of 1901, a fellow student at Colarossi arranged a meeting with Auguste Rodin at his home in Meudon.

Warrick carried an example of her sculpture, *The Man Eating His Heart*, hoping that the quality of this work would convince the artist to accept her as his student. Rodin examined the statuette and was impressed: "Mademoiselle, you are a sculptor, you have the sense of form." However, Rodin had too many students and could not add another, but he promised to come to Paris often and criticize her sculpture.

Warrick's creations become more daring in theme and execution. One of her aims had always been to explore the psychology of human emotions, a belief in the function of art that she shared with Rodin. Under his tutelage, she learned to execute such ideas with greater force. She refused to limit herself to subjects that were merely aesthetically pleasing, never avoiding portrayals because they were ugly or abhorrent.

Actually, Warrick used such imagery to make a philosophical point. The importance of duty was the theme of *Man Carrying a Dead Comrade*. The plight of the wise man who, despite his wisdom, is unable to alleviate human suffering is symbolized by *The Wretched*. The artist celebrated the 1902 Victor Hugo Centennial with a portrayal of Hugo's *Laughing Man*. The protagonist's face had been altered to resemble a grotesque mask. His mouth opened to his ears. His ears folded over his eyes. His shapeless nose heightened the effect of it all. No one could look upon this face without laughter and derision. Warrick's intention, however, was not to shock the public. She lived in an era when African Americans were portrayed as slow, lazy dullards with saucer eyes, thick lips, and wide grins: "Sambo" was the national jester. Although Warrick did not wish to specialize in African-American types, being black undoubtedly affected her world

view. Like her contemporary Paul Laurence Dunbar, she protested such stereotypes, but she did so indirectly by commenting on the black experience within the context of generally accepted visual images—in this instance, cloaked in the allegory of Hugo's *Laughing Man*.

During her last year in Paris, Warrick began holding private exhibitions and, under Rodin's sponsorship, began receiving attention. The "delicate sculptor of horrors," as the press called her, was the only American artist asked to join several French artists in a Paris exhibit. There she displayed her *Head of John the Baptist* and *The Impenitent Thief on the Cross*. Patron of such innovators as Aubrey Beardsley, Mary Cassatt, and Henri de Toulouse-Lautrec, S. Bing sponsored a one-woman show for her at his gallery, L'Art Nouveau.

In October 1902, Warrick returned to the United States and to her native city, Philadelphia. She set up a studio and continued to work but soon discovered that local art dealers were not interested in her sculpture. They claimed that they did not buy domestic pieces, but they ignored the Paris pieces as well. Warrick was convinced that the real issue was her color. She found a more appreciative public in black Philadelphia. The more she became reinvolved in black social and intellectual life, the more African-American themes shared a place with European thematic influences in her sculpture. *Two-Step* and *The Comedian* (song-and-dance-man George Walker) are examples of this transitional period. Warrick held exhibits in her studio. She also accepted invitations from community organizations and, periodically, from local art schools to contribute to their art shows.

The greater part of Warrick's patronage was local, but in 1907, upon the recommendation of Thomas Calloway, she received a commission to produce a set of tableaux for the Negro pavilion at the Jamestown Tercentennial Exposition. Her dioramas were composed of 150 figures representing black progress since the arrival of the first Africans at Jamestown, Virginia, in 1619. For this effort, she won a gold medal. Furthermore, she gained prominence as the first black woman artist to receive a federal commission.

At the turn of the century, many women did not believe it was possible to combine career and marriage. Meta Warrick was not one of these women. On February 3, 1909, she married Dr. Solomon C. Fuller. Born in Liberia, Fuller was a director of the pathology lab at Westborough State Hospital and a neurologist at Massachusetts State Hospital. The Fullers moved into a house that Dr. Fuller had built at 31 Warren Road, Framingham, Massachusetts. Meta, as her contribution, provided a frieze for the fireplace, *The Four Seasons*.

Before moving to Framingham, Meta Warrick Fuller had left her tools and sculpture in a Philadelphia warehouse, with the intention of having them shipped to her later. In 1910, a fire in that warehouse destroyed sixteen years' work that she had done in Philadelphia and Paris. Fuller was devastated and lost the urge to continue sculpting. Instead, she concentrated on her role as wife and mother. Between 1910 and 1916, she gave birth to three children—Solomon, Jr., William Thomas, and Perry.

In 1913, W. E. B DuBois, then editor of the *Crisis*, asked Fuller to reproduce *Man Eating His Heart* for the New York celebration of the Emancipation Proclamation's fiftieth anniversary. Inasmuch as this was one of the pieces lost in the fire, Fuller thought that recreating it would be too painful. Instead, she provided *Spirit of Emancipation*, a three-figured group standing eight feet in height. Fuller's emancipation piece was unlike any other of its genre. There were no discarded whips or chains, no grateful freedmen kneeling before a paternalistic Lincoln. Fuller had also not chosen to favor the female figure with Caucasian features, indicating her heightened race consciousness.

For Meta Fuller, taking up the chisel to create *Spirit of Emancipation* was the beginning of fifty prolific years of work. She turned from the grotesque of her youth and became more interested in realism and African-American themes. The change was in style rather than in substance: She did not abdicate her role as a social observer and advocate. For example, in 1915, she contributed a medallion to be sold in support of Framingham's Equal Suffrage League. Between 1914 and 1921, she dealt with a variety of issues stemming from American anxieties over the world at war—nativism, the atrocities of war, and the search for peace. Increasing violence against black Americans during this period resulted in two antilynching pieces in 1917, one based on the infamous Mary Turner case, which Walter White investigated for the **National Association for the Advancement of Colored People** (NAACP). Hoping to inspire black youth to rise above troubled times, Fuller created a relief for Atlanta, Georgia's black Young Men's Christian Association depicting a boy rising from a kneeling position to meet the morning sun. Indeed, Fuller did perceive a new level of race consciousness and pride taking shape among African Americans. Consequently, when asked to provide a sculpture for the New York City "Making of America" Festival in 1921, she responded with *Ethiopia Awakening*. She used an Egyptian motif to represent Americans of African descent, unwinding the bandages of their past, looking at life expectantly but unafraid. It was a compelling symbol of the black renaissance.

For most of this period, Fuller's attic had been her studio, but an increasing lack of space and Dr. Fuller's concern that dust in so confined an area would ruin her health made working there impractical. Consequently, in 1929, the artist designed and had a studio built on the shore of Larned's Pond, a short distance from her home. This improved setting allowed her to begin teaching as well as creating and exhibiting new works.

In the 1930s, Fuller's popularity grew. She exhibited at local libraries and churches and at the Boston Art Club. Her association with the Harmon Foundation, established in New York City to showcase the works of young black artists, was both as juror and exhibitor. Fuller's most appealing sculptures during this decade were rooted in African-American culture— *Water Boy*, based on a folksong; *Richard B. Harrison as "De Lawd"* in the popular play *The Green Pastures*; and *The Talking Skull*, derived from a folktale with African roots. During the 1930s and into the 1940s, Fuller maintained meaningful links with African America.

In 1950, Meta Fuller gave up her studio to care for her husband. Dr. Fuller died in 1953. During this time she too was ill with tuberculosis and entered a sanitarium, where she remained until 1956. Later that year, Fuller went to the Palmer Institute in Sedalia, North Carolina, in order to do a portrait of its founder, **Charlotte Hawkins Brown**. In 1957, the **National Council of Negro Women** in Washington, D.C., com-

missioned her to model heads and hands for dolls representing ten notable black women.

In March 1961, at age eighty-four, Meta Fuller was one of three artists honored in the "New Vistas in American Art" exhibit, celebrating **Howard University**'s new art building. Fuller donated several works, including *Richard B. Harrison*, to the university.

Advanced age did not dull the sculptor's creativity. Framingham Union Hospital, where her husband had practiced, commissioned Fuller to design a plaque depicting working doctors and nurses. The local women's club requested sculpture for the Framingham Center Library. The result was unveiled in 1964—*Storytime*, a mother reading to her children.

During the 1960s, Fuller contributed to the civil rights movement by donating the proceeds of art sales to the cause and by producing symbols of the era. *The Crucifixion* was her reaction to the death of four little girls in the bombing of the Sixteenth Street Baptist Church in Birmingham, Alabama, on September 15, 1963. *The Good Shepherd* was dedicated to the clergymen who marched with Martin Luther King, Jr., across the Edmund Pettus Bridge on March 9, 1965.

On Wednesday, March 18, 1968, Meta Vaux Warrick Fuller died at the age of ninety. Her funeral was held at Saint Andrew's Episcopal Church in Framingham. Afterward, her body was cremated and her ashes scattered in Vineyard Haven Sound, Massachusetts, as she had requested.

An artist whose career spanned over seventy years, Fuller was versatile and productive. At times she was a literary sculptor, at other times a creator of portraiture; and because she believed her artistic gifts were God-given, she created at least one piece of religious art a year in thanks. Her real significance, however, was in her depiction of African-American subjects. Although she once declared that she would not specialize in African-American types, Fuller was among the first artists to employ black visual aesthetics in her portrayal of African Americans. As such, she was an important precursor of the Harlem Renaissance, but, more than that, in those seventy years she presented a haunting chronicle of the black experience within the context of the American experience.

JUDITH N. KERR

G

Gafford, Alice (1886–1981)

I love to paint. It nourishes my soul as food nourishes the body. If I create something beautiful which enriches the lives of others, then my art serves a dual purpose.

Nurse Alice Taylor Gafford found it was never too late when she enrolled in art school at the age of forty-nine and became a respected figure in the world of art. (MIRIAM MATTHEWS)

Alice Taylor Gafford spent twenty-five years in the nursing profession before deciding to attend Otis Art Institute in 1935 at the age of forty-nine. She was born on August 15, 1886. One of ten children of Benjamin and Alice Armstead Taylor, she was the only one to show any interest in art even though her mother was a "Sunday painter" who had won a blue ribbon at an international exposition.

Shortly after she graduated from the Otis Art Institute, Gafford attracted the attention of the critics when she was awarded second prize for one of her paintings at the Stendahl Gallery on Wilshire Boulevard in Los Angeles. A few years later, A. Atwater Kent, a noted New York collector, purchased one of Gafford's still-life paintings at the Biltmore Galleries. Art critic Arthur Millier published a photograph of this Gafford painting in the *Los Angeles Times* with the caption, "art thrill of the week."

Alice Gafford added a third career to her list when she entered the University of California at Los Angeles (UCLA) in 1951 to earn a teaching certificate in art. She then taught art to adults in the Los Angeles county schools for five years before retiring to devote all of her time to her creative work. Today, some of her former students are accomplished artists and teachers.

From a group of five hundred artists who submitted their work for the Sixth Annual Southern California Exhibition in 1968, Alice Gafford was among the seventy-nine artists selected to participate by New York critic Clement Greenberg. Later, Gafford's *The Tea Party* was added to the collection of the Long Beach Museum.

On her eighty-first birthday, Gafford was commissioned to paint the portraits of twelve famous black Americans for the Family Savings Bank gallery.

Alice Gafford played a prominent role in the founding and development of various pioneer art groups, including the Val Verde Art and Hobby Show that now bears her name (the Alice Gafford Art and Hobby Show). She received more than twenty-five awards from the League of Allied Arts, the National Association of College Women, and various city, county, and state legislative bodies.

She died on October 27, 1981 and was buried in the Los Angeles National Cemetery next to her husband, Louis Sherman Gafford, whom she married in 1928.

MIRIAM MATTHEWS

H

Humphrey, Margo (1942–)

Early in her career, Margo Humphrey referred to herself as a "technical entrepreneur," an artist who was concerned with form as well as content. Seeking to make her work more universal, Humphrey says that "art is a relationship of symbols which formulate an idea, bringing into being thoughts of the past and present in a contemporary way which releases my vision."

Born in Oakland, California, she attended the California College of Arts and Crafts, Oakland, receiving her B.F.A. and M.F.A. from Stanford University in 1972 and 1974, respectively. Her media is primarily printmaking, but she has also worked in sculpture, and she creates site-specific installations.

In the late 1960s, Humphrey directed her focus toward the African continent, gaining inspiration and material for her creative production. A lithograph, *A Second Time in Blackness*, from the *Zebra Series* (1968), is a representation of animal and human forms distinguished from the environment by the different shades and degrees of light and tones. By the 1970s, her vibrantly colored lithographs were technically sound as she efficiently manipulated the difficulties of color registration in her prints; *Crying Ain't Gonna Help None Baby or Don't Shed Your Tears on My Rug* (1971) is an example of her mastery of this technique. We also find energized elements that comment on contemporary living as she combines fantasy images, bold color, and unique titles to narrate her special tales. In *The Last Bar-B-Que* (1989), Humphrey appropriates the Last Supper, as the source of inspiration, to state her support of black male leadership and the sharing of political and economic power. Christ and his disciples share a meal of tropical fruit, fried chicken, and watermelon.

Humphrey has traveled and taught internationally, including the University of the South Pacific; the University of Benin, Nigeria; the Tamarind Institute of New Mexico; Makala University, Kampala, Uganda; and in Senegal.

Currently a professor of art at the University of Maryland, College Park, her works are in the permanent collection of the Los Angeles County Museum; the Museum of Contemporary Art, Rio de Janeiro, Brazil; and many private and public collections in the United States. In 1988, Humphrey became the first American artist to have work included in the permanent collection of the National Gallery in Lagos, Nigeria. She has participated in numerous group and several solo exhibitions.

Humphrey received fellowships from the Ford Foundation in 1981 and from the National Endowment for the Arts and the Tiffany Foundation in 1988. Her children's book, *The River that Gave Gifts* (1992) was included in an exhibition of illustrated children's books at the National Museum of Women in the Arts Library and Research Center, Washington, D.C.

TRITOBIA HAYES BENJAMIN

Hunter, Clementine (1886–1988)

"If Jimmy Carter wants to see me, he knows where I am. He can come here." This reply, to President Carter's invitation that she come to Washington for the opening of an exhibition of her work, is vintage Clementine Hunter. Her disregard for fame and the famous was part of her special charm and did not change, even after she became known worldwide for her colorful folk paintings of black life in the Cane River region of north Louisiana.

Clementine Hunter was born on Hidden Hill Plantation, near Cloutierville, Louisiana, in December 1886. Her mother, Mary Antoinette Adams, was the daughter of a slave, brought to Louisiana from Virginia; her father, John Reuben, had an Irish father and a Native American mother. Hunter considered herself a Creole. When she was a teenager, she moved with her family from Hidden Hill to Yucca Plantation, renamed Melrose, seventeen miles south of Natchitoches, Louisiana. Hunter lived and worked at Melrose until 1970, when the plantation was sold; then she moved to a small trailer a few miles away, where she lived until her death on January 1, 1988.

Charles Dupree, the father of Hunter's first two children—Joseph (Frenchie) and Cora—died about 1914. In January 1924, Clementine married Emmanual Hunter, by whom she had five children: Agnes, King, Mary, and two who died at birth. Emmanual Hunter died in 1944. Clementine Hunter outlived all her children except Mary (called Jackie).

Hunter's mentor was François Mignon, a French writer who lived on Melrose Plantation from 1938 to 1970. According to Mignon, Hunter did her first painting in 1939. From then until a few months before her death, Hunter painted continually, on any surface she could find. Her output was prodigious; estimates are that she completed more than 5,000 paintings. Like many folk artists, however, Hunter painted the same scenes over and over. Her works fall into roughly five thematic categories: work scenes from plantation life; recreation scenes; religious scenes; flowers and birds; and abstracts. The quality of her work varies greatly, but her paintings are prized for their vibrant colors and whimsical humor.

The first exhibit of Hunter's work was at the New Orleans Arts and Crafts show in 1949. After three exhibits in the 1950s, her work received little attention until the early 1970s, when it was shown at the Museum of American Folk Art in New York City (1973) and in the Los Angeles County Museum of Art's exhibit "Two Centuries of Black American Art" (1976). In the last fifteen years of her life, Hunter had many one-woman shows at colleges and galleries throughout Louisiana, was featured on local and national television shows, included in two oral black-history projects (Fisk University, 1971 and Schlesinger Library, Radcliffe College, 1976) and was part of the photographic portrait exhibition "Women of Courage by Judith Sedwick," shown in 1985 in New York and Boston. Also in 1985, Hunter was awarded an honorary doctor of fine arts from Northwestern State University of Louisiana, in Natchitoches.

Although the quality of Hunter's paintings is uneven, the historical value of her work is beyond question.

ANNE HUDSON JONES

J

Jackson-Jarvis, Martha (1952–)

Martha Jackson-Jarvis creates abstract yet evocative sculptures in clay, mosaic, and a wide variety of other materials. Her complex themes are inspired by nature, found objects, and African imagery; she is best-known for her site-specific installations, but she has also created single vessels and, most recently, densely-layered forms that resemble tables or boxes.

Born in Lynchburg, Virginia, Jackson-Jarvis found time to draw and paint between chores on her grandparents' farm, participation in church, and schoolwork. Later she studied at the Haystack Mountain School of Crafts in Deer Isle, Maine, and in 1975 she

Martha Jackson-Jarvis creates abstract sculptures in a wide variety of materials, including clay and mosaic. She is shown here in her studio in 1993. (JARVIS GRANT)

earned a B.F.A. from Tyler School of Art in Philadelphia, followed by an M.F.A. from Antioch University in Columbia, Maryland in 1981. She is presently a resident of Washington, D.C., where she has taught at the Corcoran School of Art.

Jackson-Jarvis had majored in ceramics, and in the mid–1970s she explored a variety of approaches to clay. One series of large vessels was created by a process that combined Japanese *raku* with African dung firing, and incorporated imagery based on myths of the Bird Spirit, a motif common to many cultures. By the early 1980s she had multiplied the elements of her work and expanded its scale to fill the floor of a room, as in *Walking on Sunshine* (1982); this expansion allowed her to deal with painterly issues of composition, surface, and color, while at the same time her work became more sculptural. Throughout the decade, she created site-specific environments, such as *Legacy of a Matriarch/Notes on Death and Dying* (1986), that fused two- and three-dimensional elements in an original and expressive way.

Jackson-Jarvis also began to use fragments, found objects, and mosaic elements in her work, and after studying the technique in Italy she returned to incorporate her expertise into densely-layered objects such as *Table of Plenty* (1993) or the coffin-shaped elements of *Last Rites* (1993). More recently, she has created a series of three-dimensional wall "boxes" that mix clay, glass,

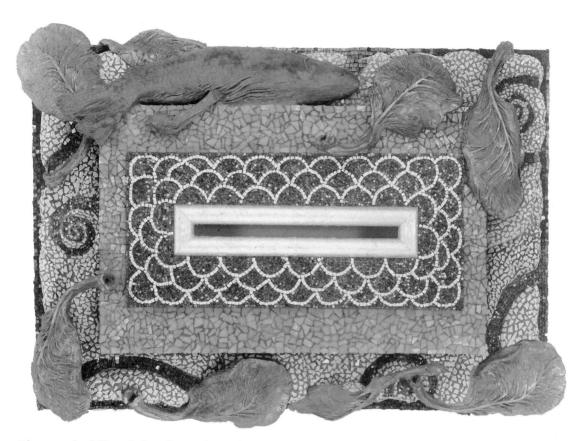

This wonderfully-titled sculpture by Jackson-Jarvis is The Sea, the Sky, the You & I (1995). (HARLEE LITTLE)

coal, wood, and other materials in unexpected and exciting combinations. Her work constantly challenges boundaries between abstraction and figuration, craft and fine art, sculpture and painting, as she moves forward in an energetic and important career.

Jackson-Jarvis's work has been seen in a wide variety of group exhibitions in museums and galleries in the United States and elsewhere; she has also had many one-artist shows, most recently a retrospective at the Corcoran Gallery in Washington, D.C. Her work is included in major private and public collections, and she has been the recipient of several private and public sculpture commissions as well as numerous awards, including a National Endowment for the Arts grant and an Arts International Lila Wallace-Readers Digest Travel Grant to Italy.

NANCY GROVE

Jackson, May Howard (1877–1931)

"There is among us one woman who is far less known than is her rightful due . . . temperamental, withdrawn, and shunning

An artist far ahead of her time, sculptor May Howard Jackson expressed in her work her fascination with the complex and varied physiognomy of black people as a result of the mixing of the races in the aftermath of slavery. (MOORLAND-SPINGARN)

publicity . . . yet endowed with unusual ability." This observation was made in *Crisis* magazine in September 1927. As is the case with great talent and vision, May Howard Jackson was a woman far ahead of her time.

She was born in Philadelphia, Pennsylvania, in 1877, the daughter of Floarda Howard and Sallie Durham. She attended public schools in Philadelphia and then entered Todd's Art School. In 1895, Jackson became the first black woman to receive a scholarship to attend the Pennsylvania Academy of Fine Arts, where she studied for four years with William Merritt Chase,

Charles Grafly, and John Joseph Boyle. After graduating in 1899, she married William Sherman Jackson, head of the mathematics department at the M Street High School in Washington, D.C., and set up a studio in their home.

Counter to the tradition of that era, Jackson did not travel to Europe for further training as a sculptor. Some critics, such as Alain Locke, speculated that this decision might have deterred the development of her technical skills, if not her recognition and credibility as an artist. Ironically, Jackson's isolation and the absence of direct European influences actually freed her, both intellectually and artistically, and thus enabled her to develop a distinctly personal style. The corpus of her work centered on Jackson's own ancestry, her fascination with the complex and varied physiognomy of black people as a result of the mixing of the races in the aftermath of slavery. Her factual execution of black subjects was not favorably received, however, especially at a time when stereotypical images of black people were rampant in the public arena. The generally negative attitude toward her work elicited in her immense frustration and anger.

In her portrait busts, Jackson tried to evoke more than the neoclassical training she had received at the Pennsylvania Academy of Fine Arts; she went far beyond the realist traditions of the day, imbuing her subjects with the psychological dimensions of the individual's personality, identity, and humanity. At a time when African Americans were considered to have nothing substantive to contribute to society, portraiture of this nature was hardly appreciated.

May Howard Jackson executed numerous portrait busts in her lifetime, among them, representations of Paul Laurence Dunbar (1919), W. E. B. DuBois, Reverend Francis J. Grimké, Kelly Miller (1929), Reverend H. M. Joseph, Sherman Jackson (1929), and W. H. Lewis. She also rendered abstract portraits, such as *Head of a Negro Child* (1929), *Mulatto Mother and Her Child* (1929), and *Shell-Baby in Bronze* (1929). Jackson was a pioneer in establishing the first stylistic movement identified by Alain Locke as a departure from "academic cosmopolitanism" in favor of a "frank and deliberate racialism." Her efforts to address, without compromise and without sentimentality, the issues of race and class, especially as they affected mulattos, make her the founder of the first movement toward an Afrocentric aesthetic.

In her active years, Jackson's successful exhibitions included the Corcoran Gallery in Washington, D.C. (1915), the Veerhoff Gallery in New York City (1919), and the National Academy of Design (1916, 1928). In 1928, Jackson won the Bronze award from the Harmon Foundation's Achievements for Negroes in the Fine Arts. The current locations of many of her sculptures are unknown, but she is represented in the Barnett-Aden Collection at Dunbar High School in Washington, D.C., and at **Howard University**, where she taught.

W. E. B. DuBois, an ardent supporter of black visual artists, eloquently eulogized Jackson in a 1931 issue of *Crisis*: "In the case of May Howard Jackson the constrictions and idiotic ramifications of the Color Line tore her soul asunder. It made her at once bitter and fierce with energy, cynical of praise, and, above all, at odds with life and people. She met rebuffs in her attempts to study and in her attempts at exhibition, in her chosen ideal of portraying the American mulatto type; with

her own friends and people she faced continual doubt as to whether it was worth while. . . . She accomplished enough to make her fame firm in our annals." Little did May Howard Jackson realize that the tenacity of her spirit, the brilliance of her vision, and the genius of her technical skills would one day make her the heir apparent to a truly original African-American imagery.

LESLIE KING-HAMMOND

In her portrait busts, May Howard Jackson went beyond the realist traditions of her day, imbuing her subjects with the psychological dimensions of individual personality, identity, and humanity. Pictured here is her bust of the Reverend Francis J. Grimké. (MOORLAND-SPINGARN)

Noted artist-educator Lois Mailou Jones is seen here in her studio, surrounded by works exemplifying her expressive, colorful, hard-edged style, which fuses abstraction with decorative patterns and naturalism. (SCURLOCK STUDIO)

Jones, Lois Mailou (1905–)

An active and acclaimed painter for more than six decades, Lois Mailou Jones enjoyed two impressive careers, one as a professor of art and the other as an artist. Her teaching gave her financial security and served as an inspiration and a challenge.

Lois Jones was born on November 3, 1905, in Boston to Caroline Dorinda Adams and Thomas Vreeland Jones. Her father was superintendent of a large office building and attended night classes at Suffolk Law School, where he received his law degree in 1915 at age forty. "I think that much of my drive surely comes from my father," says Jones, "wanting to be someone, having an ambition." Her mother was a beautician and Jones' first mentor. She filled the Jones home with color and freshly cut flowers, instilling in her daughter a love of beauty.

With the assistance of four annual tuition scholarships, Jones earned a diploma from the High School of Practical Arts (HSPA). During her high school years, she also attended the Boston Museum Vocational

Drawing Class on a scholarship. While at HSPA, she was apprenticed to Grace Ripley, a well-known costume designer and professor at the Rhode Island School of Design. She assisted Ripley in creating costumes for the Ted Shawn School of Dance and a branch of the Bragiotti School in Boston. Working on Saturdays and after school, she designed dance costumes, especially masks. She recalls that "very early I was introduced to Africa through creating the masks with the Ripley studio."

In 1923, Jones was admitted to the Boston Museum of Fine Arts, where each year from 1923 to 1927 she won the coveted Susan Minot Lane Scholarship in Design. Here she studied design concepts, life drawing, and portraiture under such artists as Anson Cross, Phillip Hale, Alice Morse, and Henry Hunt Clark. She graduated from the museum school with honors in 1927. During her last year at the museum school, Jones enrolled in evening classes at the Boston Normal Art School (now the Massachusetts College of Art), receiving a teaching certificate in 1927. That same year she won a scholarship to the Designers Art School of Boston, where she continued graduate study with Ludwig Frank, internationally known designer of textiles. Her studies were extended at Harvard University during the summer of 1928. Jones created a series of designs for cretonne—a strong, unglazed cotton or linen cloth that is used especially for curtains and upholstery—and other fabric and textile patterns.

That year, two eminent educators, Henry Hunt Clark and Charlotte Hawkins Brown, told Jones to "go south" and help her people. Jones had been disappointed by Clark when she applied for a position at the museum school; none was available, and Clark

pointed the young designer toward the South and its needs. She hesitated. Next, she applied to **Howard University**. She was informed that they had recently hired James A. Porter and had no other positions available. Then she heard Brown speak in Boston, urging college students to take their talents to the youth of the South. This time she accepted the challenge. Although thought by some to be too young and inexperienced, she was hired by Brown to develop the art department at the Palmer Memorial Institute, one of the nation's first preparatory schools for African Americans, in Sedalia, North Carolina. Jones established the curriculum, served as chairperson of the department, and provided instruction to a small, eager class. In addition to her other duties, Jones also taught dancing, coached a basketball team, and played the piano for Sunday morning worship services.

During the spring of 1930, Jones invited James Vernon Herring, founder and head of the Department of Art at Howard University, to lecture at Palmer. He was impressed by the work of her students and recruited her to serve as an instructor of design at Howard. Jones joined the Howard faculty in 1930 and remained there until her retirement in 1977. She, James A. Porter, and James Lesesne Wells constituted the art department and forged a curriculum unique among historically black colleges and universities.

For her first sabbatical Jones chose the Académie Julian in Paris. During a summer on Martha's Vineyard, she had met sculptor **Meta Warrick Fuller** and composer Harry T. Burleigh. They advised her that if she wanted to find a niche in the art world, she should travel to Paris for recognition. Also, of course, study in Paris was a tradition for

American artists who could manage the expense. With the aid of a General Education Board fellowship, Jones sailed for France on the S.S. *Normandie* on September 1, 1937. Her sojourn there marked a shift in her career from that of designer, illustrator, and teacher to that of painter. As Jones later said, the experience allowed her "to be shackle free, to create and to be myself."

Many of her works from that year were painted on location. It was during one of her painting exercises on the Seine that Jones met Emile Bernard, the father of French Symbolist painting, who encouraged her and criticized her work. Albert Smith, an African-American artist in Paris, also became a friend during Jones's stay and after her return to the United States.

Jones made such progress that, toward the end of the academic year, her friends and instructors urged her to submit paintings to the annual Salon de Printemps of the Société des Artistes Français, one of the most important exhibits of the year. Although her work of this era reveals a commitment to the organizing principles and preferred palette of the Impressionists and Post-Impressionists, her paintings were clearly personal interpretations. As James Porter, author of *Modern Negro Art*, observed: "Thus far her painting has been in the tradition, but not in the imitation of Cézanne. . . . Miss Jones wishes to confirm Cézanne but at the same time to add an original note of her own. . . . Sensuous color delicately adjusted to the mood indicates the artistic perceptiveness of this young woman."

Soon after her return to the United States in September 1938, Jones exhibited at the Robert Vose Galleries in Boston. Her work received high praise, and her reputation grew as she exhibited throughout the United States. After her return to Washington, she met Alain Locke, poet laureate of the Harlem Renaissance, or New Negro Movement, and head of the philosophy department at Howard. Telling her of his plans to include one of her Parisian street scenes in his forthcoming book, *The Negro in Art* (1940), Locke strongly encouraged her to reevaluate her subjects and take her own heritage more seriously. An early advocate of black consciousness, Locke was perhaps the most influential voice on art in the African-American community at that time. Jones' response to Locke's challenge produced works focused on the black American. The artist refers to the 1940s as her Locke period. Also during this decade, Jones took classes at Howard, receiving an A.B. in art education and graduating magna cum laude in 1945.

When Lois Jones married the noted Haitian graphic artist and designer Louis Vergniaud Pierre-Noel in 1953, both her life and her art were transformed. They took advantage of an invitation from the Haitian government to teach at the Centre d'Art and the Foyer des Arts Plastiques so that they could honeymoon in Haiti. The experience was the beginning of a new way of seeing for Jones, and, from her first visit, she "fell increasingly in love with Haiti and its people." Her early Haitian paintings explored the picturesque elements of the marketplace and its people. Although the essence of Europe was still, at the beginning, very much apparent, the palette and the formal organization of her paintings gradually evolved into a brilliantly spirited style, fresh, energetically fluid, and highly individual. This new style signaled clearly that Europe did not yield the exuberance so vital to expressing the vigor found in this African-oriented culture.

When Lois Mailou Jones married the noted Haitian graphic artist and designer Louis Vergniaud Pierre-Noel in 1953, her life and her art were transformed. From her first visit, she fell in love with Haiti and its people. Peasants on Parade *(1962) reflects her fascination with the marketplace and its people. The painting is in the collection of the artist.* (TRITOBIA BENJAMIN)

Jones' work in the 1960s drew more upon her knowledge of design techniques and her passion for color while synthesizing the diverse religious and ritualistic elements of Haitian life and culture. It showed a more expressive, colorful, hard-edged style that fused abstraction with decorative patterns and naturalism. These characteristics asserted themselves even more powerfully in the 1970s.

In 1969, Jones received a grant from Howard University to conduct research on contemporary artists in Africa. Between April and July, she compiled biographical material on African artists, photographing their work, conducting interviews, and visiting museums in eleven African countries. More than 1,000 slides were given to the Howard University archives upon completion. Jones said her trip "proved to be a revelation and a rich experience." During the 1970s and into the 1980s, she maintained an intense interest in Africa. Undoubtedly this was in part due to the African American's quest for cultural identity. The black cultural movement of these years was even more profound and widespread than that which occurred during the Harlem Renaissance.

In the summer of 1989, Jones returned to France. The works that resulted recall an earlier era. Reminiscent of the Impressionist and Post-Impressionist style abandoned by Jones more than thirty years earlier, the paintings created during that visit illustrate her continued fascination with nature and her desire to capture the fleeting beauty of place. In 1990, a major retrospective, "The World of Lois Mailou Jones," was sponsored by Meridian House International in Washington, D.C. It opened in January and traveled across the United States for two years.

Lois Mailou Jones has received innumerable awards for her work in competitions, including the National Thayer Prize for excellence in design. She has also received honorary degrees from a number of universities, including Howard. In 1954, the government of Haiti awarded her the Diplôme and Decoration de l'Ordre Nationale "Honneur et Mérite au Grade de Chevalier." Her work is represented in museums and private collections across the country and the world, including the Metropolitan Museum of Art in New York; the Museum of Fine Arts and the Museum of the National Center of Afro-American Artists in Boston; the National Museum of American Art, the National Museum of Women in the Arts, the National Portrait Gallery, and the Hirshhorn Museum and Sculpture Garden in Washington, D.C.; and the Palais Nationale in Port-au-Prince, Haiti.

Interviewed by The *Washington Post* in 1995 (at the age of ninety) Jones was asked the secret of her longevity. "Passion. . . . You have to find something in life that you love doing. You have to have some love in it. There's nothing worse that working in a position that you hate. You have to feel you have contributed to life and grow with it." And, she clearly loves her life. When the interview took place, she had just completed her first movie poster—for *Cry the Beloved Country*—and the original painting for the poster had been presented to South African President Nelson Mandela; a new book, *The Life and Art of Lois Mailou Jones*, by Tritobia Hayes Benjamin, had just been published; and two exhibitions were on view in Washington featuring her own work and that of some of her students from the forty-seven years she taught at Howard.

It is difficult to estimate the impact of any given artist during his or her lifetime. About Lois Jones, however, certain things are clear. While teaching and communicating a love of art to generations of students, she has cre- ated a body of work characterized by tech- nical virtuosity, consummate skill, versatility, elegance, vitality, structure, de- sign, and clarion color.

TRITOBIA HAYES BENJAMIN

L

Lewis, Mary Edmonia (c. 1843–?)

Her dual heritage and accomplished marble sculpture distinguish Edmonia Lewis as the first major sculptress of African-American and Native American heritage. Her early biographical circumstances are sketchily known at best. Although Lewis claimed 1854 as her birthdate, it is more likely that she was born in 1843 or 1845. Various sources, including the artist herself, have noted Greenhigh, Ohio, and Greenbush, New York, as well as the vicinity of Albany, New York, as her birthplace, but none can be verified.

Lewis' father was a full-blooded African American employed as a gentleman's servant, and her mother was a Chippewa Indian who may have been born near Albany. It was she who presumably named her daughter "Wildfire." Lewis appears to have spent little if any time with her father, and instead lived with her mother's tribe. Orphaned before she was five, Lewis remained with the Chippewa until she was about twelve years old. As "Wildfire," she learned to fish, swim, make baskets, and embroider moccasins. Typically, she sold her crafts as the tribe followed its nomadic lifestyle throughout New York State.

During the 1850s Lewis left the Chippewa because her brother "Sunrise," a California gold miner, had arranged for her schooling near Albany. Adapting to her new circumstances proved difficult, but her brother persisted in efforts to educate her.

Thus in 1859 Lewis entered **Oberlin College** in Oberlin, Ohio, with his financial assistance. This event triggered her name change, and the school's records indicate that she assumed the name Mary Edmonia Lewis. Throughout her career, however, she seldom used her new first name, as reflected in her correspondence as well as the signatures on her sculptures.

Lewis was a moderately successful student, completing the preparatory department's high-school courses and pursuing the college department's liberal arts program. Her only extant drawing, *The Muse Urania*, still in the Oberlin College Archive, was done in 1862 as a wedding present for her classmate Clara Steele Norton. She may have been inspired by optional drawing courses offered by the Young Ladies' Course. Later in life Lewis recalled that "I had always wanted to make the form of things; and while I was at school I tried to make drawings of people and things."

Although Oberlin College and its namesake village actively promoted racial harmony, Lewis became the focus of a racially motivated controversy in 1862, when two white female students accused her of poisoning them. Lewis subsequently was beaten by vigilantes. John Mercer Langston—a prominent lawyer also of African-American and Native American heritage—came to her defense and she was exonerated because of insufficient evidence. A year later she was accused of stealing art supplies. Despite her second acquittal, the college refused to allow her to graduate.

Shortly thereafter, Lewis moved to Boston, in part because her brother believed that the city's resources could support her interest in becoming a sculptor. Upon her arrival, she was greatly inspired by seeing Richard Greenough's life-size statue of Benjamin Franklin at City Hall. Using letters of introduction from Oberlin College, Lewis met William Lloyd Garrison, the abolitionist writer, who introduced her to Edward Brackett, a well-known portrait sculptor at that time. Brackett lent Lewis fragments of sculptures to copy in clay and critiqued her early efforts, then a customary alternative to academic training. Equipped only with this limited preparation, Lewis began to establish herself in Boston as a sculptor, and was listed as such in the city's directories in 1864 and 1865. According to these same directories, she worked in the Studio Building, where African-American painter Edward Mitchell Bannister and other artists maintained studios during the 1860s. To date, however, the extent of her interaction with this artistic community and specifically with Bannister has not been established.

Exposure to Edward Brackett's sculpture and the impact of the Civil War combined to determine Lewis' first sculptures—medallion portraits of white anti-slavery leaders and Civil War heroes, which she modeled in plaster and clay. She also attempted her first portrait bust during this period. Its subject was Colonel Robert Gould Shaw, the young Boston Brahmin who was killed as he led his all-black battalion in battle against Confederate forces. The city's liberal white community subsequently lionized Shaw. Lewis's bust of Shaw, and most of her early efforts, are still unlocated, despite the fact

Raised as "Wildfire" by Chippewa Indians, Edmonia Lewis was the first major sculptress of African-American and Native American heritage. She spent most of her adult life working in Europe. (SCHOMBURG CENTER)

that she made numerous plaster copies to help finance her move to Europe in 1865.

Lewis initially considered living in England because of its active abolitionist community. Following visits to London, Paris, and Florence, however, she established her studio in Rome during the winter of 1865–66. She was barely twenty years old at the time. Her interest in Italy and the decision to settle in Rome were not unique. Since the 1820s, American sculptors led by the example of Hiram Powers had been attracted by Italy's venerable artistic traditions, classical sculpture, abundant marble, and inexpensive artisan labor. Moreover, American women artists and writers considered Rome particularly congenial because it disregarded the sexist restrictions of their Anglo-American world.

Settled into a large studio near the Piazza Barberini, Lewis quickly began learning to carve in marble, experimenting with the challenge of creating full-length figures. To increase her skills, she followed the common

Edmonia Lewis' Forever Free *(1867) captures the powerful emotion of emancipation. The title adapts phrasing from Abraham Lincoln's Emancipation Proclamation.* (SCHOMBURG CENTER)

practice of copying classical sculptures in public collections. Proving adept in this direction, Lewis made copies of classical statuary, which she regularly sold to Americans who visited artists' studios in Italy as part of their European tours.

Lewis, however, shunned other customs of the art community. She avoided instruction or criticism from her peers and refused to hire native artisans to enlarge her small clay and plaster models and to carve the final marbles. Fierce pride in her heritage and the desire to achieve legitimacy as a sculptor persuaded her that her sculptures would not be considered original if she did not execute them herself. This attitude limited her production, but to date research documents forty-six different compositions. She may have done more, but in any case most of the actual works are still unlocated.

Commissions for small portrait busts in terra cotta and marble became Lewis' most reliable means of support. Patrons in Boston, especially prominent white male abolitionists and social reformers, were her most regular clients, and she shipped work to them. She also recognized the American market for "conceits" or "fancy pieces" — sculptures that used mythological children to convey human, often sentimental themes. *Poor Cupid* (or *Love Ensnared*) of 1876 (National Museum of American Art, Washington, D.C.) is probably her best-known effort in this vein.

Financial security, however, was not Lewis' principal concern. Slavery and racial oppression were the central issues of her sculptures, a focus greatly facilitated by her distance from America. It also distinguished Lewis from her fellow sculptors in Italy, who derived their ideas and images from classical literature, history, and art. Between 1866 and 1883, Lewis created at least six major figurative groups featuring either African Americans or Native Americans. *The Freed Woman and Her Child (1866; location unknown) and Forever Free* (1867; **Howard University**, Washington, D.C.), for example, both capture the powerful emotion of emancipation; the latter's title actually adapts phrasing from Abraham Lincoln's Emancipation Proclamation.

Lewis's exploration of the black figure reached as far as the African continent, when in 1868 she sculpted *Hagar*, a marble also known as *Hagar in the Wilderness* (National Museum of American Art collection). Egyptians such as Hagar, the biblical maidservant to Abraham, were considered black by the nineteenth-century western world, and in this sculpture, Lewis included the issues of gender and women's rights in her interpretation of oppression.

She also reacted against the period's negative stereotypes of Native Americans as murderous savages or a dying primitive race. Eschewing the direct social commentary and ethnographic accuracy of her black figures, however, Lewis took a more literary, sentimental approach when carving her small-scale Indian groups such as *Old Arrow Maker* of 1872, also known as *The Old Arrow Maker and His Daughter* (National Museum of American Art). Lewis was greatly influenced by the narrative poem, "The Song of Hiawatha" (1855) by Henry Wadsworth Longfellow. He posed for his portrait bust, which she began carving in Rome in 1869 and finished in 1871 (Harvard University portrait collection, Cambridge, Massachusetts).

Lewis' career in Rome coincided with those of other American women artists and writers who gathered around the neoclassical sculptor Harriet Hosmer and actress Charlotte Cushman. Both women welcomed Lewis to Rome, and it is widely believed that their influential circle greatly benefitted her. Social reformer Lydia Maria Child, one of Lewis' longtime patrons in Boston, nonetheless wondered if American artists abroad would free themselves of "American prejudice" to help Lewis when she was deeply in debt. By 1865 it had became evident that Cushman and others would not come to her aid.

During the height of her popularity in the late 1860s and 1870s, Lewis' studio was a frequent stop for those who visited American artists abroad. She was also well received during her several return visits to the United States between 1870 and 1876 when she exhibited works in Chicago, California, Boston, and Philadelphia. Perhaps the American high point of her career came in 1876 when her ambitious sculpture, *The Death of Cleopatra* (Forest Park Historical Society, Forest Park, Illinois) was exhibited and awarded a medal at the Centennial Exposition in Philadelphia.

From the outset, however, Lewis was considered "an interesting novelty . . . in a city [Rome] where all our surroundings are of the olden time." Dressed in her rakish red cap and mannish costumes, Lewis captivated both Europeans and Americans, who regularly described her as childlike, charming, and picturesque. In 1863, she had already recognized the pitfalls of her triple heritage as a black Indian woman when she asked that her sculpture not be praised solely because of her background. Unfortunately, Lewis represented a tempting opportunity to those in Boston and Rome eager to demonstrate their support of human rights, and the encouragement she subsequently received ranged from sincere belief in her talents to well-meant but misguided indulgence.

Equally diverse, if not confused, were the interpretations of Lewis' appearance. Some described her hair as being black and straight like an Indian's and associated her complexion and willfully proud character with her mother's ancestry, while others believed that her facial features and hair reflected her father's background. Lewis herself was amused by a Bostonian's observation that "as her father had been a 'man of color' it would have seemed as though she ought to have been a painter, had it not been that her mother was a 'Chippe-e-way' Indian, and that made it natural for her to be a sculptor."

In 1883, Lewis received her last major commission, *Adoration of the Magi* (location unknown), for a church in Baltimore, no doubt a reflection of her conversion to Catholicism in Rome in 1868. After 1883, demand for her work declined, as it did for neoclassical sculpture in general. Her presence in Rome was reported in 1911, but the activities of her final decades are barely documented and the date and place of her death are unknown even today.

Following a visit to Lewis' studio, an anonymous American writer wondered in 1867 if "the youthful Indian girl" would create a "distinctive if not original style in sculpture." Lewis indeed represented a fresh approach to the neoclassical sculpture tradition, injecting as she did timely yet universal human rights issues and developing a more emotional, naturalistic style than her contemporaries.

LYNDA ROSCOE HARTIGAN

M

Maynard, Valerie (1937–)

Valerie Maynard enjoys working in various media ranging from prints and collage to gouache and sculpture. The dominant theme in her work is communication, emanating from her philosophy of "forming an aesthetic which I hope speaks to the seriousness of my message and hopefully my audience sees the irony and wit and humor along with the cutting edge of my work."

Born in Harlem, New York, Maynard began her career as an artist when she was a high school senior, exhibiting as one of the outdoor artists in the Greenwich Village section of New York. By 1959, as she turned twenty-one, Maynard lived and worked among artists of the "East Village." Through a part-time job with the Parks Department, she formed friendships with actors and actresses who encouraged her abilities as a designer of costumes, posters, and stage sets. She was very prolific during those years, producing many drawings and paintings daily.

When her brother was incarcerated in 1968 for a crime that he did not commit, Maynard worked tirelessly in his defense, but she also remained focused on her art until his release in 1974. During this time, she taught printmaking at the Studio Museum in Harlem to groups from ages eight to 80. While spending a summer in Vermont, she began a new facet of her art career—sculpture. As she recalled, "At Vermont, I began carving a piece called *Justice Blinded* and it was based on my brother's situation. . . . I knew then I was a sculptor. . . . One turns to sculpture because one tries to draw around paper—to see people as sculptures. . . . Artists are constantly trying to make the message clearer and I'd work until I couldn't say anything more in a given medium. Now I'm with form and I hope it'll always be that way."

Maynard studied painting, drawing, and printmaking at the Museum of Modern Art and the New York School for Social Research, New York City. She received her M.A. degree from Goddard College, Plainfield, Vermont in 1977.

In 1974, Maynard created *I See the Beauty In You*, a ceramic sculpture mural for the facade of the Social Services Center for the Community Association of East Harlem Triangle. A two-year project involving Maynard's talents as a designer and incorporating her feeling about being a Harlem resident, it was a monumental achievement and a personal tribute to that community. Maynard sought to create a single visual statement which by its theme and execution would be timeless, reflecting the history of the Harlem community and the progress of African Americans.

Her spray-painted acrylics-on-paper series, *No Apartheid*, of approximately 250 images, have been created over the last several years and shown at the Guadalupe Theater Gallery in San Antonio, Texas, and at the Hammonds House Gallery in Atlanta,

215

Sculptor Geraldine McCullough has exhibited widely. She is shown here working on her 1973 piece Our King. *(TRITOBIA BENJAMIN)*

Georgia. Maynard has been a resident fellow at the McDowell Colony, Petersborough, New Hampshire, the Women's Studio Workshop, Rosendale, New York, and twice as artist-in-residence at the Blue Mountain Center, New York.

A strict disciplinarian in the studio, Maynard has taught printmaking and sculpture at **Howard University**, Washington, D.C.; Jersey City State College, New Jersey; Northeastern University, Chicago; Baltimore School of the Arts, Maryland; and the College of the Virgin Islands, St. Thomas. In 1980, she was both a finalist in the National Sculpture Competition and honored with the Bedford-Stuyvesant Arts Award. On Commission, she created the Communica-

tions Excellence to Black Audiences (CEBA) Award statuette. The subject of several films, Maynard has exhibited throughout the United States and abroad in Stockholm, Sweden; Cali, Colombia; Lagos, Nigeria; and Berlin, Germany.

TRITOBIA BENJAMIN

McCullough, Geraldine (1922–)

Geraldine McCullough became the subject of an interesting and unusual success story when in 1964, she won the prestigious George D. Widener Memorial Gold Medal at the 159th annual exhibition of the Pennsylvania Academy of the Fine Arts. The award was an artistic coup for the sculptor; it was the first time she had shown in a major national exhibition, and the Academy exhibition was one traditionally dominated by invited established artists. The prize-winning work was McCullough's powerful 250-pound welded metal called *Phoenix*. The sculpture suggests several views of a mutilated form struggling to free itself from its moorings, surging against the force that tries to smother the fire out of which it is being reborn.

A native of Edinburgh, Arkansas, Geraldine moved to Chicago with her parents when she was very young. She attended the Frances E. Willard grade school and then the Hyde Park High School, where she was active in art organizations and as the artist for the school newspaper. She married young, then entered the Chicago Art Institute to study painting and art education. She graduated in 1948, and received a masters of art education from the Institute in 1955.

Her initial interests were expressed in abstract painting, which she pursued after-hours as an art teacher at Chicago's

Wendell Phillips High School. She won a few prizes but was the first to admit that a promising career as a painter appeared remote. Then, when a young apprentice (Richard Hunt, who is now an internationally renowned sculptor) encouraged her to make small sculptures, McCullough began sculpting by welding bits of scrap metal into small objects. Initially, she made simple wire constructions. Later, assisted by her husband, himself a journeyman welder, she began working in solid metals. He taught her the rudiments of welding, purchased tanks, torches, pipes, and other gear which the couple had installed in their high-ceilinged home, a converted coach house in suburban Oak Park, Illinois.

Since receiving the Widener Award in 1964, McCullough has been prolific as an artist. Her works have been on exhibit in museums and galleries throughout the United States, and she has received numerous commissions. Perhaps the best known among them is *Our King* (1973), located at the entrance of the Martin Luther King, Jr., Plaza on West Madison Street and Kedzie Avenue, in Chicago, the scene of massive rioting after King's death. The controversial work was a seven-foot high formulated bronze interpretation of the leader presented in the ceremonial dress of a king of Benin, one of the great West African kingdoms which existed from antiquity until the end of the nineteenth century. The dress includes a crown, anklets, a tunic, and other adornments of Beninese chiefs of state during formal court ceremonies. Because of King's nonviolent philosophy, the artist included a broken sword and a Tibetan prayer wheel, held in each hand, and a dove of peace which hovers symbolically above the head. The portrait of King is a faithful rendering; the statue weighs just under a ton.

In a more playful mood, McCullough's *The World's Biggest Mousetrap*, commissioned for the Village of Oak Park, Illinois (1976), is a 20-foot high abstract welded metal inspired, as the artist says, "by that old saying 'If you build a better mousetrap, people will beat a path to your door.'" Other commissioned work can be found at the Johnson Publishing Company, Chicago, Illinois, *(Oracle)*; the Maywood Civic Center Plaza, Maywood, Illinois (*Phoenix Rising*); the DuSable Museum of African American History, Chicago (*DuSable's Chicago*); and Oak Park, Illinois.

Mccullough has exhibited frequently in the Chicago area; the San Jose Museum of Art, California; the Brooklyn Museum of Art, New York; Cornell University, Ithaca, New York; Washington, D.C.; and Atlanta, Georgia. She is Professor of Art and Chair of the Department of Art at Rosary College, River Forest, Illinois.

TRITOBIA HAYES BENJAMIN

Moutoussamy-Ashe, Jeanne (1951–)

"Research on black women is a difficult task, but . . . historical research on the black woman photographer seemed impossible," stated Jeanne Moutoussamy-Ashe in the introduction to her book *Viewfinders* (1986). Nonetheless, she devoted herself to that task in the mid–1980s, producing a work that documents the lives and work of black female photographers as far back as 1860. Even prior to the publication of *Viewfinders*, she had visually recorded the cultural heritage of the South Carolina coastal region in the book *Daufauskie Island* (1982) and had developed a series of lectures and a traveling exhibit around that photo essay.

Jeanne Moutoussamy was born in Chicago, Illinois, in 1951. Both of her parents were active professionals in the visual arts and nurtured their daughter's interest and talent. She moved to New York City to attend Cooper Union, where she earned a B.F.A. in photography in 1975. She then worked in television photojournalism for both WNBC and WNEW in New York and for *PM Magazine*. In addition to her books, she has had several individual and group exhibits in New York City, Boston, Chicago, Houston, Washington, D.C., Detroit, Los Angeles, London, Florence, and Paris and has contributed photographs to numerous magazines and newspapers, including *Life*, *Smithsonian*, *Sports Illustrated*, *People Weekly*, *Ebony*, *Black Enterprise*, *World Tennis*, *Self*, and *Essence*. She has also done official photo-portraits of several U.S. cabinet members, including **Patricia Roberts Harris**. Her work has received awards and is in the permanent collections of several museums.

Moutoussamy-Ashe's husband, Arthur Ashe, died in 1993. She lives in New York City with their daughter Camera. Much of her current work focuses on the black family. She is a founding member of the Black Family Cultural Exchange, a group of African-American women from New York City and nearby Connecticut who have organized a series of successful book fairs for and about black children. Profits are contributed to scholarship funds and to book funds for local community centers.

ADELE LOGAN ALEXANDER

O

Owens-Hart, Winifred (1949–)

The ceramic sculpture of Winnie Owens-Hart addresses the issues of injustice observed in daily life. Distinguished as one of America's leading female ceramicists, Owens-Hart uses her artistry as a didactic socio-political tool, drawing attention to problems of racism and sexism. Born in Washington, D.C., Owens-Hart has been called a "messenger in clay," a community artist who uses herself as a medium, a transmitter through which the African-American experience can be heard.

As a young child, Owens-Hart was fascinated with African culture and dreamed of visiting her ancestral homeland. After graduating from the Philadelphia College of Art where she majored in crafts and studied metal- and wood-working, printmaking, painting, and philosophy, she taught ceramics at the Ile-Ife Black Humanitarian Center. There she was introduced to Yoruban (Nigerian) culture. She immediately began to incorporate their images into her ceramic work. As a student, she created utilitarian vessels to supplement her income.

Owens-Hart learned of the new black-consciousness underway at **Howard University** in Washington, D.C., and she applied to the graduate program. Her master's thesis on ceramic drums drew upon the recently learned imagery of the Yoruba. After graduation, she studied at the Haystack Mountain School of Crafts in Maine.

At the suggestion of Nigerian sculptor Agbo Folarin, Owens-Hart visited the women's pottery village in Ipetumodu. She surprised and delighted these female potters when she revealed her knowledge of their technique—working without the potter's wheel, kiln, or chemicals. In 1977, she received a grant from the National Endowment for the Arts for an apprenticeship with the Nigerian potters; there she learned other techniques different from Western ceramicists. She combined wheel-throwing and hand-built shapes using African motifs and patterns in her utilitarian pottery. Eventually, however, Owens-Hart felt the limitations of functional objects. "There were a lot of things I wanted to express," she said, "so I drifted away from cups, bowls, and plates and started making statements in clay that deal with being an African American in this time and place."

In the late 1970s, Owens-Hart began the series *Scream . . . You're Black and In America*, a reaction to the racism and negativity existing in the United States. As she stated "the Scream series symbolized how I feel . . . like screaming sometimes about the way I have been treated in this country because of my color. And when I say 'I' . . . I mean all African Americans."

Owens-Hart used her own body in the series on African-American women; she could not find a willing model. She insists, however, that the series is not autobiographical but symbolic. *Initiations: African*

American (1978), the best-known work in this series represents, on one side, the African woman before she was enslaved and brought to America; the other side represents the acculturation of the African woman in America with skin color variations from dark to beige, illustrating the mixture with other races.

In 1980, Owens-Hart traveled to Haiti as a CARE consultant; in 1982 she was a ceramic instructor at the Haystack Mountain School of Crafts. In 1989-90, she began to conduct research for a book, *Black on Brown: African American Clay Workers and Their Impact on American Culture* while a James Renwick Fellow in American Crafts at the Renwick Gallery in Washington, D.C. Her studies and research continued as a visiting scholar at the Smithsonian Institute (1988–89, 1990–91) and at the National Museum of American Art (1992–93). She has participated in numerous group and solo exhibitions, and served as artist-in-residence throughout the United States. The National Museum of Women in the Arts honored her with a lifetime achievement award in 1993. Owens-Hart is currently professor of ceramics at Howard University, where she began teaching in 1976.

TRITOBIA HAYES BENJAMIN

P

Pindell, Howardena (1943–)

Howardena Pindell has made significant contributions to the visual arts as well as to scholarship on racism in the art world. She was born on April 14, 1943, in Philadelphia. Her art training began at the age of eight years old when she was enrolled in free Saturday morning classes at the Fleischer School. In 1965 she received a B.F.A. from Boston University's School of Fine and Applied Arts and in 1967 an M.F.A. from Yale University's School of Art and Architecture. After graduating from Yale she moved to New York City where she began working at the Museum of Modern Art as an exhibition assistant. She held three other curatorial titles there before leaving the museum in 1979 to teach at the State University of New York at Stony Brook.

Pindell was trained as a figurative painter at Yale, where she produced urban landscapes and studied skeletal forms. While she was in New York City, the necessity of maintaining full-time employment impeded her art-making because she could not devote as much time to it. By the time she finished work in the evenings there was very little natural light, so she would experiment with color, light, and texture using dots and grids, and because of space constraints her work remained small and abstract.

Pindell's distinctive abstract style was inspired by many sources throughout the 1970s. She initiated this style by making stencils or templates of punched-out holes and then spraying paint through them. The product of so many hole punches was bags and bags of tiny dots, which she began to add to the surfaces of her works. In addition, she numbered many of these dots and then arranged them randomly over an underlying grid of graph paper. In these numbered works she was toying with notions of distance, size, mass, quantity, and identification. The use of numbers was partly influenced by her father's odometer books in which he would keep track of mileage on family road trips, and by Pindell's experiments in surface light and shadow, randomness, and interpretation. She chose numbers for their visual quality instead of their associative value.

The unnumbered dot works became studies in accumulation of color, space, and surface texture, tension, and contrast. The effects were three-dimensional and sculptural. The surfaces were built upon a regimented grid which accentuated the juxtaposition of the random and the rigid. Pindell used the grid as a metaphor for technological society with its square computers, televisions, and vertical and horizontal format. Her abstract works of the 1970s can be categorized as having a very tactile quality, and clearly deal with issues of confinement, control, order, and the elusive quality of boundaries. As Pindell began to move away from the strict confines of the stretched canvas, and still utilizing the basic structure of the grid, she began to experiment with sewing her canvases. The sewing added an internal geometry and tension as well as a physical quality.

Pindell's abstract works of the 1970s were indicative of many of her personal struggles during this time. They were reflective of issues that affected her experience as a black woman artist. The racism, sexism, discrimination, exclusion, isolation, and rejection that she experienced in her life translated into an obsessive quality in her works that was her means of escape and avoidance. The tedious process of her work was meditative and the aesthetic quality of her product was a means to deal with her anger by making everything beautiful.

Ironically, this abstraction in itself created problems for her because it placed her work in a limited category. Since she was not using explicit political imagery in these works, they were considered by black art institutions to be invalid. She found temporary acceptance in the women's movement and helped to found a collective alternative exhibition space for women artists called Artists-in-Residence Gallery. Still, she was frustrated with a primarily white women's movement that did not address issues relevant to her situation as a black woman.

These factors, along with her feelings of powerlessness to help other black artists and women artists despite her position at the museum, led to disillusionment and to the realization that her work was masking her pain and anger. Almost simultaneous with these recognitions, her move toward open political activism was reinforced by a black art community protest of a show at Artists Space in New York City in 1979 entitled "Nigger Drawings." Pindell was active in this protest and her own outrage led to a decisive change in her visual imagery. Her video work *Free, White and 21* (1980) seems to mark this change and the beginning of more explicitly political content in many of her

works. In this important twelve-minute work, Pindell focuses on the image of herself as she recounts experiences in her life that clearly demonstrate racial prejudice and reactions to skin color.

Along with the changes that took place in 1979, Pindell was also in a serious car accident from which she experienced memory loss. This experience led her to use artistic production as an exercise in memory. She began to use the postcards and photographs she had collected in her extensive travels to recreate her impressions of places she had visited. From this time, memory and personal experience became integral parts of her artistic vision.

In 1982, Pindell traveled to Japan on a United States–Japan Friendship Commission Creative Artist grant for about eight months. The works inspired by her experience in Japan are more circular and organic in shape than her earlier works and they tend to focus on nature and landscape while reflecting the rigidity she found in that culture. The work *Hiroshima Disguised: Japan* (1982) is asymmetrical, oddly shaped, and maze-like. The surface is built up so that its texture resembles a Japanese ornamental dry garden and is reminiscent of her dot works. It consists of ten separate canvases arrayed like the islands and its pale lavender tone resembles ash. The surface is embedded with shattered metal and cut glass and contains small photographic images that make reference to the devastating effects of nuclear war. This work is characteristic of her near-far style which, when viewed from afar, gives the impression of abstraction while upon close scrutiny revealing its political content.

Pindell traveled to India in 1984 on a National Endowment for the Arts painting fellowship. Her works from this period became more sinuous and S-shaped, like coiled snakes or flowing rivers. They have a meditative quality and reflect a spirituality with an undercurrent of poverty and suffering. The works from India and Japan resemble travelogues of her personal physical and emotional journeys.

Pindell's *Autobiography* series presents a coming together of her past focuses and a distinct emphasis on personal identity and self-definition. This series focuses on key issues, such as notions of self, racial heritage, women of color, hierarchical imagery, omission, appropriation, and stereotyping. These works utilize near-far contrast in both canvas and photographic mediums. They deal with public as well as private spheres and both comment and reflect upon issues of history, culture, politics, personal experience, and identity.

The Autobiography series, for which she received a College Art Association award in 1990, and her extensive published research on art world racism attest to her prominence as a key black woman artist. Her work addresses multifaceted aspects of her experience and her multiple consciousness as a black woman. Through her work she expresses her rejection of superimposed categories and definitions and emphasizes that black women define themselves in diverse manners in response to their own personal experience. Her visual and written works battle against the silencing of people of color by omission and promote inclusive and egalitarian practices in art history and in the art world at large.

NADINE WASSERMAN

Piper, Adrian (1948–)

Adrian Piper is a philosopher, writer, educator, and important conceptual and performance artist. She is internationally recognized for work that challenges racism, sexism, and xenophobia at every level by means of verbal presentations and visual installations in a variety of media.

Piper made her entrance as an artist in the early 1970s, with the *Catalysts* series, performances of antisocial but nonviolent acts in the streets and other public places. During these activities she wore masks and alienating disguises (such as dirty clothes) to emphasize her "otherness" and prevent communication between herself and spectators. She also sometimes assumed the identity of the androgynous *Mythic Being*, a sometimes hostile or threatening person with reflective sunglasses and a pencil mustache who allowed her to explore and/or escape other aspects of herself.

In the late 1970s Piper created *Three Political Self-Portraits*, posters with texts in which she discussed her own experiences of gender, race, and class conflicts. She grew up in an upper-middle-class family in Harlem, where her neighbors called her "paleface" and a hostile fifth-grade teacher in the private school she attended on scholarship asked her mother, "Does she know she's colored?" She attended New York's School of Visual Arts (where a professor asked a friend of hers, "Is she black? She's so aggressive.") and received a B.A. from City College of New York; she went on to earn an M.A. and a Ph.D. in philosophy from Harvard University.

Beginning in 1983 Piper traveled with a series of performances called *Funk Lessons*, in which she spoke about the origins of Funk and then gave dancing lessons to the audience. The highly effective performances used music and dance to break down barriers of difference. In 1986 she began an ongoing group of charcoal drawings layered over *New York Times* articles on racial topics or over advertisements; collectively called *Vanilla Nightmare*, the images depict powerful African Americans dominating whites in political and sexual situations. That year Piper also created *My Calling (Card) #1*, politely subversive printed rectangles that could be used to confront racism in situations where she was not perceived as African-American. The card began, "Dear Friend, I am black. I am sure you did not realize this when you made/laughed at/agreed with that racist remark. . . ." It ended, "I regret any discomfort my presence is causing you, just as I am sure you regret the discomfort your racism is causing me."

Piper has continued to explore social transformation through the self, articulating rage with exquisite politeness in installations such as *Cornered* (1988), in which the artist challenges—from a video screen in a corner behind an overturned table—the audience's unexamined assumptions about race. Currently a professor of philosophy at Wellesley College, Piper has received awards from the National Endowment for the Arts (1979, 1982), Art Matters, Inc. (1987), John Simon Guggenheim Memorial Fellowship (1989), New York State Council on the Arts (1989) and Awards in the Visual Arts (1990). She has had numerous solo gallery exhibitions and has presented performances at many museums and schools in the United States and Europe. Piper's work has been shown in many group exhibitions in galleries and in museums such as the New Museum of Contemporary Art and Museum of Modern Art in New York, the Seattle Art Museum, Chicago Museum of Contemporary Art, Cincinnati Art Museum, Stadtisches Museum, Leverheusen, Germany, and the Musée d'Art Moderne, Paris.

NANCY GROVE

Pogue, Stephanie (1944–)

Grounded in traditional art scholarship, the works of Stephanie Pogue have explored a number of themes in the wide range of media offered in the discipline. Working primarily with color etchings from the beginning of her career in the late 1960s, Pogue explored mythology, landscapes, semi-abstract compositions, and the human figure. In the early 1970s, using the color viscosity technique, her work moved away from a naturalistic treatment of subject matter and became more abstract. Color and texture were the focus of her compositions.

Born in Shelby, North Carolina, Pogue received a B.F.A. from **Howard University**; an M.F.A. from Cranbrook Academy of Art; and an M.A. degree in art history from Vanderbilt University. She has been consistently focused on exploring the breadth and depths of graphic arts.

In 1966, Pogue traveled throughout Europe, where she studied early Christian and Byzantine mosaics and paintings. Her prints reflected her knowledge and fascination with this artistry, creating semi-abstract compositions with jewel-like qualities and symbols similar to the work of that era. During the summer of 1981, under the auspices of a Fulbright-Hayes Fellowship, Pogue traveled throughout India for the purpose of studying the architecture and sculpture of that country. Pogue recalls that "it was just about the most exciting experience I have had—one is constantly bombarded by the light of the bright sun, exotic sights and sounds, and breathtaking vistas of ancient temples." After her travels in India, her color etchings expanded to include architectural elements (windows, doors, and passageways) and she began to use the color black for dramatic contrast. Works from this period rely on a recognizable and more naturalistic treatment of forms, but retain an abstract quality not present in the prints of the late sixties.

In transitional pieces begun in the late eighties, Pogue expanded her work to include egg tempera, mixed media, and collage with handmade paperwork. More recently, she has begun to explore planar relationships and the "sense of freedom" resulting from the release of her creations from the two-dimensional format. This interest has involved a third and final consideration—exploration of various combinations of material in what is for her a new and nontraditional manner: tearing prints and reassembling them, making handmade paper forms, and combining egg tempera, wax crayons, and pastels with the reassembled prints and handmade paperworks.

Her focus in 1989 and the early nineties was with monotypes, exploring the inner psychological self, evoking such titles as *Self Portrait: Venus*; *Self Portrait: Off-Balance*; *Self-Portrait: Awakening*, and others, which examine her inner being and self revelations.

Pogue has participated in numerous solo and group exhibitions throughout the United States, and in Japan, Germany, Belgium, and Poland. Her prints are in the collections of the Whitney Museum of American Art, the Studio Museum in Harlem, as well as the Xian College of Art, China. She is professor of art and chairperson of the Department of Art at the University of Maryland, College Park.

TRITOBIA HAYES BENJAMIN

Powers, Harriet (1837–1911)

There is only one way to understand the significance of Harriet Powers, and that is to look at her quilts (one of which is pictured here). Their originality and joyful spirit cannot be described. On seeing them, one experiences an undeniable feeling that this woman was an artist.

Harriet Powers was born a slave on October 29, 1837, in Georgia. Her maiden name is unknown, as are the circumstances of her birth and childhood. She was married to Armstead Powers and had three children, two of whom were born in slavery; the third was born in 1866, just after the end of the Civil War. Most of this information comes from the 1870 census, which also states that Powers's occupation was keeping house and that her husband was a farmhand.

The family was fairly prosperous. They owned animals and tools and, sometime in the 1880s, bought two two-acre plots of land. In 1873, they were living in the Buck Branch, Winterville, district of Clarke County, Georgia. At other times between 1870 and 1894, when Armstead seems to have left the farm, they lived in the Sandy Creek district. Harriet Powers remained in that district, living an independent and reasonably comfortable life until her death in 1911.

Powers' existence and her quilts are known to us because of Jennie Smith, a white artist from Athens, Georgia, who was head of the art department of the Lucy Cobb School. Smith first saw a Powers quilt at the Athens Cotton Fair of 1886. She was enormously impressed and resolved at once to find its maker. She visited Powers at her farm and offered to buy the quilt, but Powers refused to sell. Then, in 1890, the Powers family went through a very difficult time financially. A year later they would have to sell off one of their pieces of land. Smith received word that she could now buy the quilt. Unfortunately, she was unable to do so. The next year, Smith sent word to Powers that she was ready to buy the quilt if it was still for sale. At the end of this back-and-forth communication, Powers brought the quilt, carefully wrapped, to Smith's home and handed it over in return for five dollars. Before she left, she related to Smith the story of each of the quilt's fifteen squares. The quilt depicts events of her lifetime that Powers considered significant, such as a dark day apparently caused by forest fires in New York and Canada. Smith wrote down and preserved what she had been told. Powers returned a number of times to Smith's house to visit her quilt.

It was Smith's plan to exhibit the quilt in Atlanta at the Cotton States Exposition of 1895. The black community had raised

Born into slavery, Harriet Powers went on to live an independent and reasonably comfortable life, and to create quilts characterized by originality and a joyful spirit. The quilt illustrated here is The Creation of the Animals, *dated 1895–98 and made in Athens, Georgia, of pieced and appliquéd cotton with plain and metallic yarns.* (BEQUEST OF MAXIM KAROLIK; COURTESY, MUSEUM OF FINE ARTS, BOSTON)

$10,000 for a special building at the exposition, and there were exhibits from eleven southern states. Powers' name is not on the list of exhibitors, but there is evidence that her quilt was there; in 1898, a group of faculty wives from Atlanta University commissioned Powers to create a second quilt as a gift for Reverend Charles Cuthbert Hall, president of Union Theological Seminary.

The quilt owned by Smith passed, at her death, into the hands of a friend, Hal Heckman. He kept the quilt for some time and then gave it to the Smithsonian Institution, where is now on exhibit. The quilt owned by Hall was inherited by his son, Reverend Basil Douglas Hall, who sold it to collector Maxim Karolik. Karolik gave it to the Museum of Fine Arts in Boston in 1964. Entitled *The Creation of the Animals*, it is reproduced here. Powers dictated her explanation of this quilt to Jennie Smith as well.

Looking at these two quilts today causes profoundly mixed feelings. It is wonderful to see the work of an artist preserved, but it is impossible not to feel great sadness that Harriet Powers was denied the opportunity to fulfill her potential.

KATHLEEN THOMPSON

Prophet, Nancy Elizabeth (1890–1960)

Nancy Elizabeth Prophet was a master sculptor who studied in Europe and taught at Atlanta University and Spelman College. Prophet was born March 19, 1890, apparently the only child of William H. Prophet and Rose Walker Prophet, in Providence, Rhode Island. Her father was employed by the city. Her mother was a housewife. Prophet attended public school in Providence and as she advanced through the system, she exhibited an exceptional aptitude for art. Encouraged by her teachers and friends, she entered the renowned Rhode Island School of Design, often working as a domestic to pay her tuition.

After graduation, Prophet lived for a brief period of time in New York City. This was the age of the Harlem Renaissance, and she wanted to go to France where she could study with master teachers and exhibit her work in the salons of Paris. With financial assistance from Gertrude Vanderbilt Whitney, Prophet went to Paris in 1922. She studied at l'Ecole Nationale des Beaux Arts from 1922 to 1925. While in Europe, Prophet came to the attention of Henry Tanner, who was so impressed with her talent that he recommended her for the Harmon Foundation prize. She won this prestigious award, which included money she could use to support herself while she continued her studies.

Prophet returned to the United States in 1932 and was received in Newport, Rhode Island, society as a master sculptor. One year later, on the advice of her friend W. E. B. DuBois, she accepted a teaching position at Spelman College. By 1939, however, she had left Spelman and was working in the art department at Atlanta University. Prophet ostensibly realized that there was virtually no opportunity for her, as a black woman, to become a part of the art community in Atlanta. And so, in 1945, she returned to Providence, where she expected to make a comeback. Unfortunately, she had lost contact with many of her supporters over the years. She could not obtain the financial backing needed to allow her to live as a sculptor. Having no other means of support, Prophet went to work as a domestic, just as she had done as a student twenty years earlier.

Prophet's most productive years were between 1920 and 1930, and she received

Although her work was exhibited at Paris salons and at the Whitney Sculpture Biennial, Nancy Elizabeth Prophet ended her life working as a domestic, and few of her works survive. (NATIONAL ARCHIVES)

several awards; for example, her *Head of a Negro* earned the Harmon Foundation prize for best sculpture in 1930. In 1932, at the annual meeting of the Newport Association, she won first prize (the Richard Greenbough Prize) for her sculpture *Discontent*, but because she was not a member of the association, she was initially ineligible to receive the award. The association hurriedly elected her to membership minutes before the show opened. This was a special honor for Prophet, because the exhibition included over 200 works by forty-one artists. Prophet's three other head carvings at this exhibit received excellent reviews from the judges.

Her work was exhibited in the Paris August Salons from 1924 to 1927 and at the Salon d'Automne in 1931 and 1932. In the United States, Prophet's work was included in group exhibitions throughout the 1930s at the Harmon Foundation and the Whitney Sculpture Biennial. In 1978, her pieces were part of the "Four from Providence" exhibit at the Bannister Gallery of Rhode Island College. Other group exhibitions include the Bellevue Art Museum and the Art Association of America tour in 1985. Prophet's only known one-person exhibit was in 1945 at the Providence Public Library.

Prophet sculpted in both marble and stone. Her surviving sculptures are heads carved in wood in a style described as "stark, aggressive" and "naturalistic and non-sentimental." Her subjects were always black. Prophet's best-known sculpture is *Congolaise,* which she completed in 1930. It is not known who posed for this piece or for any of her other works, or even if she used a model. *Congolaise* is described as very similar to a Masai tribesman, and this strong African influence is characteristic of the heads she sculpted. Prophet's other works include *Silence* and *Head in Ebony.* She eventually destroyed some of her pieces, and others rotted out-of-doors because she could not afford to pay for storage. Consequently, very few of her works survive. Some of those that do are housed in the Black Heritage Society of Rhode Island in Providence, the Rhode Island School of Design, and the Whitney Museum of American Art in New York City.

Elizabeth Prophet died in 1960 in Providence in poverty and obscurity. In her lifetime she overcame the barriers of sex and race to become a respected sculptor, whose surviving works are a testimony to her special talent and race consciousness.

GLORIA V. WARREN

R

Ringgold, Faith (1930–)

"I don't want the story of my life to be about racism, though it has played a major role," wrote Faith Ringgold in her recent autobiography. "I want my story to be about attainment, love of family, art, helping others, courage, values, dreams coming true." From her earliest years in Harlem to today, when she ranks as one of America's most important and beloved artists, those have been the qualities that have shone from her life and work. She has harassed the white male art establishment as fervently as she has reached out to young black children. And she has been part of the transformation of what we in the United States call art.

Faith Ringgold was born on October 8, 1930, in Harlem. Her parents were Andrew Louis Jones, Sr., and Willie Edell Posey Jones. She was surrounded by a large and loving extended family all during her childhood. Her father, a truck driver, remained an important part of her life even after his separation from her mother, when Faith Ringgold was three years old. Her paternal grandfather was a minister, and her mother, after the separation, became a fashion designer.

Young Faith Jones suffered from asthma and so frequently stayed home from school. She and her mother went to museums, parks, or, sometimes, the legendary Apollo Theater, where she saw the great black performers, including Cab Calloway, **Billie Holiday, Ethel Waters,** and **Lena Horne.**

The family spent summers at Atlantic City, New Jersey, swimming and going to the amusement park. On hot evenings in the city, they had picnics on the roof of the apartment building, or "Tar Beach."

The Jones children—Faith, her brother Andrew, and her sister Barbara—began

An activist as well as an artist, Faith Ringgold has had her work exhibited widely and is now an enormously successful author and illustrator of children's books. (FAITH RINGGOLD)

Faith Ringgold is best known for her quilts. This 1988 work is entitled Church Picnic. (FAITH RINGGOLD; COLLECTION OF HIGH MUSEUM)

their education at an all-black public school. Then, when Faith was in the second grade, they transferred to the racially mixed P.S. 186. There, Faith's interest in and talent for art were discovered. She went to George Washington High School in Washington Heights, graduating in 1948. From there she went to City College, still in New York.

"Once I made the commitment," Ringgold wrote in her memoir *We Flew over the Bridge*, "I never for one moment doubted my ability to become an artist." She found at City College that learning the methods and techniques of art came easily to her and she was soon very competitive with the other students. There were, however, complications in her life. In 1950, at the age of twenty, she secretly married pianist Robert Earl Wallace. In January of 1952, she had the first of her two children, Michele. Before the year was out she had her second, Barbara. In 1954, she and the children moved out and she began divorce proceedings.

Ringgold graduated from City College in 1956 with a bachelor's degree in fine art and became a teacher in the New York City public schools. She then earned her master's degree. In the meantime, her mother had become one of Harlem's most successful designers, and her daughters were growing up. The family of women formed a close and caring unit. They were all stricken by grief when Ringgold's brother, Andrew, died in 1961 of a drug overdose.

In 1962, Faith married Burdette Ringgold. As a painter, she was beginning to develop the style she called "super realism" and in 1963 she completed the first of her American People series, *Between Friends*. The next year, she tried to join Spiral, a black artists' group made up of "the old men of black art"—Romare Bearden, Charlse Alston, Norman Lewis, Hale Woodruff, and others. There was only one woman in the group, Emma Amos, and Ringgold did not become the second.

In 1966, Ringgold was included in a group show entitled *Art of the American Negro*, curated by Romare Bearden for the Harlem Cultural Council. It was her first gallery appearance and was followed by an invitation to join the Spectrum Gallery. She was able to work in the gallery, which was closed during the summer months and, in

December she had her first one-person show. At this show she exhibited the entire American People series. It received high critical acclaim for its powerful depiction of racial violence and suffering. In 1970, she exhibited the Black Light series, again at Spectrum, and again the work was well received. Still, there were few sales.

During the late sixties and early seventies, Ringgold was involved in activist politics on behalf of black artists and, later, women artists. In 1971, she cofounded Where We At, an organization for black women artists. That same year, she did *For the Women's House*, a mural for the Women's House of Detention. The following year, she began to use tankas, soft cloth frames, on her paintings. Her mother helped her create the tankas, which were her first important use of fabric.

In 1973, Ringgold quit her teaching job to become a full-time artist. She continued to explore fabric as a medium in her dolls, *Family of Woman* masks, and tankas for her *Slave Rape* series of paintings. Soon she was making soft sculptures that hung from the wall and using paintings as environments for more sculptures. Her work looked less and less like standard American painting. She was exploring new ways of expressing her heritage as an African American and as a woman. Ringgold's art took another step away from the conventional in 1975 when she began using her art in performance.

Ringgold's first quilt, *Echoes of Harlem*, came out of a collaboration with her mother in 1980. However, it was not until 1983 that she made her first story quilt. As the 1980s progressed, she began to gain more serious recognition of her work, teaching at the University of California at San Diego and showing her work regularly. In 1990, the exhibit *Faith Ringgold: A Twenty-Five-Year Survey*, which opened at the Fine Arts Museum of Long Island, went on a thirteen-museum tour.

Ringgold's career as an artist entered a new phase in 1991 when she published the children's book *Tar Beach*, inspired by those summer picnics on the roof. The quilt on which the book was based was purchased and donated to the Guggenheim Museum. It is not, however, on exhibit. As a result, children from all over the country drag their parents to the museum to see it and go away puzzled and disappointed. "I don't know what it would take," says Ringgold, "to have this totally Eurocentric male-dominated Guggenheim Museum exhibit a painted story quilt by an African-American woman. So I don't hold my breath, but it was the innocence of children that initially broached the subject. And if *Tar Beach* ever hangs on the walls of the Guggenheim, it will be due to the children."

In recent years, Ringgold has written and illustrated a number of children's books. She also continues to create her story quilts. She

Passionately dedicated to fighting the racism and sexism black women face, Faith Ringgold has a strong commitment to the tradition of which she is a part. This quilt (entitled The Black Family Dinner Quilt *depicts Mary McLeod Bethune, the founder of the National Council of Negro Women, and Dorothy Height, the current president.* (FAITH RINGGOLD; COLLECTION OF THE NATIONAL COUNCIL OF NEGRO WOMEN)

has received numerous honorary doctorates and in 1995, published her autobiography. Her daughter **Michelle Wallace** has become and important and controversial writer. Her daughter Barbara is a linguist.

"Painting is the ultimate magic act," says Ringgold, "in which you transform a flat surface into a three-dimensional illusion of form and space. Time and place disappear as you begin to see your ideas materialize. Yes, painting is a thoroughly self-absorbed activity, but you still need someone to look with you, to see what you see." In her life and her career, Ringgold has drawn millions of people to see what she sees, from those closest to her to those half a world away.

KATHLEEN THOMPSON

Roberts, Malkia (1923–)

Since her first trip to Africa in 1966, Malkia Roberts has created art that is colorful, energetic, rhythmical, and vibrant. Her encounter with the culture and the people made a substantial impact on her emotionally as well as aesthetically. She has returned to Africa several times, and her art has become more richly endowed with iconographical references and motifs from the continent.

Born in Washington, D.C., and originally named Lucille, she was given the name Malkia, a Swahili word meaning *black and queenly one,* while traveling in Tanzania during the late 1960s. She attended the **Howard University** Department of Art for her undergraduate degree, maintaining a family tradition; her father, had also taught there early in his career. Later, she returned to her alma mater to teach painting and design from 1976 to 1985.

Roberts has traveled extensively in Africa, Canada, Europe, Mexico, and the Far East, extracting elements of her choice for her artistry. Contact with the broad spectrum of these cultures has reaffirmed her sense of the spiritual connection between peoples of color wherever they are found. But it is evident that Africa has had the strongest impact on her work.

In her engaging abstract forms, human figures of varying types emerge through the plethora of color and sweeping brush strokes, revealing patterns of light, reflecting the emotional and spiritual reactions of the places and peoples she has seen around the world. "My gathered visions are evoked and implied rather than realistically delineated in the traditional sense," says Roberts about her work.

After a trip to the American Southwest, Roberts created *The Guardian,* a figure of a woman who stands as "the guardian or the keeper of the flame . . . one capable of overcoming a multiplicity of odds." *Masai Woman* and *Africa Oye,* inspired by the African continent, resemble spiritual creatures who rise from the textured environment of warm and cool colors, pulsating with as much intensity as the background. These paintings have been an exploration of the experiences of peoples of color throughout the world, powered also by the varied streams of black music.

Malkia Roberts was named a Fellow of the Black Academy of Arts and Letters in the late 1970s, in addition to receiving the keys to the cities of Savannah and Miami in 1987 and 1988. "I thought so much about my father, who grew up in the South. He would not believe that his daughter would receive the keys to two major southern cities," recalls Roberts. In addition to exhibitions in those cities, Roberts has shown in Maryland, at the W. E. B. DuBois Institute at Harvard University; Pennsylvania State University; Atlanta, Georgia; and Washington, D.C.

Retired as professor of design and water-color painting from Howard University, Roberts has served as docent at the National Gallery of Art, the National Museum of African Art, and the Hirshhorn Museum and Sculpture Garden.

TRITOBIA HAYES BENJAMIN

S

Saar, Alison (1956–)

Well-known sculptor Alison Saar addresses humanity through archetypal images that reach audiences from backgrounds as ethnically and culturally diverse as her own. She is the daughter of the important mixed-media artist **Betye Saar**, who has African-American, Native American, and European ancestors, and art conservator Richard Saar, whose origins are German and Scottish. Raised in the outskirts of Los Angeles, she went to area museums, but also visited Simon Rodia's famous *Watts Towers* and Grandma Prisbrey's *Bottle Village*; the visionary artists' ability to create beauty from discarded materials had a profound effect on her.

As a student at Scripps College, she studied art history with Dr. Samella Lewis, noted scholar of African and Caribbean art, and wrote a thesis on southern African-American folk art, which has also been a major influence on her work. Like folk artists, Saar lacks formal technical training in sculpture, although she earned an M.F.A. from the Otis/Parsons Art Institute in Los Angeles. Her approach to materials is inventive and unselfconscious, but her sense of scale, ability to mix media, and layering of meanings reveal her thorough knowledge of African, Latin American, and Caribbean (particularly Haitian) art and religion. She has also relied increasingly on found objects, because: "I like the fact that found metals and found pieces of wood have a history. . . . they had another function at one time and that ghost is still hanging around."

Soul Service Station (1986) was a mixed media public sculpture that combined a sign, gas pump, cheerful attendant, and friendly dog; it offered "Petrol for the Soul, Spirit Tuneups, Blues Flushout and Ol' Tickets Changed." It was inspired by Latino roadside shrines that invited passersby to honor their dead ancestors, and by the vastness of the New Mexico landscape, where she had been an artist in residence. Such works were followed by *Shamans, Saints and Sinners*, a series of large, vertical black-and-white portrait drawing scrolls framed by fragmented images from old encyclopedias. The subjects, such as "Juju Eugene," "Python Lady," and "El Bato Loco," were spiritual powers within their own communities, and Saar described the series as "modern fetishes of the magic and mystery of the urban underground."

In 1988 Saar had a solo exhibition called "Zombies, Totems, Rootmen, and Others" that included small carvings, totems, and an installation about the power of love dominated by *Love Potion #3: Conkerin' John*, a six-foot wooden statue rising proudly from a tangle of roots. Recently she created majestic male and female figures called *Tree Souls* and *Stone Souls* that were exhibited at the Brooklyn Museum; the installation was titled *The Woods Within*, suggesting that within trees and stones there are spirits that give them supernatural qualities and connect their lives to ours. The powerful sense of visual narrative in Saar's work invites us to look beyond its compelling surfaces to explore the meanings hidden within. Alison Saar has also had solo exhibitions at, among others, the Whitney Museum at the Philip Morris headquarters and the Studio Museum in Harlem, New York; the Hirshhorn Museum and Sculpture Museum, Washington, D.C.; the New Gallery, Calgary, Canada; the Cleveland Center for Contemporary Art, Ohio; the Addison Gallery of American Art, Andover, Massachusetts. She has received numerous grants and artist residencies, and her work has been included in many important group shows, including the 1993 Biennial at the Whitney Museum of American Art, New York; she also shared a retrospective with Betye Saar at the Wight Gallery of the University of California at Los Angeles in 1990–91.

NANCY GROVE

Saar, Betye (1926–)

Betye Saar is a visual artist with more than thirty years of experience. Her artistic style is distinguished by her use of assemblage in forms ranging from three-dimensional frames to installations.

She was born in Pasadena, California, in 1926. She earned a Bachelor of Arts degree in design from the University of California at Los Angeles in 1949, and did graduate work in printmaking at California State University at Long Beach (1958-62) and the University of Southern California (1962). At the time, black students were not encouraged to enter art programs except in design.

Saar's work of the early 1960s was inspired by her training in graphics and by her experience as mother and wife. Her visual representations frequently depicted her children, women, women and children, and nature. From an early age Saar had been a collector, so her progression from printmaking to mixed media was natural. After finding an old leaded window, she experimented with filling each panel with a print or drawing. When she saw an exhibition of works by Joseph Cornell, she realized the potential of assemblage.

Although Saar's work has gone through many stylistic changes, it always conveys history, memory, ritual, cultural diversity, and spirituality. Her *Black Girl's Window* (1969) marks her move toward collage and assemblage, as it combines a window frame with prints as well as photographs and three-dimensional objects. The theme revolves around Saar's own life and encompasses elements of the past, present, and future. A central panel contains skeletal images that refer to the death of her father when she was six years old, but the panel relates to death as part of the cycle of life. The bottom panel depicts Saar herself as a silhouette of a young black girl peering out into the world. Her palms contain astrological symbols that represent destiny or fate. The overall work explores Saar's quest for enlightenment through her identity as a black woman and in a collective human identity that is revealed through diverse cultural practices. The imagery seems inspired by Saar's lifelong fascination with mysticism and ritual.

Saar's combination of elements has its source in the African ritual notion of vital force or collective energy. She generally combines thrift store objects that have a history of their own, to create a powerful charm. Saar uses the idea of accumulation as an extension of an African cultural heritage, and her work reflects a tie to cultures that relate to the earth, nature, and mysticism.

Prominent artist Betye Saar creates distinctive assemblages that convey issues of history, memory, ritual, cultural diversity, and spirituality. (TRACEY SAAR)

As an artist Saar acts as a shaman, combining special ingredients and found objects into charms or mojos. She alters, manipulates, recycles, and transforms her materials into boxes, altars, and installations. The products come together like allegorical stories for which she is the author or griot. Each work is a vehicle for conveying human spirit and emotion. She sounds a collective chord in the public by focusing on issues of memory and personal experience. Saar's work touches her audience both at the heart and in the mind by projecting a familiar space through intimate emotions. She reaches into the depths of human memory and retrieves sentimental images and fragments of the past, making her viewers feel as if they are returning to the comforts of childhood, taking a sentimental sojourn triggered by the recognition of objects that were once familiar but had been forgotten.

By communicating her own emotions and experiences as a black woman, Saar reveals commonalities in cultures and histories and exposes the mystical in time and space. Her work attempts to break through the barriers of time, space, energy, history, culture, memory, and human emotion.

During the 1960s and 1970s, when African Americans were concerned with cultural awareness, civil rights, and a search for identity, Saar began to focus on her anger and hurt due to the negative imagery projected in popular culture. Saar's work contributed a strong political statement of protest, such as *The Liberation of Aunt Jemima* (1972), which focused on the historical use of derogatory images of black people. By using commercial images, Saar calls to question the mechanisms of racism and exposes how deeply they are embedded in our culture. This particular work raises the consciousness of her viewer as well as asserts her control of her own image as a black woman. Her use of derogatory images was a vehicle not only for transformation but also for empowerment through self-proclaiming and exposing.

Saar takes the familiar image of Aunt Jemima and transforms her into a woman in active pursuit of her own liberation. She is taking initiative and is capable and self-reliant. The traditional symbol of Aunt Jemima is reclassified to demonstrate how black women can and do control their own identities despite the images imposed upon them by traditional Western notions of black womanhood.

In this series of works, Saar infiltrates stereotypical images with messages of reality. *The Liberation of Aunt Jemima* is a box assemblage that contains the powerful image of Aunt Jemima in a vibrant and assertive red dress. Saar manipulates Jemima's role as servant and raises her to a postion of power. By exposing the objectification of black people and by confronting white American exploitation, this representation rattles the very

foundations of racism. Jemima is proud, confident, and self-assured. Saar actively reclaims the history of her foremothers and her cultural heritage.

In the 1970s, Saar's work became more introspective, as she began to focus more on her own personal history. Her Aunt Hattie, who had been like a grandmother to her, died in 1974. With her death Saar felt a resurfacing of feelings of pain and sadness similar to those she had felt at the loss of her father. This inspired a new body of work based in private, intimate memories. From Aunt Hattie she inherited drawers and closets full of clothing and objects. Unlike found objects from thrift stores with unknown histories, Aunt Hattie's memorabilia inspired a nostalgic vision of a real woman from recent time past. Saar captured the power and magic elicited from everyday, ordinary lives in these works. They were testaments to Aunt Hattie as well as a celebration of black history and heritage, and they evoke memories of a collective past in which there is a shared emotional spirit.

After this series of works Saar made a stylistic switch from boxes to altars. The viewer was often invited to participate physically by the ritual leaving or exchanging of offerings. In the 1980s Saar again expanded her vision by creating installations, often incorporating her altars into these sites. These walk-in versions of her smaller works break free of boundaries by magnifying the intimacy of her boxes. They evolve as ritual by combining old, familiar objects with nature and personal energy. She continues to focus on shared emotion and experience, and in a recent body of works she returns to the power of nostalgia and memory by combining found objects with old photographs in order to reconstruct the identities of the people in the photographs, whom she does not know. She continues to pursue the notion of a collective identity in which there is a shared emotional space.

Saar's philosophical content is consistent throughout her body of work. With each progression, her ideas become more intricate and informed. Her work is continuously evolving along with the events in her life. She is a prominent artist whose significant contributions are underscored by her many achievements, exhibitions, awards, and commissions.

NADINE WASSERMAN

Savage, Augusta (1892–1962)

Augusta Savage is one of the most enigmatic figures in American art. Although she was one of the most influential individuals in Harlem during the later part of the Harlem Renaissance, her life and career remain a somewhat sketchy mystery. She championed social and political causes and effected cultural and economic opportunities, particularly for African-American artists and the Harlem community in the 1930s, but chose to leave that community later in life.

Her efforts in establishing the Harlem Community Art Center, where black people had the unprecedented and rare opportunity to study fine arts, was heralded throughout the nation. The center was one of the most exciting programs of its kind in America. It became a model for other urban centers and a symbol of race pride, as did her best known work, *The Harp*, which she produced for the 1939 World's Fair.

Cast in plaster and painted, this sixteen-foot-high sculpture stood in the court of the Contemporary Arts Building on the fair grounds. The sculpture depicted a choir sup-

ported by the arm and hand of the Creator. The kneeling figure held a bar of musical notes and the text of James Weldon Johnson's poem "Lift Every Voice and Sing." The work received wide publicity and became well known nationally throughout black communities.

Augusta Savage was one of four women artists, and the only black artist, to receive a commission from the Fair Corporation. She was awarded twelve hundred dollars to design and produce the sculpture. *The Harp*, which became popularly known as *Lift Every Voice and Sing*, executed at the pinnacle of her career, represented Augusta Savage's most

A groundbreaker in the creation of a vital black artistic community, Augusta Savage was the first director of the Harlem Community Art Center, the only black artist to receive a commission for the 1939 World's Fair, and the only director of the Salon of Contemporary Negro Art in Harlem. (NATIONAL ARCHIVES)

monumental achievement. Regrettably, there were no funds to cast the work and it was destroyed at the close of the fair.

Augusta Savage made a tremendous personal sacrifice to be an artist and a teacher. She had to fight for virtually everything that she believed in and wanted to be. From the outset, she fought her father's disapproval of making art, and as a young single woman in New York, she fought against racism, sexism, and discrimination. Yet, in spite of the early deaths of two husbands, another short-lived marriage that ended in divorce, and the constant emotional demands placed on her by her family, she managed to live a life of artistic intensity and exert great influence on younger artists.

Born Augusta Christine Fells in 1892, in Green Cove Springs, Florida, she was the seventh of fourteen children. Her father was a carpenter, fisherman, farmer, and minister and disapproved of her making "graven" objects. Savage indicates in her autobiographies that she came from a hard-working family. Her early years were spent working in the house with her mother, going to school, and making small clay objects. As she says:

at a very early age, [I] demonstrated the artistic talent which shaped my career. . . . From the time I can first recall the rain falling on the red clay in Florida, I wanted to make things. When my brothers and sisters were making mud pies, I would be making ducks and chickens with the mud.

Her father was not impressed with her fascination and love for making clay objects. She later stated that her parents "practically whipped the art out of me."

At the young age of fifteen, Augusta married John T. Moore, her first husband, and a year later had her only child, Irene Connie Moore. Her husband died a few years after the birth of their daughter.

In 1915, Augusta's father moved the family to West Palm Beach, Florida. At this time she gave up clay making. However, she resumed modeling in clay when a school principal who recognized her talents persuaded her to teach a clay modeling class in the black high school for a term. This experience inspired her to be a teacher and she enrolled at Tallahassee State Normal School (now Florida A&M University) for one year. She returned to West Palm Beach and entered the county fair there. Her work was greatly admired. Fairgoers, including many northern tourists, purchased her work. Impressed by her entries, George Graham Currie, superintendent of the fair, suggested that she go to New York to study. But Augusta moved to Jacksonville, Florida, where she attempted to earn a living sculpting portrait busts of prominent black Americans. She soon discovered that this plan was not feasible. The expected patronage did not materialize and after a few months, she moved to New York City.

In 1921, at the outset of the Harlem Renaissance, Augusta arrived in New York. She was twenty-nine and had not yet formally studied sculpture or art. Currie provided Augusta with a letter of introduction to his friend, sculptor Solon Borglum, founder of the School of American Sculpture. Since Augusta could not afford the tuition of the school, Borglum directed her to Kate L. Reynolds, principal of Cooper Union, where tuition was not required.

Savage was accepted into the program and began a formal course of study with portrait sculptor George Brewster. To support herself, Savage took a job as an apartment caretaker.

By her second year at Cooper Union, she was taking fourth-year courses but had financial difficulties. After losing her job, she informed Reynolds that she would be unable to complete her studies. Reynolds found temporary employment for her and special funds to pay for her living expenses.

In 1923, Savage was engulfed in a controversy over a scholarship for foreign study. She sent an application to an American summer program for architects, painters, and sculptors at the Palace of Fontainebleau near Paris. She was accepted in the program, but the scholarship was withdrawn when two Alabama women who also won scholarships complained to the committee that they could not be expected to travel or room with a "colored girl." Herman MacNeil, president of the National Sculpture Society and a member of the committee, attempted to reverse the decision of the committee, but their minds could not be changed. Ashamed of their decision, he invited Savage to study privately that summer with him at his studio in College Point, New York.

The incident was extensively published in the press. It brought Augusta Savage sympathetic public attention and notoriety. On the political front she had the support of W. E. B. DuBois and other prominent and distinguished people. It was during this time that she met and married Robert Poston, a Garveyite and brother of journalist Ted Poston. Robert Poston died five months after their marriage.

DuBois arranged for Savage to receive a working scholarship to Italy. Sponsored by Countess Irene Di Robilant, manager of the Italian-American Society in New York, the scholarship covered tuition and materials at the Royal Academy of Fine Arts in Rome. Unable to raise the money for travel and living expenses, she had to postpone the trip. What she earned working at a laundry was sent to West Palm Beach to care for her father, who was now paralyzed. She eventually brought her parents to New York to live with her and postponed her trip indefinitely.

Although she worked and cared for her parents, she was able to continue her art work. She succeeded in producing several important works, such as *Green Apples* and a bust of musician Theodore Upshure. She exhibited periodically with the Harmon Foundation and at the 135th Street branch of the New York Public Library. She also participated in major group exhibitions that included the works of artistic giants, painter Henry O. Tanner and sculptor **Meta Warrick Fuller**.

Another family tragedy struck. A brother drowned in a flood in the aftermath of a Florida hurricane. Savage then had to shoulder the cost of bringing the remainder of her family to New York to live with her.

As a recipient of the Julius Rosenwald Fellowship, Savage was finally able to study abroad. She departed for Paris in 1929. Because she had won a consecutive award, she was able to stay for two years. The initial award was for her sculpture titled *Gamin*. Using her nephew Ellis Ford as a model, she captured the quintessential character of youth. The work expresses the tenderness and streetwise sharpness of the boy. *Gamin*, in the collection of the Schomburg Center for Research in Black Culture, is a work that straddles the boundary between portraits and types. It is an important marker in the shift of African-American art toward the representation of black people by black artists.

The work reflected the new realism that was beginning to emerge.

While in Paris, she studied with Félix Beauneteaux at the Grande Chaumière and Charles Despiau. She exhibited at the Salon d'Automne, at the Grand Palais, Salon Printemps, and at the Société des Artistes Français Beaux Arts. During this period, she also received a Carnegie Foundation grant that allowed her to travel to Belgium and Germany.

Shortly after returning to New York at the age of forty, she opened her own school—the Savage Studio of Arts and Crafts, located at 163 West 143rd Street in Harlem. She attracted young artists Ernest Crichlow, Norman Lewis, William Artis, and others. By the mid–1930s, her school, through an association with the State University of New York, had become the largest art school of its type in New York and had attracted the attention of both the Carnegie Foundation and the Federal Art Project of the Works Progress Administration (WPA).

By 1936, Savage became an assistant supervisor for the WPA Federal Art Project and became an advocate for other black artists. She was responsible for bringing many of them onto the rolls as art instructors and studio artists. Her vigor and advocacy led to her appointment as the first director of the Harlem Community Art Center in 1937.

Savage took a leave of absence in 1938 from the Harlem Community Art Center in order to execute the commission for the World's Fair. During her absence, her position was taken over by artist and writer Gwendolyn Bennett.

Following her triumphant success at the World's Fair, she was awarded a silver medal by the Women's Service League of Brooklyn in recognition of her pioneering efforts. She was the first black member of the National Association of Women Painters and Sculptors, the first director of one of the most important art centers in the nation, the only black artist to receive a commission for the World's Fair, and the first and only director of the first black-owned corporation to open a gallery devoted to the work of black artists.

The gallery, named the Salon of Contemporary Negro Art in Harlem, opened in 1939. It was the culminating project in Savage's long career of promoting black artists and art, and of her efforts to build economic support and opportunities for them. Over thirty artists participated in the show. Among the more popularly known women artists were Meta Warrick Fuller (exhibiting for the first time in twenty years), Gwendolyn Knight, Sara Murrel, Georgette Seabrooke, **Lois Mailou Jones**, Grace Mott Johnson, **Selma Burke**, and Elba Lightfoot. However, because of a lack of funding, the gallery closed after a few months.

Savage's attention shifted away from the intense involvement that characterized her work, and in 1945, she moved to Saugerties, New York. There she supported herself with odd jobs, taught art to children in local summer camps, wrote short stories, and reestablished ties with her daughter Irene. During this time, her artistic production was virtually nonexistent, although she completed a few works.

Her influence as a teacher was demonstrated often when her students were praised and awarded for their excellent work and achievements. Norman Lewis, Gwendolyn Knight, Ernest Crichlow, Morgan Smith, and Marvin Smith are among the many talented artists that she nurtured artistically and intellectually. They were the direct beneficiaries of her personal sacrifice, dedication, and love.

Savage contributed substantially and uniquely to the shaping of African-American art. She was among the earliest African-American artists to consistently and sympathetically use black physiognomy in her work. She is most appreciated for her ability to give dignity to her subjects in spite of the obstacles of racism, sexism, and discrimination. She gave her sitters quiet will and perseverance like her own.

DEIRDRE BIBBY

Sklarek, Norma Merrick (1928–)

It is seldom that a groundbreaker is quite so far ahead of the pack as architect Norma Merrick Sklarek. Born on April 15, 1928, in New York City, she is the daughter of Amelia Willoughby and Walter Merrick. She attended Barnard College of Columbia University, receiving a bachelor's degree in architecture there in 1950. In 1954, she was the first black woman to become licensed as an architect in the state of New York. She was hired in 1955 by the distinguished firm of Skidmore, Owings & Merrill and remained there for five years. At the same time, she was on the architecture faculty of City College of New York. In 1960, she moved to Los Angeles to join the firm of Gruen and Associates and to join the architecture faculty of the University of California at Los Angeles. She was the first black woman to be licensed as an architect in California, passing the examination in 1962; it would be twenty years before another black woman would achieve that status.

Six years after joining Gruen, Merrick became director of architecture, managing a large staff of architects. She was the first woman to hold that position. In 1966, she became the first woman honored with a fellowship in the American Institute of Architects, but she was not yet a partner at Gruen. She married Ralf Sklarek in 1967 and had two sons. She remained with Gruen and Associates for twenty years.

From 1980 to 1985, Sklarek was vice president of Welton Becket Associates, leaving to form her own firm with two women partners. In 1984, her husband died and in 1985 she married her second husband, physician Cornelius Welch. In 1989, she became a principal in the Jerde Partnership.

Among Sklarek's important works are the American Embassy in Tokyo, the Pacific Design Center, Terminal One of the International Airport in Los Angeles, and Fox Plaza in San Francisco.

KATHLEEN THOMPSON

T

Thomas, Alma (1891–1978)

Alma Thomas, an abstract artist of world renown, was born in Columbus, Georgia, in 1891. She moved to Washington, D.C., with her family in 1907, and two years later graduated from Armstrong Technical High School, where she studied art and architectural and mechanical drawing. She then attended normal school in Washington, D.C., and after two years went to teach in Wilmington, Delaware. Returning to Washington in 1921, she enrolled at **Howard University**, where she became part of the newly organized art department and its first graduate in 1924. She later received an M.A. in education (1934) from Teachers College, Columbia University, New York, and was organizer and director of the School Art League Project which encouraged an appreciation of art among black students, between 1936 and 1939. For the next twenty years Thomas continued teaching while pursuing her own art and organizing exhibitions by African-American artists in galleries in Washington, D.C., most notably the Barnett-Aden Gallery, which was one of the city's first commercial art galleries.

Thomas created her most important and exciting work after she retired from teaching in 1960 and devoted herself full-time to painting. For the next eighteen years she created distinctive abstract compositions in oil paint and watercolor that featured vertical, centrifugal, and horizontal cascades of individual strokes of color. The marks left by Thomas as her strokes accumulated on the surface of canvas or paper exhibited a poetic quality of involvement by the hand. Each form sat in rows that lost their regularity as the length of the stroke varied or shifted into another direction. The pristine white of the under-surface peered through, between her battalions of gesture, evoking at once an optical delight and a landscape phenomenon.

In a work such as *Red Roses Sonata* (1972, Metropolitan Museum of Art, New York), the curtain of red daubs covers a green background, which sets up a vibrating visual effect between the complementary colors. In addition, two vertical bands of a lighter green color are laid within the background, creating a minimalist composition that recalls the composition of Barnett Newman within the dense articulation of the surface. In a 1973 composition, *Wind and Crepe Myrtle Concerto* (National Museum of American Art), the differentiated bands lie on the surface of the rose over-painting, contrasting with the lighter pink. Underneath is a more intricate landscape of yellows and greens, which looks like a sunny glade overhung by a curtain of rose petals. This work indicates how Thomas was able to loosen the gridlike tendency of her compositions and produce, in the words of Merry A. Foresta, "an atmospheric quality" (1981). As Foresta observes, "despite our propensity to read these compositions on multiple layers, attempting to discern what

244

seems to be happening behind the surface, in fact Thomas intends no specific spatial illusion. Edges are merged and blended by the brushwork so that the surface constantly shifts in an evocation of fluttering and falling leaves."

Thomas' later work was informed by her earlier compositions from the 1950s and 1960s as she followed the trend toward gestural abstraction. Compositions such as *Untitled (Study for a Painting)* (1964, watercolor on paper, collection of Michael G. Fisher, Washington, D.C.) show an intense accumulation of distinctly applied brushfuls of paint that recalls the dense painterly articulations of Hans Hofmann at the end of his career. Another, *Watusi (Hard Edge)* (1963, acrylic on canvas, Hirshhorn Museum and Sculpture Garden, Smithsonian Institution, Washington, D.C.), shows unexpected arrangements of what seem to be uncut shapes of paper whose irregular borders nonetheless suggest squares, trapezoids, and parallelograms. These shapes are arranged seemingly helter-skelter against a white background, reminiscent of Jean Arp's Dada compositions created through the seemingly random tossing of bits of paper onto a surface. What is evident is that Thomas had readily absorbed the language of a variety of abstract idioms and was able to synthesize them quickly into a highly individual style.

Her work of the 1960s is characterized by a shortening and regimentation of strokes, as well as a restriction of the palette (individual colors are nonetheless brilliant and translucent), which is well suited to the more discrete surfaces and the objectification of the creative process that marked the artistic phenomena of the decade, Minimalism and Color-Field Painting. Thomas was working in Washington, D.C., at the time, and it is evident that the evocative abstractions of Morris Louis and the so-called Washington Color School, which gave rise to such talents as Gene Davis and Sam Gilliam, were a prime influence on her work. Thomas never divorced the trace of her hand from her work, however. Instead, she created "curtains" of color composed of individual irregular strokes of paint that interact optically with one another. This interweaving of visual patterns is as accomplished in her watercolors as in her oils. The powerful sense of luminosity that emanates from her oil paintings, particularly those that have white in the background, is readily achieved in the watercolors, which themselves are distinctive by virtue of Thomas' use of intensely saturated hues.

Toward the end of her career, Thomas' individual tesserae of color become even more sharply defined as individual squares, rectangles, and parallelograms that occasionally curve around on one edge to conform to the more circular arrangement of her color. The forms function alternately as individual pieces of tile or ceramic and as pictograms with distinct personalities. The regularity and density of the surface also begin to break up. In *Hydrangeas Spring Song* (1976, acrylic on canvas, collection of Harol Hart, New York), a passageway seems to have been cleared in the wake of an unexpected clearing of white color, which moves up the composition from the center of the bottom edge to the upper right-hand corner. Not only is the population of hieroglyphs much more sparse, but the forms themselves seem to be breaking up into individual forms. This adds a decidedly dynamic character to the pleasant regimentation of forms in a grand scheme that is established in each one of Thomas' compositions. If, as Foresta suggests, this was a strategy to counter accusations of decorativeness in her work, it was a development that sadly was left incomplete because of Thomas' frail health during the last year of her life.

Alma Thomas was the first African-American woman to achieve critical acclaim within an abstract medium. She had her first one-person exhibition at the Whitney Museum of American Art in New York City in 1972, making her the first African-American woman to have an individual show in that institution. That same year the Corcoran Gallery of Art in Washington, D.C., opened a retrospective of her work, and she also received the Two Thousand Women of Achievement award for her life's work.

Thomas died in 1978 at the age of eighty-six from complications following heart surgery.

LOWERY S. SIMS

W

Waring, Laura Wheeler (1887–1948)

Laura Wheeler Waring, painter and educator, was acknowledged as a significant artist during her lifetime and continues to be appreciated today for her technical skill and imagination. Although best known for portraits, she also produced highly original landscapes and other important paintings.

Born in 1887 in Hartford, Connecticut, Laura Wheeler grew up with the advantages available to the black upper-class of the time. She showed promise as an artist early in her life and, after graduating from high school, chose to study at the Pennsylvania Academy of Fine Arts in Philadelphia, where she remained for six years. In 1914, she received a scholarship that allowed her to pursue her artistic interests in Europe, where she spent a large part of her time at the Louvre. These studies were interrupted by the outbreak of World War I, and Wheeler returned to the United States where, soon afterward, she was asked to direct the art and music departments at Cheyney Training School for Teachers in Philadelphia. Although her work at Cheyney was interrupted by two more trips to Europe for study and for exhibition of her work, she continued to teach there for thirty years.

After her second European trip, Wheeler's reputation as an artist grew rapidly. Her work began to be shown at major American galleries, including the Philadel-

Painter and educator Laura Wheeler Waring was acknowledged as a significant artist during her lifetime and continues to be appreciated today for her technical skill and imagination. (MOORLAND-SPINGARN)

phia Museum of Art, the Corcoran Gallery in Washington, D.C., and the Art Institute of Chicago. During her third European trip, Wheeler, who was now Laura Wheeler Waring, and married to Professor Walter E. Waring of Lincoln University, exhibited her work at the Galerie du Luxembourg.

Many of Waring's most famous paintings are portraits of celebrated figures, such as W. E. B. DuBois, James Weldon Johnson, and Marian Anderson. Others are considered socially significant; for example, *Mother and Daughter* depicts a mixed-race woman and her child. Late in her life, Waring produced a series of paintings, including *Jacob's Ladder* and *The Coming of the Lord*, interpreting various Negro spirituals.

Waring died on February 3, 1948, after a long illness.

JAN GLEITER

An Associated Press story about Beulah Woodard's 1935 one-person show at the Los Angeles County Museum brought her sculpture to the attention of the entire country and resulted in the earliest of many important commissions. (MIRIAM MATTHEWS)

Woodard, Beulah Ecton (1895–1955)

Beulah Ecton was born on November 11, 1895, near Frankfort in rural Ohio. The William P. Ecton family, including the youngest daughter, Beulah, migrated to California and settled near Los Angeles in what is now the city of Vernon. Through the years many unusual visitors came to the Ecton home, but none aroused Beulah Ecton's interest as much as the native African she met when she was twelve years old. This was the beginning of her lifelong interest in all things African.

While at Polytechnic High School, Ecton began showing an interest in sculpture. Possessing a natural talent that probably would have found expression even without formal training, she developed her artistic ability with courses at the Los Angeles Art School, Otis Art Institute, and the University of Southern California. She was tutored by Felix Piano, David Edstrom, Glen Lukens, and Prince Troubeskoy.

Following her marriage to Brady E. Woodard, she set to work in an improvised studio in the rear of their home. The earliest public recognition of her work came when James Rodney Smith, publisher of *California News*, exhibited her sculpture in the window of his newspaper office and advertised it in the paper's columns.

A short time later Miriam Matthews, head librarian of the Vernon Branch Library, invited Woodard to display her work at the branch and later arranged an exhibition for her at the Los Angeles Central Library downtown. This exposure led to a one-person show at the Los Angeles County Museum in fall 1935. As she was the first black artist to be so honored, Los Angeles metropolitan newspapers headlined the event and ran photos. The Associated Press story appeared in newspapers across the nation.

Soon Woodard was in great demand throughout southern California as a lecturer, especially in educational institutions from elementary to university graduate schools. The artist received important commissions to sculpt busts of John Anson Ford, a member of the Los Angeles County Board of Supervisors; Irving Lipsteitch, a noted philanthropist; Thomas Evans, the first executive secretary of the University Religious Conference at the University of California at Los Angeles; and others. She won a number of awards, including first prize for sculpture at the third All-City Art Festival in 1953, and her work is in the permanent collections of various museums and in private collections on two continents.

Despite her full work schedule, Woodard always found time to support worthwhile community causes and to promote the work of other artists. She was a principal organizer of both the Los Angeles Negro Art Association in 1937 and the Eleven Associated Artists Gallery in 1950. She also stimulated public interest in the work of local and national artists, both black and white.

Woodard died at the age of fifty-nine on July 13, 1955, just before what might have been her greatest triumph—an exhibition of her work scheduled for several German museums.

MIRIAM MATTHEWS

Chronology

1812
Elleanor Eldridge opens a weaving business with her sister in Warwick, Rhode Island.

1836
In the earliest documented painting or drawing by an African-American woman anywhere in the United States, **Sarah Douglass**, a schoolteacher in Philadelphia, contributes a signed painting of a rose-dominated bouquet to an album belonging to Elizabeth Smith.

1837
Harriet Powers is born in Georgia.

1845
Sculptor **Edmonia Lewis** is born.

1855
Annie E. Anderson (Walker) is born in Flatbush, then a suburb of Brooklyn, New York.

1860
Fifteen percent of free black women are dressmakers.

1864
Edmonia Lewis' bust of Colonel Robert Gould Shaw is exhibited at the Boston Fair for the Soldiers' Fund.

Elizabeth Keckley, dress designer to Mary Todd Lincoln, designs Mrs. Lincoln's inaugural ball gown, which is now on display at the Smithsonian Institute in Washington D.C.

1877
May Howard (Jackson) is born in Philadelphia on May 12th.

Meta Vaux Warrick (Fuller) is born in Philadelphia on June 9th.

1886
Harriet Powers, one of America's most famous quiltmakers, exhibits one of her quilts at the Athens Cotton Fair. The quilt is now on display at the Smithsonian Institute.

1890
Alma Woodsey Thomas is born in Columbus, Georgia.

1892
Augusta Savage is born in Green Cove Springs, Florida.

1895
Annie E. Anderson Walker graduates from Cooper Union for the Advancement of Science and Art in New York City.

Harriet Powers, Georgia quiltmaker, is believed to have exhibited her quilt *The Creation of the Animals*, at the Cotton States Exposition in Atlanta.

Beulah Ecton Woodard is born in Ohio.

May Howard Jackson wins a scholarship from the Philadelphia Public Schools to study at the Pennsylvania Academy of Fine Arts. She is the first black woman to study at the Academy.

1896

Annie Anderson Walker's drawing "La Parisienne" is exhibited in the Paris Salon of 1896.

1899

Meta Vaux Warrick Fuller begins her studies at the Ecole des Beaux-Arts and sculpture at the Colarossi Academy.

1900

Selma Hortense Burke is born in Mooresville, North Carolina.

1901

At twenty-four years of age, Meta Vaux Warrick Fuller has an appointment with Auguste Rodin, the most famous and respected sculptor of the time. He expresses admiration of her work and informally becomes her mentor.

1903

Meta Vaux Warrick Fuller has several of her works exhibited in the Paris Salon.

Eliza Hawkins, a design student at Cooper Union, exhibits her designs for wallpaper and book covers and her architectural drawings at the Samuel O. Collins Gallery at 11 Gay Street in Greenwich Village.

1905

Lois Mailou Jones is born in Boston, Massachusetts.

1906

Meta Vaux Warrick Fuller exhibits her sculpture *Portraits from Mirrors* in the 101st Annual Exhibition at the Pennsylvania Academy of Fine Arts.

1907

Meta Vaux Warrick Fuller is commissioned to sculpt fifteen figurines of African Americans for the Jamestown Tercentennial Exposition. She is the first black woman artist to receive a federal commission. She receives a gold medal for these works.

1910

A fire in a Philadelphia warehouse destroys sixteen years of Meta Vaux Warrick Fuller's work.

1913

W. E. B. DuBois commissions Meta Vaux Warrick Fuller to reproduce *Man Eating His Heart,* lost in a warehouse fire, for the Emancipation Proclamation's fiftieth anniversary in New York. Instead of replicating this piece, she creates *Spirit of Emancipation.*

1915

Meta Vaux Warrick Fuller creates a medallion for Framingham's Equal Suffrage League.

May Howard Jackson exhibits at the Corcoran Gallery of Art, Washington, D.C.

1916

May Howard Jackson exhibits at the National Academy of Design in New York City.

1918

Nancy Elizabeth Prophet graduates from the Rhode Island School of Design (RISD).

1919

Meta Vaux Warrick Fuller sculpts a figure representing the infamous Mary Turner case.

The Tanner Art Students Society is organized at all-black Dunbar High School in Washington, D.C. Their first exhibition displayed thirty paintings and six sculptures, including works by Meta Vaux Warrick Fuller, May Howard Jackson, and Laura Wheeler Waring.

May Howard Jackson exhibits at the Veerhoof Gallery in Washington, D.C.

Dunbar High School commissions May Howard Jackson to sculpt a portrait bust of Paul Laurence Dunbar.

1921

At the age of twenty-nine, Augusta Savage enters Cooper Union, a tuition-free art school, for instruction. Within a month, she is advanced to the third-year class.

Meta Warrick Fuller exhibits a twelve-inch statuette of *Ethiopia Awakening* at the Making of America Exposition in New York City. The work is later cast life-size in bronze.

1922

Friends of the Schomburg Library commission Augusta Savage to sculpt a bust of W. E. B. DuBois.

Nancy Elizabeth Prophet enters the Ecole des Beaux-Arts in Paris and remains in France for ten years, where she participates in several salons and receives exceptional reviews.

1923

Augusta Savage receives a scholarship from the French government to attend summer school in Fontainebleau, France. Two other recipients protest traveling with Savage, and the scholarship is withdrawn. The resulting publicity elicits an invitation from Hermon MacNeil, president of the National Sculpture Society, to study privately with him.

1924

Alma Woodsey Thomas receives the first B.S. degree in fine arts from Howard University.

1925

Augusta Savage receives a working scholarship to the Royal Academy of Fine Arts in Rome but does not have enough money for travel and living expenses. She receives her first Rosenwald Fellowship to study in France.

1926

The Harmon Foundation begins its support of African-American writers, artists, and professionals. May Howard Jackson serves as a juror in their second exhibition this year and Laura Wheeler Waring wins the gold medal.

1927

Laura Wheeler Waring receives a Harmon Foundation award for her portrait of Ann Washington Derry.

1928

May Howard Jackson wins the bronze medal in the Harmon Foundation exhibition. Meta Warrick Fuller is one of the jurors.

1929

Augusta Savage wins a Rosenwald grant for her sculpture *Gamin*.

1930

Lois Mailou Jones begins her forty-seven-year teaching career in the department of art at Howard University.

1931

Augusta Savage creates several important sculptures this year, including *Martiniquaise*, *After the Glory*, and *Envy*.

Nancy Elizabeth Prophet's *Head of a Negro* wins the Harmon Foundation prize for best sculpture.

1932

Augusta Savage establishes the Savage Studio of Arts and Crafts. Some of the brightest young artists around, including Ernest Crichlow, Gwendolyn Knight, Jacob Lawrence, Morgan and Marvin Jones, William Artis, and Norman Lewis, become her students.

Elizabeth Prophet's *Congolaise* is purchased by Gertrude Vanderbilt Whitney for the Whitney Museum Collection.

1933

The Public Works of Art Project and the Federal Art Project of the Works Progress Administration are created. Among the artists who are commissioned to create public works of art is Augusta Savage.

1934

Elizabeth Prophet joins the art department at **Spelman College,** introducing sculpture into the curriculum.

1935

Beulah Ecton Woodard has a one-woman exhibition of her sculpture at the Los Angeles County Museum of Art.

1937

Augusta Savage opens and is the first director of the Harlem Community Arts Center.

Zelda Jackson "Jackie" Ormes initiates her first cartoon strip, "Torchy Brown in Dixie to Harlem" in the Pittsburgh Courier; Ormes becomes the first nationally syndicated black woman cartoonist.

1939

Augusta Savage is commissioned by the World's Fair Corporation and creates a sixteen-foot sculpture called *The Harp*. She and the composer William Grant Still are the only black artists represented in the Fair.

1940

Elizabeth Catlett receives the first M.F.A. in sculpture from the University of Iowa. She studied with Grant Wood.

1941

Lois Mailou Jones wins the Corcoran Gallery of Art Robert Woods Bliss Prize for Landscape of the Society of Washington Artists. With this award, Jones breaks the color barrier at the Corcoran.

1943

Selma Burke, winning a national competition sponsored by the Fine Arts Commission, is commissioned to create a profile of President Franklin Delano Roosevelt. The image she creates becomes the basis for the image on the Franklin dime.

1945
Elizabeth Prophet mounts a solo exhibition at the Providence Public Library.

1946
Elizabeth Catlett completes her graphic series, fifteen linocuts that configure real images of black women, which she titles *Negro Woman*. The series is exhibited in her first solo show the following year.

1953
Lois Mailou Jones travels to Haiti; the visit introduces a new element into her style.

1954
Norma Merrick (Sklarek) becomes the first black woman architect licensed in New York. She is hired the following year by Skidmore, Owings, and Merrill, one of the largest and most successful firms in the United States.

1959
Elizabeth Catlett heads the sculpture department of the National School of Fine Arts at the Universidad Nacional Autónoma de México.

1961
Margaret Taylor Burroughs and her husband open the Ebony Museum of Negro History, later to become the DuSable Museum of African-American History, in Chicago.

1963
Norma Sklarek is licensed as an architect in California, where she works for twenty years with Gruen Associates, rising to the position of director of architecture.

1964
Geraldine McCullough wins the prestigious Widener Prize.

1967
The Studio Museum is established in Harlem.

1968
The Museum of the National Center of Afro-American Artists is founded in Boston, Massachusetts, by Elma Lewis.

1969
Elizabeth Catlett's linocut *Malcolm Speaks for Us* is critically acclaimed and widely popular.

1970
Filmmaker Madeline Anderson's documentary *I Am Somebody* is produced.

Faith Ringgold cofounds the Women Students and Artists for Black Liberation.

1971
Betye Saar is among the artists featured in "Contemporary Black Artists in America," an exhibit at the Whitney Museum of American Art.

Faith Ringgold is commissioned to paint a mural for the Women's House of Detention at Riker's Island. It is called *For the Women's House*.

Where We At, Black Women Artists, Inc. founded in New York City to provide a showcase for black women artists.

1972

Alma Thomas is the first African-American woman to have an individual show at the Whitney Museum of American Art, in New York City.

Betye Saar creates *The Liberation of Aunt Jemima*.

1973

Lois Mailou Jones is the first African-American to have a solo exhibition at the Museum of Fine Arts in Boston.

Elizabeth Catlett executes *Phillis Wheatley*, a life-size bronze sculpture at Jackson State College in Mississippi.

1974

Valerie Maynard creates *I See the Beauty in You*, a ceramic sculpture mural for the facade of the Social Services Center for the Community Association of East Harlem Triangle.

1976

Louis Armstrong, a ten-foot bronze statue by *Elizabeth Catlett* is presented at the U.S. bicentennial celebration in New Orleans.

1978

Barbara Chase-Riboud is named the Academic of Italy with a gold medal for sculpture and drawing.

1980

Forever Free: Art by African-American Women, 1862-1980, edited by Arna Bontemps is published. It is the first major exhibition catalogue devoted to black American women.

Faith Ringgold creates her first quilt, *Echoes of Harlem*. She would later become famous for her work in this art form.

1982

After a United States-Japan Friendship Commission eight month travel grant **Howardena Pindell** creates *Hiroshima Disguised: Japan*, consisting of ten separate canvases arrayed like the islands of Japan. Its pale lavender tone resembles ash. The surface is embedded with shattered metal and cut glass and contains small photographic images that make reference to the devastating effects of nuclear war.

1983

Filmmaker Julie Dash produces, writes, and directs *Illusions*, a thirty-four-minute black-and-white film.

1985

Sharing Traditions, Five Black Artists in Nineteenth Century America opens at the National Museum of American Art. Edmonia Lewis is one of the artists.

Clementine Hunter is included in Judith Sedwick's photographic portrait exhibition *Women of Courage*, which opens in New York and Boston and travels around the country.

1986

Jeanne Moutoussamy-Ashe publishes her pathbreaking book *Viewfinders: Black Women Photographers, 1839-1985*.

1988

Adrian Piper exhibits her installation *Cornered*, in which she challenges (from a video screen in a corner behind an overturned table) the audience's unexamined assumptions about race.

1989

Barbara Brandon's cartoon strip "Where I'm Coming From" makes its appearance in the *Detroit Free Press*.

Julie Dash's film *Illusions* is named the Best Film of the Decade by the Black Filmmakers Foundation.

1990

Betye Saar's retrospective, *Secrets, Dialogues, Revelations*, shared with her daughter **Alison Saar**, opens at the Wight Gallery of the University of California at Los Angeles and goes on tour.

Faith Ringgold's first children's book, *Tar Beach*, is published. *Faith Ringgold: A 25-Year Survey*, a comprehensive retrospective exhibition of her work begins a national tour.

Black Women in the Arts exhibition opens at Montclair State College Gallery, Upper Montclair, New Jersey.

The World of Lois Mailou Jones exhibition opens at The Meridian International Center, Washington, D.C. This retrospective exhibition of seventy-six works from the years 1919 to 1989 tours the country for five years.

Lowery Stokes Sims curates *The Next Generation: Southern Black Aesthetic* for the Southeastern Center of Contemporary Art, Winston-Salem, North Carolina.

Elizabeth Catlett continues work on her commission for a 36 x 10 foot bronze bas-relief for the Atlantic City, New Jersey, City Hall (1989-1991). She also serves as Artist-in-Residence, at the University of Michigan, Ann Arbor.

Adrian Piper exhibits her *Vanilla Nightmares* series in *Artworks: Adrian Piper* at the Williams College Museum of Art.

1991

Barbara Brandon's "Where I'm Coming From" is nationally syndicated, making her the first black woman to have a syndicated cartoon strip in the mainstream white press.

Mary Schmidt Campbell, the former director of The Studio Museum in Harlem, is appointed dean of the Tisch School of the Arts at New York University, becoming the first black women to head a major arts school.

1992

Geraldine McCullough has a solo exhibition of sculpture and wall hangings at Isoble Neal Gallery in Chicago.

The film *Daughters of the Dust*, by **Julie Dash** is released to great critical acclaim. It is the first feature-length film by an African-American woman.

Free Within Ourselves, an exhibition of works by African-American artists in the Collection of the National Museum of American Art begins a two year tour. It includes works by Edmonia Lewis, Augusta Savage, and Elizabeth Catlett.

Elizabeth Catlett is commissioned to do six lithographs for an edition of **Margaret Walker**'s book *For My People* by The Limited Editions Club.

Betye Saar receives the Brandywine Association's Van Der Zee Award.

Faith Ringgold has a solo exhibition at the Bernice Steinbaum Gallery in New York City.

1993

Winnie Owens-Hart is awarded a lifetime achievement award from the National Museum of Women in the Arts.

The Hampton University Museum acquires a collection of 73 prints from

Elizabeth Catlett, dating from 1946 to 1993.

Images of African-American lesbians are presented in *Keepin' On*, an exhibition produced by the Lesbian Herstory Educational Foundation in New York City.

The exhibition *Uncommon Beauty in Common Objects: The Legacy of African American Craft Art* opens at the National Afro-American Museum and Cultural Center, Wilberforce, Ohio. It includes the work of over twenty black women.

Sylvia A. Boone, an art historian and critic and the first black woman to receive tenure at Yale University, dies.

1994

Barbara Chase-Riboud has a one-woman exhibition at Kiron Arts and Communication in Paris.

Betye Saar and John Outterbridge represent the United States at the 1994 São Paulo Biennal with three-dimensional assemblage works. The exhibit is curated by Lizzetta Lefalle-Collins, an independent African-American curator from California.

1995

Barbara Chase-Riboud is commissioned by the United States government to execute a sculpture for the African Burial Ground Memorial in New York City. In October, she receives the Brandywine Association's Van Der Zee Award.

Lois Mailou Jones and Her Former Students: Seven Decades of American Art opens at Howard University and Fondo del Sol in Washington, D.C. The exhibition travels to Boston in June of 1996, the birthplace of the ninty year old artist. Jones is commissioned to illustrate the poems of Léopold Senghor for The Limited Editions Club.

Selma Hortense Burke dies on August 29th in New Hope, Pennsylvania.

Geraldine McCullough has a one-woman exhibition at the Essie Green Gallery in New York City.

Elizabeth Catlett's sculpture is included in the 20th Century American Sculpture installation at the White House, First Lady's Garden, as well as in *The Listening Sky: An Inaugural Exhibition of The Studio Museum in Harlem Sculpture Garden*, New York City. She receives an honorary Doctor of Fine Arts degree from Spelman College.

Leslie King-Hammond, art historian and dean of graduate studies at the Maryland Institute, College of Art (Baltimore), becomes the first African American elected to head the College Art Association, the nation's largest body of arts professionals.

Tangled Roots, a site-specific installation by Betye Saar opens at the Palmer Museum of Art at Pennsylvania State University.

Martha Jackson-Jarvis has a one-woman exhibition at the Corcoran Gallery of Art in Washington, D.C.

Three Generations of African-American Women Sculptors: A Study in Paradox opens at the Afro-American Historical and Cultural Museum in Philadelphia. The exhibition will travel through 1999 and includes the work of Edmonia Lewis, Meta Warrick Fuller, May Howard Jackson, Beulah Woodard, Augusta Savage, Selma Burke, Elizabeth Prophet, Elizabeth Catlett, Geraldine McCullough, and Barbara Chase-Riboud.

Bearing Witness, an exhibition of the work of over twenty-five African-American Women artists opens at the Spelman College Museum of Fine Art. It will travel through 1999.

Barbara Chase-Riboud is made a Knight of the Order of Arts and Letters by the

Ministry of Culture in Paris.

Faith Ringgold's autobiography, *We Flew Over the Bridge: The Memoirs of Faith Ringgold* is published. A forty-year retrospective of her work opens at the ACA Galleries in New York City.

Bibliography

GENERAL BOOKS USEFUL TO THE STUDY OF BLACK WOMEN IN AMERICA

Reference Books

African-Americans: Voices of Triumph. Three volume set: Perseverance, Leadership, and Creative Fire. By the editors of Time-Life Books, Alexandria, Virginia, 1993.

Estell, Kenneth, ed. The African-American Almanac. Detroit, Mich., 1994.

Harley, Sharon. The Timetables of African-American History: A Chronology of the Most Important People and Events in African-American History. New York, 1995.

Hine, Darlene Clark. Hine Sight: Black Women and The Re-Construction of American History. Brooklyn, New York, 1994.

Hine, Darlene Clark, ed.; Elsa Barkley Brown and Rosalyn Terborg-Penn, associate editors. Black Women in America: An Historical Encyclopedia. Brooklyn, New York, 1993.

Hornsby, Alton, Jr. Chronology of African-American History: Significant Events and People from 1619 to the Present. Detroit, Michigan, 1991.

Kranz, Rachel. Biographical Dictionary of Black Americans. New York, 1992.

Lanker, Brian. I Dream a World: Portraits of Black Women Who Changed America. New York, 1989.

Logan, Rayford W., and Michael R. Winston, eds. Dictionary of American Negro Biography. New York, 1982.

Low, W. Augustus, and Virgil A. Clift, eds. Encyclopedia of Black America. New York, 1981.

Salem, Dorothy C., ed. African American Women: A Biographical Dictionary. New York, 1993.

Salzman, Jack, David Lionel Smith, and Cornel West. Encyclopedia of African-American Culture and History. Five Volumes. New York, 1996.

Smith, Jessie Carney, ed., Notable Black American Women. Two volumes. Detroit, Mich., Book I, 1993; Book II, 1996.

General Books about Black Women

Giddings, Paula. When and Where I Enter: The Impact of Black Women on Race and Sex in America. New York, 1984.

Guy-Sheftall, Beverly. Words of Fire: An Anthology of African-American Feminist Thought. New York, 1995.

Hine, Darlene Clark, Wilma King, and Linda Reed, eds. "We Specialize in the Wholly Impossible": A Reader in Black Women's History. Brooklyn, N.Y., 1995.

Jones, Jacqueline. Labor of Love, Labor of Sorrow: Black Women, Work, and the Family from Slavery to the Present. New York, 1985.

Lerner, Gerda, ed. Black Women in White America: A Documentary History. New York, 1972.

BLACK WOMEN IN DANCE

Haskins, James. Black Dance in America: A History Through Its People. New York, 1990.

Long, Richard A. *The Black Tradition in American Dance*. New York, 1989.

Stearns, Marshall & Jean. *Jazz Dance: The Story of American Vernacular Dance*. New York, 1968.

BLACK WOMEN IN SPORTS

Ashe, Arthur, Jr. *A Hard Road to Glory: A History of the African-American Athlete*. Three Volumes. Volume 1, 1619–1918; Volume 2, 1919–1945; Volume 3, Since 1946. New York, 1988.

———. *A Hard Road to Glory: The African-American Athlete in Track & Field*, etc. Paperback edition of the above three-volume set divided topically into the following five volumes: *Baseball, Basketball, Boxing, Football, Track & Field*.

Condon, Robert J. *Great Women Athletes of the 20th Century*. Jefferson, North Carolina, 1991.

Davis, Michael D. *Black American Women in Olympic Track and Field*. Jefferson, North Carolina, 1992.

Eitzen, D. Stanley and George H. Sage. *Sociology of American Sport*. Dubuque, Iowa, 1978.

Green, Tina Sloan, Dr. Carole A. Oglesby, Dr. Alpha Alexander and Nikki Franke. *Black Women in Sport*. Reston, Virginia, 1981.

Guttmann, Allan. *Women's Sports: A History*. New York, 1991.

Nelson, Mary Burton. *Are We Winning Yet?* New York, 1991.

Oglesby, Carole A. *Women in Sport: From Myth to Reality*. Philadelphia, Pennsylvania, 1978.

Page, James A. *Black Olympic Medalists*. Englewood, Colorado, 1991.

Woolum, Janet. *Outstanding Women Athletes*. Phoenix, Arizona, 1992.

BLACK WOMEN IN VISUAL ARTS

Bank, Mirra. *Anonymous was a Woman*. New York, 1979, 1995.

Bontemps, Jacqueline F. *Forever Free: Art by African American Women, 1862–1980*. Alexandria, Virginia, 1980.

Dover, Cedric. *American Negro Art*. Greenwich, Connecticut, 1960.

Gumbo Ya Ya: Anthology of Contemporary African-American Women Artists. New York, 1995.

Henkes, Robert. *The Art of Black American Women: Works of Twenty-Four Artists of the Twentieth Century*. Jefferson, North Carolina, 1993.

Lewis, Samella. *African American Art and Artists*. Berkeley, California, 1990.

Contents of the Set

(ORGANIZED BY VOLUME)

Dance, Sports, and Visual Arts

Dance

Sports

Visual Arts

Education

Science, Health, and Medicine

Contents of the Set

(LISTED ALPHABETICALLY BY ENTRY)

271

Index

Page numbers in **boldface** indicate main entries. *Italic* page numbers indicate illustrations.